Thomistic Principles and Bioethics

Thomas Aquinas is one of the foremost thinkers in Western philosophy and Christian scholarship, recognized as a significant voice in both theological discussions and secular philosophical debates. Alongside a revival of interest in Thomism in philosophy, scholars have realized its relevance when addressing certain contemporary issues in bioethics. This book offers a rigorous interpretation of Aquinas's metaphysical and ethical thought, and highlights their significance to questions in bioethics.

Jason T. Eberl applies Aquinas's views on the seminal topics of human nature and morality to key questions in bioethics at the margins of human life – questions which are currently contested in academia, politics, and the media, such as:

- When does a human person's life begin? How should we define and clinically determine a person's death?
- Is abortion ever morally permissible? How should we resolve the conflict between the potential benefits of embryonic stem cell research and the lives of human embryos?
- Does cloning involve a misuse of human ingenuity and technology?
- What forms of treatment are appropriate for irreversibly comatose patients? How should we care for patients who experience unbearable suffering as they approach the end of life?
- What ethical mandates and concerns underlie the practice of organ donation?

Thomistic Principles and Bioethics presents a significant philosophical viewpoint which should motivate further dialogue amongst religious and secular arenas of inquiry concerning such complex issues of both individual and public concern. It will be illuminating reading for scholars, postgraduate and research students of philosophy, metaphysics, ethics, bioethics, and moral theology.

Jason T. Eberl is Assistant Professor of Philosophy at Indiana University-Purdue University Indianapolis (IUPUI). He is an affiliate faculty member of the Indiana University Center for Bioethics, and co-director of IUPUI's Master of Arts in philosophy program. He has published articles in the journals: *Bioethics, Journal of Medicine and Philosophy*, *The National Catholic Bioethics Quarterly*, and *Review of Metaphysics*.

Routledge Annals of Bioethics

Series Editors:

Mark J. Cherry
St Edwards University, USA

Ana Smith Iltis
Saint Louis University, USA

Bioethics has become a truly international phenomenon. Secular Western bioethics in particular lays claim to a universal account of proper moral deportment, including the foundations of law and public policy, as well as the moral authority for national and international institutions to guarantee uniformity of practice, secure basic human rights, and promote social justice.

Through foundational philosophical, religious, and cultural perspectives, clinical case studies, and legal analysis, the books in this series document, review, and explore emerging bioethical viewpoints as well as the state of the art of this global endeavor. Volumes will critically appreciate diverse legal, moral, cultural, and religious viewpoints representing the various regions of the world, from mainland China and Hong Kong, Taiwan, Japan, India and East Asia more generally, to Europe, the Middle East, Australia and New Zealand, to South America and North America. Moral perspectives range from Orthodox Christianity, Roman Catholicism, and contemporary Protestant Christianity, to Orthodox, Conservative and Reformed Judaism, to Islam, Buddhism, Confucianism, Hinduism, and so forth, to secular liberalism.

The *Annals of Bioethics* compasses monographs and edited volumes on moral theory, normative health care practice, case studies, and public policy as well as volumes documenting and assessing legal, religious, and cultural responses to specific aspects of the fast-paced developments in health care and medical technology.

Thomistic Principles and Bioethics

Jason T. Eberl

Routledge
Taylor & Francis Group

LONDON AND NEW YORK

First published 2006
by Routledge
2 Park Square, Milton Park, Abingdon, Oxon OX14 4RN

Simultaneously published in the USA and Canada
by Routledge
711 Third Ave, New York, NY 10017

First issued in paperback 2013

Routledge is an imprint of the Taylor & Francis Group, an informa business

Typeset in Bembo by
Newgen Imaging Systems (P) Ltd, Chennai, India

British Library Cataloguing in Publication Data
A catalogue record for this book is available from the British Library

Library of Congress Cataloging in Publication Data
A catalog record for this book has been requested

ISBN13: 978–0–415–77063–7
ISBN13: 978-0-415-65457-9 (pbk)

To my parents Robert (1936–2001) and
Betty – "Bear" and "Tiny"

Contents

Acknowledgments

A number of colleagues have contributed to this volume's development at various stages and in myriad ways. I began working on Aquinas's metaphysical account of human nature as a graduate student at Arizona State University, under Prof. Michael White, and then at Saint Louis University, under Prof. Eleonore Stump. Their careful attention to detail and generous giving of their time in reviewing my work were invaluable. Prof. White first helped me to see the connection between historical and contemporary analytic approaches to philosophical issues. Prof. Stump assisted me greatly in developing this connection in my research, and continues to be a *mentor* to me in the truest and most complete sense of the word. My interest in applying Aquinas's thought to issues in bioethics was inspired by Fr John Kavanaugh, S.J., who has also mentored me through graduate studies and beyond, and has been a continual source of wisdom and learning. My initial work on this volume as part of my doctoral dissertation owes much to each of them, as well as to Fr Theodore Vitali, C.P., whose zealous regard for the success of his students is quite evident and infectious.

Research for this volume began while I participated in an exchange program at the Johann Wolfgang Goethe Universität in Frankfurt am Main, Germany. I am grateful to the Philosophisch-Theologische Hochschule Sankt Georgen for their hospitality, to Prof. Matthias Lutz-Bachmann for his guidance and an invitation to deliver a presentation to his graduate colloquium, and to Prof. Jan Aertsen, Prof. Ludger Honnefelder, Andreas Niederberger, and Stephanie Vesper for their helpful discussions.

I completed drafts of Chapters 2 and 3 while visiting the Center for Philosophy of Religion at the University of Notre Dame. I wish to thank the fellows and faculty of the Center and the Philosophy Department, particularly Profs Kelly Clark, Fred Crosson, Thomas Flint, Jaegwon Kim, Brian Leftow, Hugh McCann, Alvin Plantinga, Michael Rea, David Solomon, and Peter van Inwagen.

Research for Chapters 4 and 5, and completion of this volume, has been accomplished at Indiana University-Purdue University Indianapolis. I greatly appreciate my colleagues' vital contributions, particularly Prof. Michael Burke's detailed reading and commentary on the entire manuscript, Prof. John Tilley's careful reading of Chapter 5 and late-night discussions of ethics, and Prof. Eric Meslin's professional guidance and support from the Indiana University Center for

Bioethics. Others who deserve special recognition for helping to shape my thinking on Aquinas's philosophy and issues in bioethics are Prof. Thomas Cavanaugh, Prof. James DuBois, Prof. Colleen McCluskey, Michael Allen, Chris Brown, Bryan Cross, Miguel Endara, Jennifer Hart Weed, Eric LaRock, Michael Rota, and Kevin Timpe. Acknowledging these contributions to this volume should not be taken to indicate agreement with the arguments therein or responsibility for any errors, which are solely my own.

This volume came to fruition through the kind efforts of Profs Mark Cherry and Ana Iltis, editors of the *Annals of Bioethics* series, Martin Scrivener from Swets & Zeitlinger Publishers, and Terry Clague, Lizzie Catford, and Emma Davis from Routledge. I am most grateful to all of them for their assistance at various stages of the writing and publishing process. I would also like to thank Michelle Ruben for her valuable editorial assistance.

Portions of this volume have benefited from being presented at the following professional conferences and I wish to express my gratitude to the audience members and commentators at each conference: 2003 Central Division Meeting of the American Philosophical Association, 2003 International Conference on Ancient and Medieval Philosophy at Fordham University, 2003 "Formation and Renewal" Conference at the University of Notre Dame, 7th Annual International Conference on Bioethics at Trinity International University, and the 36th and 38th International Congresses on Medieval Studies at Western Michigan University.

Finally, but most importantly, this volume would not have been possible without the love and support of my wife, Jennifer Vines, and my daughter, August Claire Eberl.

The author and publishers would like to thank the following for granting permission to reproduce material in this work:

Blackwell Publishing/*Bioethics* for permission to reprint Eberl, J.T. (2000), "The beginning of personhood: A Thomistic biological analysis," *Bioethics*, 14: 134–57; © 2000 Blackwell Publishers Ltd.

Blackwell Publishing/*Bioethics* for permission to reprint Eberl, J.T. (2005) "A Thomistic understanding of human death," *Bioethics*, 19: 29–48; © 2005 Blackwell Publishing Ltd.

The National Catholic Bioethics Center for permission to reprint Eberl, J.T. (2003) "Aquinas on euthanasia, suffering, and palliative care," *The National Catholic Bioethics Quarterly*, 3: 331–54; © 2003 The National Catholic Bioethics Center.

The Review of Metaphysics for permission to reprint Eberl, J.T. (2004) "Aquinas on the nature of human beings," *The Review of Metaphysics*, 58: 333–65; © 2004 *The Review of Metaphysics*.

Taylor & Francis Ltd/*Journal of Medicine and Philosophy* for permission to reprint Eberl, J.T. (2005) "Aquinas's account of human embryogenesis and recent interpretations," *Journal of Medicine and Philosophy*, 30: 379–94; © 2005 Taylor & Francis.

List of Aquinas's works and abbreviations

Abbreviations for Aquinas's works

CDP	*Collationes in decem praecepta*
CT	*Compendium theologiae*
DAM	*De aeternitate mundi*
DEE	*De ente et essentia*
DME	*De mixtione elementorum*
DUI	*De unitate intellectus contra Averroistas*
In BDT	*Expositio super librum Boethii De trinitate*
In I Cor	*Commentarium super Epistolam Primam ad Corinthios*
In DA	*Sententia libri De anima*
In DGC	*Sententia super libros De generatione et corruptione*
In Job	*Expositio super Job*
In M	*Sententia super Metaphyisicam*
In NE	*Sententia libri Ethicorum*
In Ph	*Sententia super Physicam*
In Rom	*Commentarium super Epistolam ad Romanos*
In Sent	*Scriptum super libros Sententiarum*
In II Thes	*Reportatio super Epistolam Secundam ad Thessalonicenses*
QDA	*Quaestio disputata de anima*
QDM	*Quaestiones disputatae de malo*
QDP	*Quaestiones disputatae de potentia*
QDSC	*Quaestio disputata de spiritualibus creaturis*
QDV	*Quaestiones disputatae de veritate*
SCG	*Summa contra gentiles*
ST	*Summa theologiae*

Latin texts of Aquinas's works

Nearly all of Aquinas's works cited in this volume can be found in the Leonine critical edition published by the Vatican:

Commissio Leonina (ed.) (1882–) *S. Thomae Aquinatis Doctoris Angelici Opera Omnia*, Rome: Vatican Polyglot Press.

The following are editions of Aquinas's works cited in this volume that have not yet appeared in the Leonine critical edition:

Cai, R. (ed.) (1953) *Super Epistolas S. Pauli lectura*, 2 vols, Turin: Marietti.
Cathala, R. and Spiazzi, R. (eds) (1950) *In duodecim libros metaphysicorum Aristotelis expositio*, Turin: Marietti.
Mandonnet, P. and Moos, M. (eds) (1929–47) *Scriptum super sententiis magistri Petri Lombardi*, 4 vols, Paris: Lethielleux.
Spiazzi, R. (ed.) (1949) *De spiritualibus creaturis*, in *Quaestiones disputatae*, vol. 2, Turin: Marietti.
—— (1949) *Quaestiones disputatae de potentia dei*, in *Quaestiones disputatae*, vol. 2, Turin: Marietti.

English translations of Aquinas's works

While I have preferred my own translations in this volume, unless otherwise indicated, I found consulting the following English translations of Aquinas's works helpful:

Bobik, J. (trans.) (1965) *Aquinas on Being and Essence*. Notre Dame: University of Notre Dame Press.
English Dominican Fathers (transs) (1952) *On the Power of God*, 3 vols, Westminster: Newman Press.
—— (1981) *The Summa Theologica of St. Thomas Aquinas*, 5 vols, Westminster: Christian Classics.
Foster, K. and Humphries, S. (transs) (1994) *Commentary on Aristotle's De Anima*, Notre Dame: Dumb Ox Books.
Macierowski, E. (trans.) (1998) *Thomas Aquinas's Earliest Treatment of the Divine Essence: Scriptum Super Libros Sententiarum, Book I, Distinction 8*, Binghamton: Center for Medieval and Renaissance Studies and Institute for Global Cultural Studies.
McInerny, R. (trans.) (1993) *Aquinas Against the Averroists*, West Lafayette: Purdue University Press.
Maurer, A. (trans.) (1968) *On Being and Essence*, 2nd ed, Toronto: Pontifical Institute of Mediaeval Studies.
Mulligan, R., McGlynn, J., and Schmidt, R. (transs) (1952–4) *The Disputed Questions on Truth*, 3 vols, Chicago, IL: Henry Regnery.
Pasnau, R. (trans.) (1999) *A Commentary on Aristotle's De Anima*, New Haven, CT: Yale University Press.
Pegis, A., Anderson, J., Bourke, V., and O'Neil, C. (transs) (1975) *Summa Contra Gentiles*, 5 vols, Notre Dame: University of Notre Dame Press.
Robb, J. (trans.) (1984) *Questions on the Soul*, Milwaukee, WI: Marquette University Press.
Rowan, J. (trans.) (1995) *Commentary on Aristotle's Metaphysics*, Notre Dame: Dumb Ox Books.

Introduction

This volume presents an application of the philosophical views of the medieval philosopher and theologian Thomas Aquinas to contemporary issues in bioethics. Though Aquinas lived and wrote in the thirteenth century, scholars continue to find merit and relevance in his ideas. Several distinct movements of "Thomism" throughout the twentieth century bear witness to Aquinas's enduring influence in both philosophy and theology. For Aquinas, these disciplines are not in fundamental conflict with one another, as some scholars in both Aquinas's time and even today contend. Aquinas was open to the results of pure rational inquiry and did not perceive such inquiry to be a threat to his Christian faith.

Due to Aquinas's trust in human beings' rational capacity, it is appropriate, for certain purposes, to set aside Aquinas's theological views and concentrate solely on his philosophy. I do so in this volume in order to introduce the Thomistic perspective into the realm of secular bioethics. Bioethics, of course, has a strong historical foundation in what is called "moral theology," as Albert Jonsen recognizes in his history of the discipline (Jonsen, 1998). Nevertheless, contemporary bioethicists and others involved in public policy debate often dismiss those views which are founded upon a set of theological tenets; not because such views are necessarily mistaken or incoherent, but due to the fact that their appeal is limited to those who hold certain "faith" beliefs. It is difficult to either affirm or argue against such views unless one shares the religious beliefs upon which they are based. The most one can do, unless the religious beliefs in question are rationally incoherent, is simply to assert that one does not share the relevant beliefs and thus cannot accept any argument based on them. This generally precludes theologically based views from having a significant voice in secular bioethics; or, if they are given such a voice, it is not without criticism. Geneticist Richard Lewontin and bioethicist Ronald Green both criticize President Clinton's National Bioethics Advisory Commission for hearing testimony from representatives of various religious traditions on the controversial subject of cloning. Green quotes Lewontin as saying:

> By giving a separate and identifiable voice to explicitly religious views the commission has legitimated religious conviction as a front on which the issues of sex, reproduction, the definition of the family, and the status of fertilized eggs and fetuses are to be fought.

> (Green, 2001, p. 116)

Green himself contends, "Specific religious or moral beliefs not grounded in publicly defensible values cannot be allowed to dominate this process" (Green, 2001, p. 169) – the process being one of "objective assessment and peer review" to determine public policy. While Green is correct that religious views should not "dominate" the process of determining public policy, the question remains whether such views can offer a "legitimate" voice in public policy debate.

Philosophical views, on the other hand, require only a shared capacity for reason among those who would debate them; which, of course, does not mean that everyone will agree with the philosophical premises that form the basis of various arguments and conclusions. But such premises can be subjected to rational scrutiny and thereby demonstrated to be more-or-less true, or more-or-less reasonable; theological premises cannot be subjected to such scrutiny if they are ultimately based on faith. Therefore, in order to introduce Aquinas's views into contemporary bioethical debates, his theologically based positions and arguments must be set aside despite being a key component of his overall thought. In saying this, I am by no means asserting that Aquinas's theological views are not worthy of discussion. In fact, a great deal of significant scholarship attests to the value of Aquinas's theological insights to Roman Catholic and other Christian philosophers, theologians, and bioethicists.

Certain Thomistic scholars, who have offered contributions to bioethical debates, have associated Aquinas's views with the magisterial teachings of the Roman Catholic Church (McCormick, 1991; Vacek, 1992; Ashley and Moraczewski, 2001; Haldane and Lee, 2003a). This is quite understandable because Aquinas was a Roman Catholic priest – a friar in the Dominican Order to be precise – and the Catholic Church has long taught the value of Aquinas's thought as a primary foundation for its teachings (Leo XIII, 1879; John Paul II, 1998). Nor is it fallacious for scholars to associate Aquinas's views with Roman Catholic teachings as there is sure to be a great deal of agreement. Nevertheless, it is not given that everything Aquinas wrote is reflected in what the Church teaches today, and Aquinas himself recognized that there is a difference between what can be rationally demonstrated and what can be known by faith alone. For example, Aquinas argued, in agreement with his intellectual ancestor, Aristotle, that it is not rationally demonstrable that the universe had a beginning "in time." In other words, it may be the case that the universe is without a temporal beginning or end – as some contemporary physicists and cosmologists argue as well (Hawking, 1996, ch. 8). Aquinas, however, also argued that it is not rationally demonstrable that the universe did *not* have a beginning in time. He thus concluded that what Christians believe regarding the origin of the universe – that it was created at the beginning of time by God – is rationally consistent even if it is not rationally demonstrable (DAM; Torrell, 1996, p. 114). Despite this conclusion in favor of Christian belief, the bishop of Paris, Stephen Tempier, condemned this argument and several of Aquinas's other "heterodox" arguments on December 10, 1270 (Torrell, 1996, p. 185).[1]

Hence, Aquinas was able to distinguish when one of the Church's teachings or his own religious beliefs was knowable as a matter of faith alone, and when it was rationally demonstrable and thus arguable to those outside of the Christian faith.

It is solely the rationally demonstrable aspects of Aquinas's thought that I will concern myself with in this volume. My goal is to present an *arguable* Thomistic perspective to contemporary bioethicists – both religious and secular. In doing so, I do not make it my task here to argue for the conclusion that Aquinas's views are superior to the alternatives; although I endeavor to point out important contrasts between his views and certain contemporary positions on various issues.

What I do argue for in this volume are particular interpretations of Aquinas with respect to the bioethical issues that will be discussed. Thomistic scholars, as will be seen, differ in their interpretations and applications of Aquinas's philosophy to issues of the day; an obvious reason for this being that many such issues are not even touched upon in Aquinas's writings. Aquinas, for example, clearly could not have even imagined the issues of embryonic stem cell research, cloning, withdrawal of artificial life support, or organ donation. He did, however, write about the inherent value of human life, the individual nature of human persons, the complex nature of human intentionality, and the moral imperative to be charitable; each of which, respectively, bears on the ethical evaluation of these issues.

Therefore, it is possible to identify certain relevant *principles* – that is, general philosophical conclusions – that Aquinas espouses and which are applicable to various bioethical issues. Such principles are both metaphysical and moral in nature. As will be elucidated in the following chapters, certain principles are fundamental to Aquinas's account of human nature and moral action and are thus quite general, such as, "Human beings are composite entities constituted by a rational soul informing a material human body"; "The morality of human action is judged with respect to what fulfills humanity's proper natural inclinations"; "Human life has a fundamental intrinsic, but not absolute, value"; "Some actions may be morally permissible even if they result in a negative consequence." Other principles are more specific metaphysical and ethical conclusions derived from these general principles, such as, "A human being comes into existence when there exists a body with an active potentiality for rational thought"; "A human being's death occurs when their[2] body is no longer an integrated living organism"; "Not every means that prolongs a human being's biological existence must be utilized."

My intention is not to present definitive conclusions to the difficult bioethical issues that will be discussed, but to offer an interpretation of one significant philosopher's viewpoint for the purpose of engaging bioethical debate in the secular arena. The particular issues that I address in Chapters 4 and 5 relate to the margins of human life: abortion and the use of abortifacient contraceptives, embryonic stem cell research, cloning, care of patients in a persistent vegetative state, euthanasia, and organ donation. Before treating these issues, I offer a metaphysical analysis in Chapters 2 and 3 of when a human being's life begins and ends. First, though, I elucidate Aquinas's metaphysical view of human nature, his systematic moral philosophy, and his account of intentional action.

1 Aquinas's account of human nature and natural law theory

Introduction

The past century has witnessed a revival of interest in the thought of Thomas Aquinas across various schools in philosophy. In the latter half of the twentieth century, Aquinas's metaphysics, ethical theory, and philosophy of religion have been introduced into contemporary debates in analytic philosophy. Concurrently, scholars have utilized Thomism as a basis for addressing certain issues in bioethics. Some, for example, have appealed to Aquinas's metaphysical account of human nature and human embryogenesis to argue for distinct points at which a developing human embryo may be considered to have a rational soul, and thus to be a person (Donceel, 1970; Ashley, 1976; Ford, 1988; Grisez, 1989; McCormick, 1991; Heaney, 1992; Eberl, 2000a). Others have appealed to Thomistic natural law theory to evaluate issues such as abortion and euthanasia (Grisez and Boyle, 1979; Gómez-Lobo, 2002; Eberl, 2003).

In this chapter, I will outline the fundamental principles of Aquinas's thought regarding the metaphysical nature of human persons and the natural law which governs human moral behavior. These principles are well-known to Thomistic scholars and have served as a foundation for the Roman Catholic Church's approach to addressing various issues in bioethics. Nevertheless, to the wider community, Thomistic philosophical principles are generally either unknown or misunderstood. I thus endeavor, in the chapters that follow, to address certain bioethical issues using the Thomistic philosophical principles elucidated here.

Aquinas's account of human nature[1]

Aquinas's metaphysical account of human nature includes, though it is not limited to, three interrelated theses: a human person is a substance composed of an immaterial soul informing a material body; a human person is not identical to an immaterial, spiritual substance; and "animality" is fundamental to human nature. I will further elucidate each of these theses.

According to Aquinas, a human being is a *person*. He adopts the definition of personhood developed by Boethius: "An individual substance of a rational nature"

(ST, Ia.29.1; cf. Boethius, 1918). Being of a rational nature – that is, having an intellective mind[2] – distinguishes human beings from other material substances (QDA, III; SCG, II.60; In NE, I.10, X.10). A human being, though, is not only rational, but is also a sensitive, animate, and corporeal substance; human beings have a material nature (In BDT, V.3). Aquinas thus distinguishes human beings from other types of persons[3] as "rational animals" (In M, VII.3.1326).

Aquinas refers to human beings as essentially animal, because we share certain essential qualities with other members of the animal genus. The primary exemplification of such similarity is the capacity for sense-perception. A human body, though, is unique among various kinds of animal bodies in that it is organized not only to support the capacity for sense-perception, but also the capacity for rational thought. The disposition of a human body is determined by its having a *rational* soul as its "substantial form."[4] As a substantial form, a rational soul is responsible for the existence of a human being, the actualization of the matter that composes a human being, and the unity of existence and activity in a human being (SCG, II.68; In DA, II.2). One way to understand the notion of a rational soul as a substantial form, in contemporary terms, is to think of it as a "principle of organization" for a human body. A human body is an "organic" construct. It has a variety of parts that both operate independently and function collectively to support the existence and activity of a living, sensing, and thinking being. Both the independent operation of one of a body's organs, and its functional unity with the body's other organs, are governed by the formal, or *functional*, unity of the organism itself.

A rational soul and the material body of which it is the substantial form are not two separately existing substances. A substantial form is the actualization of a material body. Aquinas asserts:

> Body and soul are not two actually existing substances, but from these two is made one actually existing substance. For the body of a human being is not actually the same in the soul's presence and absence; but the soul makes it to be actually.

(SCG, II.69)

The intrinsic unity of matter and substantial form – body and soul – is responsible for a human being's unified existence. Aquinas contends, "If you say that Socrates is not one simply, but one due to the aggregate of mover and moved, many incoherencies follow" (DUI, III). The primary incoherency is that Socrates would not be one being unqualifiedly [*unum simpliciter*] (ST, Ia.76.1). If Socrates is not *unum simpliciter*, then he cannot count as a substance.[5] The idea that Socrates is an aggregate of a mover and that which it moves is analogous to the aggregate of sailors and the ships they pilot. One would not say that sailors and their ships compose one being; analogously, one would not say that Socrates's soul – the mover – and his body – the moved – compose one being.[6]

A human being is not merely an aggregate of body and soul, for neither alone counts as a substance. A human being does not naturally exist without being composed of both a material body and a rational soul. As Armand Maurer describes it:

> The human person, according to Aquinas, contains a dualism of body (matter) and soul (form): two incomplete components of the person's essence, unified by the person's one complete *esse* ["being" or "existence"]...there is but one *esse* of the whole composite. Accordingly the soul is not united to the body as one being to another. If it were, the person would not have a substantial but an accidental unity. Nor is the whole human personality present in the soul.
>
> (1993, p. 511)

Typically, when matter is informed by a rational soul, a new ontological entity comes into existence: a human being.[7]

An analogous example is salt. The elements sodium and chloride, which are substances in themselves, come together to form a new substance: salt. When salt comes into existence, the sodium and the chloride each ceases to exist as a distinct substance, though both persist "virtually" as parts of the new substance (DME; SCG, IV.35; In M VII.17.1680). Salt has a set of properties that is not merely the result of combining the sets of properties had by sodium and chloride, respectively. The composition of a human being by soul and body is not exactly the same as the case of salt, for soul and body do not exist as distinct substances prior to composing a human being. Soul and body, however, like sodium and chloride, do not exist as distinct ontological kinds in a composite human being. Neither is it the case that the set of properties had by a human being is merely the result of combining the sets of properties had by their soul and body, respectively. Once again, a human being is an individual entity composed of a rational soul informing a material body.

Aquinas rejects the Platonic "substance dualist" account of human nature, in which a rational soul is understood as akin to a sailor guiding a material vessel (QDSC, II; Pegis, 1978, pp. 147–68; Pasnau, 2002, pp. 73–9). Aquinas's basic complaint against Platonism is based on his contention that humans beings cannot be identified with their souls alone, because such identification would deny them ownership of those activities of their souls that depend upon bodily organs to operate (ST, Ia.75.4). If human beings live, sense, and act through physical behavior, then, since such activities are identified with capacities of the soul that depend upon bodily organs for their operation, human beings cannot be identified with their souls alone. Rather, human beings are composed of both their souls and bodies:

> There cannot be one operation of things that are different in being...Now, although there is some operation belonging to the soul in which the body does not share – such as understanding – nevertheless, there are some operations common to it and the body – such as fear and anger and sensation and the like; for these occur according to some transmutation in a determinate part of the body, from which it is clear that they are operations of the soul and body together. Therefore, it must be that one thing is made from soul and body, and that they are not diverse according to being.
>
> (SCG, II.57)

Therefore, Aquinas's account is not representative of substance dualism, as it is sometimes mischaracterized (Moreland and Rae, 2000, pp. 201–6). The fundamental difference between Aquinas's account and substance dualism concerns the questions of whether a rational soul is a complete substance and whether human beings are identical with their souls. According to substance dualism, a human being is their soul, which is a complete substance on its own, and their body is merely something to which they are joined between birth and death (Swinburne, 1997; Foster, 2001). This is not Aquinas's position.

Aquinas does argue that a rational soul has a mode of being that distinguishes it from all other substantial forms of material substances (In Sent, I.8.v.2.ad 1) owing to its rational capacities, which are not dependent upon any material body for their operation (Klima, 2001). A rational soul's special mode of being, however, does not entail its complete independence from its material body. Some capacities of a rational soul – namely, its vegetative and sensitive capacities that nonhuman animals also have – act through material organs. A rational soul thus requires a material body to function completely – that is, for all of its capacities to be actualizable. Aquinas further argues that a rational soul communicates its being to a material body such that there is one being of the composite substance: a human being. Hence, a soul must be *immediately* joined to such a body (QDA, I.ad 1; White, 1995). Additionally, while a soul's rational operation does not itself require a bodily organ (QDV, X.5; ST, Ia.78.4), the objects of rational operation – what the mind thinks about – are universal, intelligible forms abstracted from phantasms.[8] The mind has such phantasms through sense-perception of particular material substances. Since the activity of sense-perception requires proper material organs – eyes, ears, nose, etc. – a human mind does have need of a material human body (QDA, II; ST, Ia.101.2; SCG, II.83).

Furthermore, a rational soul is naturally united to a particular material body as its substantial form (In DA, II.2; SCG, II.68; ST, Ia.76.1). Aquinas contends that it is not a mind itself that understands, nor the soul which is the foundation for the mind's rational capacities. Rather, *human beings* understand by means of the rational capacities they have by virtue of their souls; just as they see by means of the capacity for sight they have by virtue of their eyes and visual cortex (SCG, II.76; In DA, III.7; DUI, II, IV). Hence, because a human being naturally exists as composed of both soul and body, a rational soul's existence and operation are most properly in union with a particular material body.

By virtue of its rational capacities, which do not intrinsically depend upon any physical organ to operate, Aquinas argues that a rational soul can subsist without need of a physical body (QDA, II; ST, Ia.75.2; Eberl, 2000b). Although it is capable of subsisting apart from its body, a human rational soul does not subsist in such a state as a complete substance (QDP, III.10; ST, Ia.90.4). For one thing, a rational soul's other capacities – vegetative and sensitive – depend upon bodily organs for their operation (ST, Ia.77.5). Furthermore, a human mind, according to Aquinas, is designed to operate by abstracting universal, intelligible forms from phantasms generated through sense-perception of particular concrete objects (ST, Ia.85.1); the mind thus depends on well-functioning sense organs for its rational operation

(ST, Ia.84.6–8). As Etienne Gilson asserts, "Human intelligence simply must be a soul and must profit from the advantages which union with a body can bring it" (Gilson, 1956, p. 191). Aquinas could be labeled a "dualist" of sorts, because he argues that a rational soul is immaterial (ST, Ia.75.5), incorruptible (ST, Ia.75.6), and capable of subsistence apart from a material body. Nonetheless, this characterization does not equate Aquinas's account with what is today known as "*substance dualism*" (Stump, 1995).

Since Aquinas is not a substance dualist and contends that a rational soul is the substantial form of a material human body, it appears that he would define a human being as fundamentally a biological organism. In fact, Aquinas explicitly asserts that a human being is an "animal":

> "Animal" is predicated of a human being essentially, not accidentally, and "human" is not placed in the definition of an animal, but conversely. Therefore it must be the same form by which something is animal and by which it is human. Otherwise, a human being would not truly be that which is animal, such that "animal" would be essentially predicated of a human being... so neither is Socrates human by one soul and animal by another, but by one and the same.
>
> (ST, Ia.76.3)

Aquinas, however, does not agree with the *reduction* of a human being to their "animality."[9] While a well-functioning cerebral cortex is required for a human mind's operation, due to the mind's dependence upon phantasms generated through sense-perception, it is not essential for the mind's operation of cognizing the universal, intelligible forms abstracted from phantasms (SCG, II.62; QDA, II).[10] Aquinas argues that a human mind is not reducible to the functioning of a human brain. A mind is not identical to a brain, nor is rational operation merely the firing of neurons in a cerebral cortex; a human being's rational capacity cannot be wholly explained in merely neurophysical terms.

This does not entail, however, that there is no relationship between a human being's mind and their brain. In fact, Aquinas describes a very intimate relationship between the two. First, Aquinas recognizes that certain cognitive functions are localized in the brain. These are the cognitive functions that human beings share with nonhuman animals and include what Aquinas terms the "estimative" capacity, by which animals are able to determine what is good versus what is harmful to them (ST, Ia.78.4).

Second, a mind depends on sense-perception for gaining knowledge. Unlike Plato, Aquinas contends that a mind is a *tabula rasa* at its creation; it has no innate knowledge. A human being's natural source of knowledge is sensory experience of their surrounding environment (ST, Ia.84.3). Sense-perception is a mental capacity humans share with all other animals, and is a function of the brain along with the sense organs that are connected to it. When damage occurs to the brain or sense organs, rational operation is affected (ST, Ia.76.5, Ia.84.7).

Finally, given current discoveries in neurobiology, it is reasonable to conclude that a *correlation* exists between rational activity and neural activity. Asserting such a correlation is not antithetical to Aquinas's account so long as the correlation is not explained in terms of rational activity being identical with, or reducible to, neural activity (LaRock, 2001).

To summarize, a rational soul, while separable from its body by virtue of one of its essential capacities, is naturally united to a human body for the sake of its other capacities because it is the body's substantial form. Because of this natural unity, a human body's organic structure is disposed toward subserving the rational soul's capacities, including the mind (In DA, II.1, II.19; QDA, X.ad 1–2; ST, Ia.91.3).

Although a rational soul is capable of existing on its own, because it is the substantial form of a material body, it does not subsist with a complete specific nature; a soul alone is not completely "human" (QDSC, II.ad 5; QDP, V.10; ST, Supp.93.1). Since a rational soul alone does not have a complete human nature, it cannot be identical to a human being (ST, Ia.29.1.ad 5; ST, Ia.75.4.ad 2).

Neither a rational soul nor the matter it informs is a complete substance on its own. Rather, the two together compose a complete substance: a human being who is not identical to either their soul or their informed material body. Rather, a human being is *composed* of their informed material body. Aquinas concludes, "A human being is said to be from soul and body just as from two things a third is constituted that is neither of the two, hence a human being is neither soul nor body" (DEE, II; cf. ST, Ia.75.4). Having described the basic theses of Aquinas's metaphysical account of human nature, I will now elucidate the natural law principles that, Aquinas argues, follow from this account.

Aquinas's natural law theory

Aquinas's ethical theory involves two components: the Aristotelian concept of "virtue" and the concept of "natural law." Although Aquinas devotes much more attention to the discussion of virtue in his *Summa theologiae* – 170 questions versus the 19 questions that comprise his "Treatise on Law" – contemporary ethicists typically classify Aquinas as a natural law theorist. Without stipulating that Aquinas is either primarily a virtue theorist or a natural law theorist, I have elected to focus on his natural law ethic because it provides a set of formal principles that have clear bioethical implications.[11] As a preliminary, though, it is important to note the close relationship between Aquinas's understandings of virtue, natural law, and human nature.

Virtues, according to Aristotle, whom Aquinas closely followed, are habits cultivated in order to define a moral agent's "character." If, for example, a human being develops the virtue of courage, then they will be considered a courageous person. On a virtue theory construal of human morality, the goal is not necessarily to do virtuous actions, but rather to become a virtuous person. A human being, however, becomes a virtuous person only by cultivating specific virtues, which is accomplished by doing virtuous actions. A human being thus becomes courageous by performing acts of courage, generous by performing acts of generosity, etc.

Since a human being's moral development depends upon doing virtuous actions, it is necessary to understand what counts as a "virtuous" action in order to know whether it should be done. According to Aristotle and Aquinas, a virtuous action is whatever action that, if done, will promote a human being's "flourishing" – that is, the fulfillment of their "nature" (ST, Ia-IIae.18.5, Ia-IIae.49.2, Ia-IIae.71.1). A human being's nature, as described above, is determined by their substantial form, which provides the set of capacities – vegetative, sensitive, and rational – that define them as a "rational animal." Human flourishing involves actualizing these definitive capacities such that a virtuous human being is the most "perfect" – that is, most complete or fully actualized – human being there can be.

Natural law enters the picture when considering what a human being's definitive capacities are. Aquinas argues that everything has goodness to the degree that it has being (ST, Ia.5.1); the convertibility of being and goodness is the primary metaethical foundation for Aquinas's moral theory (MacDonald, 1991; Stump, 2003, p. 62). Aquinas's concept of goodness includes the notion of "desirability": the more goodness something has, the more it is objectively desirable. Based on this premise, Aquinas argues that all substances have a set of "natural inclinations" to pursue whatever they perceive to be good – that is, what is desirable to them. In particular, all substances are naturally inclined toward whatever they perceive that can increase their own goodness – that is, whatever will help actualize their definitive capacities. Natural law, as will be explained in detail later, includes a set of principles which, if followed, will satisfy a human being's natural inclinations and thus lead to their perfection as a human being. By acting in accordance with the principles of natural law, a human being will perform virtuous actions and thereby become a virtuous person. Aquinas thus refers to natural law principles as "nurseries" of virtue:

> Virtue is natural to a human being as it is inchoate. Such is the case with respect to the specific nature, insofar as in human reason there are by nature certain naturally known principles of knowledge and action, which are the nurseries of intellectual and moral virtues.
>
> (ST, Ia-IIae.63.1; cf. ST, Ia-IIae.27.3.ad 4,
> Ia-IIae.51.1, Ia-IIae.63.2.ad 3)

The relationship between natural law and virtue can be understood, in a simple and direct fashion, in terms of the natural law principles providing the formal guidance – that is, the rule or measure (ST, Ia-IIae.63.2) – for a human being to choose what actions to perform which will lead to their perfection as a human being. For example, if I desire to be a virtuous person, I must understand that, as a rational being, I need to actualize my capacity for rational thought. I thus choose to do those actions which involve actualizing that capacity, such as getting an education, reading intellectually stimulating books, conversing with intelligent and wise people, etc. By developing a habit of doing those actions and other actions that involve applying what I learn in beneficial ways, I thereby become an intellectually virtuous person. Having briefly outlined the relationship between natural law and the cultivation of virtue in Aquinas's overall ethical theory, I will now focus on the natural law itself in order to illuminate how Aquinas formulates certain normative principles based on his metaphysical understanding of human nature, and exactly what these principles are.

Aquinas defines "law" as "nothing other than a certain ordinance of reason for the common good, made by whoever has care of the community, and that is promulgated" (ST, Ia-IIae.90.4). In order for some principle to count as a law, it must fulfill all four of these criteria. For example, a law against driving while intoxicated is a valid law because it is made by a legitimate legislative government, the members of which used their collective reasoning capacity to determine that it would promote the common good if people were not allowed to drive while their judgment is impaired by alcohol consumption, and is announced to the citizenry so that they are aware that this law is binding upon them.

This example represents one type of law Aquinas recognizes: human law, also known as civil or positive law (ST, Ia-IIae.91.3, Ia-IIae.95–96). Aquinas defines three other types of law: eternal law (ST, Ia-IIae, 91.1, Ia-IIae.93), natural law (ST, Ia-IIae.91.2, Ia-IIae.94), and divine law (ST, Ia-IIae.91.4–5, Ia-IIae.98–108). Eternal law is the ultimate foundation for all other types of law. It is formulated in the mind of God, who has care of everything that exists, for the good of the entire created universe. It is the inherent order of the universe created by God and governed by God's providence. According to Aquinas, God creates the universe with a specific order that is manifested in the laws of nature – for example, the laws of physics, such as gravity – and the natural inclinations of the various species that populate the universe – for example, a plant's natural inclination to take in nourishment and grow in the direction of sunlight. Aquinas thus asserts, "It is evident that all things participate to some extent in eternal law; namely, insofar as from its impression on them they are inclined toward their proper acts and ends" (ST, Ia-IIae.91.2).

Aquinas describes human beings as able to participate in eternal law more fully than other material beings by virtue of having the capacity for rational thought. Human beings are able to understand, albeit imperfectly, the eternal law; nonrational beings are unable to do so. It is the human understanding of eternal law which Aquinas terms "natural law." Natural law is one of two ways in which eternal law is promulgated to rational creatures. The second way is through direct revelation, which Aquinas terms "divine law" and which he considers, due to his Christian heritage, to consist of the so-called "Old" and "New" Laws found in the Hebrew and Christian Scriptures.

Natural law principles, as will be shown below, are quite general so as to be universally applicable to all human beings, no matter what their cultural background or station in life. Aquinas thus recognizes the need for what he terms "human law," which is the particular determination of general natural law principles made by human legislators using prudent practical judgment. Human laws are crafted with respect to particular communities to help train each community's members in becoming virtuous; in this sense such laws can be considered culturally relative because the same human laws would not be appropriate for every community. "The general principles of natural law cannot be applied in the same way to all, because of the great variety of human affairs. And accordingly there appears a diversity of positive [human] laws among diverse people" (ST, Ia–IIae.95.2.ad 3). Aquinas further notes the important role that "custom," relative to different communities, plays in specifying and applying natural law principles (ST, Ia–IIae.97.3).

Nevertheless, human laws must be crafted in accordance with the general principles of natural law that are universal and thus binding upon all human beings regardless of culture or circumstance. Any valid human law, Aquinas contends, must be somehow derived from the natural law; otherwise, it would be a "perversion of law" (ST, Ia–IIae.95.2). For example, a law permitting racial segregation is not a valid human law because it violates the natural law mandate to treat all human beings justly and maintain social harmony. Racial segregation does not treat all human beings justly and leads to a fundamentally disharmonious social state. Even if such a practice has the force of "custom" supporting it, Aquinas maintains that the customs of human communities, useful as they may be in specifying and applying the natural law, cannot change the universally binding principles of natural law and must yield when they conflict (ST, Ia–IIae.97.3.ad 1). In what follows, I will focus on Aquinas's concept of natural law, its metaethical foundation, and the general principles of which it consists to guide moral behavior and the formulation of valid human laws.[12]

Aquinas defines natural law as "nothing other than the participation in eternal law by rational creatures" (ST, Ia–IIae.91.2). By virtue of our capacity for rational thought, human beings are able to understand the general principles which underlie the existence of particular beings, actions, and events. For example, everything that exists is governed by the principle of noncontradiction, which states that the same thing – whether it is a substance, action, or event – cannot both *be* and *not be* at the same time, in the same place, in the same respect. Hence, it cannot be both raining in this very spot at this very moment and not raining in this very spot at this very moment. As another example, I can be both tall with respect to my 7-year-old daughter and not tall with respect to an NBA basketball center; but I cannot be both tall and not tall with respect to my daughter at this very moment.

Just as there are general principles that underlie what Aquinas terms "speculative" matters, such as the nature of reality, mathematics, geometry, etc., there are also general principles that underlie what Aquinas terms "practical" matters, such as what a moral agent ought to do in a particular situation (ST, Ia–IIae.94.2; QDV, XVI.1). Some of these general principles are "self-evident" because they are immediately knowable by the human mind without any empirical investigation required. Everyone acts, for example, on the principle of noncontradiction, even if they had never seen it formulated before reading the earlier paragraph. No one in their right mind would think that, if Vladimir Putin is the current president of Russia, that it is true that Vladimir Putin is not the current president of Russia. By the same token, Aquinas thinks that certain general practical principles are self-evident to any rational mind.

This leads Aquinas to formulate the first, fundamental principle of natural law that is understood by the human mind: "Good is to be done and pursued, and evil avoided" (ST, Ia-IIae.94.2). He then contends, "And upon this are founded all other principles of natural law; such that everything which practical reason naturally apprehends to be good [or evil] for human beings belongs to the natural law principles to be done or avoided" (ST, Ia-IIae.94.2). Hence, natural law mandates us to use our reasoning capacity to determine what is "good" in accordance with our nature as rational animals and go after it, and avoid whatever we determine to be "evil" because it is opposed to our flourishing as human beings. While Aquinas provides one of the most determinate formulations of natural law, he certainly did not invent the concept, nor was he the first to exhort that laws made by human legislators were subject to immutable, universal moral principles founded upon a metaphysical conception of human nature and the universe as a whole. The pre-Socratic philosopher Heraclitus argued that there is a fundamental order in nature to which human reason conforms in making laws – both descriptive laws about nature and prescriptive laws guiding human behavior – and that such laws derive their authority from the unchanging and eternal law of nature (Rommen, 1948, pp. 5–6). This basic concept of natural law persisted throughout the Greek philosophical tradition, coming to fruition in the Stoic school that most prominently influenced the great thinkers of the Roman Empire, such as Cicero and the emperor Marcus Aurelius. Due to the influence of Cicero and other Roman jurists that followed him, the relationship between human law and natural law became more refined as it was enacted in Roman jurisprudence and adopted by notable figures in early Christian thought (Rommen, 1948, pp. 21–45). The refinement of the natural law theory culminated in Aquinas's account as described earlier.[13]

This basic understanding of Aquinas's natural law ethic prompts the consideration of its metaethical foundation. What is required in order for Aquinas's theory of natural law to be coherent and sound? As noted above, the most fundamental metaethical foundation is the convertibility of being and goodness. More must be said, however, to allow for a fully developed and sound theory of human morality based on human natural inclinations.

Anthony Lisska (1996, p. 120) highlights five concepts that Aquinas requires as necessary conditions for a coherent account of natural law:

1   the possibility of essences or natural kinds;
2   a dispositional view of essential properties determining the content of a natural kind;
3   a metaphysics of finality determining the obligatory ends central to human well-being;
4   an adequate epistemological apparatus providing an awareness of essences or natural kinds in the individual;
5   a theory of practical reason undertaking the ends to be pursued in terms of human nature.

These concepts, in addition to the convertibility of being and goodness, provide a foundation for Aquinas's natural law theory. If the concepts are themselves sound, then there are definable specific natures of things in the world; each nature is defined by a set of essential properties that incline each individual of that nature to pursue certain fulfilling ends; and, for rational natures at least, it is possible for individuals to understand their own nature and that of other things in the world such that they can choose which ends to pursue in order to satisfy their natural inclinations. Aquinas concludes:

> Therefore, natural law is nothing other than a concept naturally instilled in a human being by which he is directed toward acting in accord with his proper actions; whether they are suitable to him from his generic nature, such as to procreate, to eat, and the like, or from his specific nature, such as to reason and the like.
>
> (ST, Supp.65.1)

If these concepts form the metaethical foundation of Aquinas's natural law theory, then what remains for a human moral agent to reason about are the ends they should pursue that are fulfilling to their nature as a rational animal. To discover the relevant ends, they must consider first their specific nature as a rational animal, which I elucidated in the first half of this chapter, and then what natural inclinations they have as a rational animal.

After conducting such a reflection, Aquinas cites the following "goods" with respect to human nature toward which human beings are naturally inclined: life, sexual intercourse, education of offspring, knowing the truth about God, and living in society (ST, Ia-IIae.94.2; Armstrong, 1966, pp. 47–50). Aquinas acknowledges that this list is not complete and exhorts the prudent use of practical reason to determine the set of goods and evils relative to human nature, and then to define the principles of natural law which promote the goods while avoiding the evils.[14] For example, since human beings are "social" by nature (In NE, I.9), it is good for us to live in community; fulfilling this good requires that we be honest with one another and keep our promises (ST, IIa-IIae.88.3.ad 1), avoid deception (ST, IIa-IIae.110.3), as well as respect others' property and not injure one another (SCG, III.129; Armstrong, 1966, p. 77). As a general natural law principle to guide human beings in our relationships with each other for the sake of forming a stable society, Aquinas cites the Golden Rule: "Do not have done to another what you do not wish to be done to you" (ST, Supp.65.1.ad 7). R. A. Armstrong notes several more specific natural law principles that can be derived from this general principle:

> But from this general precept, we see that we have the duty not only to refrain from murder, but also to avoid injuring one another. More positively we have the duty of aiding the preservation of health, of preventing avoidable unhappiness and pain... Contemplation of this principle shows us the wrongness of slavery and the wrongness of using other people for medical experimentation.

Likewise we see the wrongness of masochism, sadism, the inflicting of bodily harm, torture and suicide.

(1966, p. 111)

As mentioned above, it also follows from our social nature to treat each other justly and not segregate different racial groups from one another.

Aquinas cites further specific natural law principles that follow from the natural inclination to educate one's offspring. Such education is not simply the imparting of knowledge, but the more general sense of "upbringing" that includes moral education and everything else a child needs to learn in order to pass successfully into adulthood (SCG, III.122–3; ST, IIa-IIae.57.4). Thus, for example, one ought not to engage in "simple fornication" – that is, casual sex – that may result in a pregnancy for which one does not intend to take responsibility. Lack of parental responsibility, on the part of both fathers and mothers, hinders the fulfillment of a child's upbringing (ST, IIa-IIae.154.2).

Aquinas contends that various natural law principles can be known by the human mind either immediately, with little reflection, or only with a great deal of reasoning (ST, Ia-IIae.100.1). Nevertheless, it is expedient, on Aquinas's view, for God sometimes to reveal directly certain general natural law principles. As a prime example, the Decalogue, or "Ten Commandments," contain a number of natural law principles which, though divinely revealed, are discoverable by human reason alone (ST, Ia-IIae.100.3; CDP). As Heinrich Rommen explains:

> The Decalogue contains the most essential conclusions [from the first principle of natural law] for the simple reason that its precepts do not result from an arbitrary arrangement made by God, but from the fundamental distinction of good and evil. The first table of the Decalogue (first three Commandments) embraces the moral norms that relate to the worship of God; these required a special promulgation, in the view of St. Thomas, because they are not so evident as the laws found in the second table. The latter (the last seven Commandments), which are derived from the mutual relations among men and from the essence and goal of human nature, are, on the other hand, known more readily and with greater evidence.
>
> (1948, pp. 51–2)

The natural law thus includes prohibitions against murder, theft, adultery, covetousness, lying, and dishonoring one's parents.[15]

In addition to the human goods and correlative natural law principles Aquinas himself enumerates, contemporary natural law theorists have cited other goods and principles that arguably follow from the Thomistic understanding of human natural inclinations. Gerard Hughes lists food, shelter, proper medical treatment, affection, support, and "a fairly clear role in society" as necessary for a human being to fulfill their proper "function" as a rational, social animal (Hughes, 1976, p. 35). John Finnis identifies seven "basic forms of good for us": life, knowledge, play, aesthetic experience, sociability/friendship, practical reasonableness, and religion

(Finnis, 1980, pp. 86–94). While only some of these items are found explicitly in Aquinas's writings, a case can be made for all of them being in the "spirit" of Aquinas's natural law ethic.

An important issue that I can address here only briefly concerns the relationship of Aquinas's concept of natural law and the existence of God. Is God's existence necessary for a coherent and sound Thomistic account of natural law? Does the nature of God's relationship to human morality, if there is a relationship, entail a "divine command ethic"? Lisska answers the first question negatively when he argues, "The existence of God is, in a structural sense, neither a relevant concept nor a necessary condition for Aquinas's account of natural law" (Lisska, 1996, p. 120; see Finnis, 1998, pp. 304–12). This is an important consideration because Aquinas's moral theory is often taken to be theologically defined due to his description of natural law as rational beings' participation in God's eternal law. It thus seems that we must add eternal law as a necessary metaethical foundation for Aquinas's natural law theory. But the fact that Aquinas cites God as a metaethical foundation of human morality, just as he cites God as the metaphysical foundation of human existence, does not entail that the nature of human existence or morality requires divine determination. It is the consideration of human natural inclinations that grounds our understanding of natural law principles, and not an arbitrary set of revealed divine commands (ST, Ia-IIae.94.2). Even the commandments of the Decalogue *reflect* what is in accordance with the natural law as opposed to *defining* morality.[16] Despite Aquinas's appeal to God as a metaethical foundation for human morality, actual belief in God and divinely revealed law is not required for moral knowledge or the validity of natural law principles.

For Aquinas, God is the creative source by which beings in the universe have a specific essence or belong to a natural kind, have certain dispositional properties relative to their essence, and have obligatory ends that promote their well-being relative to their essence. God also provides rational beings with the epistemological apparatus and practical reasoning capacity required to be aware of their essence and the ends to be pursued that promote their well-being. Aquinas, however, argues that the human mind cannot apprehend the eternal law itself, because we are not God (ST, Ia-IIae.19.4.ad 3, Ia-IIae.93.2). Therefore, apprehension of natural law principles must be based upon something knowable by the human mind – namely, human natural inclinations. One could respond that the revealed divine law provides a better epistemological foundation for moral awareness, and that morality is thus best understood as theologically defined. Aquinas, though, contends that divine law is something distinct from natural law that is added to it, and in fact presupposes natural law (ST, Ia-IIae.99.2.ad 1). Therefore, the existence of natural law principles knowable by the human mind is logically prior to the principles of divine law, which serves to define more clearly and enforce natural law.

This completes my brief elucidation of Aquinas's natural law ethic. My goal here has been simply to show how Aquinas grounds his moral theory and systematically formulates certain foundational moral principles. In Chapters 4 and 5, I will apply some of the natural law principles described above, and additional relevant secondary principles, to bioethical issues at the margins of human life. In the remainder of this chapter, I address an additional issue regarding Aquinas's moral theory: whether he holds the Principle of Double Effect (PDE), which is often appealed to in order to justify certain forms of medical treatment that will be discussed in Chapters 4 and 5.

Aquinas and the principle of double effect[17]

I will begin by offering a simple formulation of PDE, which states that an action taken to produce some consequence, that is a "good" *per se*, may be permissible even if the action produces a foreseen negative consequence, that is *per se* morally impermissible. This principle holds provided that the relative value of the negative consequence does not outweigh that of the good consequence, and the negative consequence is not *directly intended* as an end or the means by which the good consequence is brought about.

I argue that Aquinas's account of intentional action allows one to hold this formulation of PDE. As Gareth Matthews and Thomas Cavanaugh both indicate, it is not evident that Aquinas would assent to many contemporary formulations of PDE (Cavanaugh, 1997; Matthews, 1999). Cavanaugh contends that the oft-quoted passage in which Aquinas appears to express PDE is limited to only certain restricted types of cases involving self-defense. I will begin by examining what Aquinas says in the key passage from ST, IIa-IIae.64.7, which concerns the permissibility of killing an aggressor in defense of one's own life. I will highlight a general principle expressed in this passage that allows one, together with other principles of Aquinas's account of intentional action, to derive the formulation of PDE given above.

Many contemporary scholars claim that Aquinas holds PDE based on this passage:

> Nothing prohibits one act from having two effects, only one of which is in the intention, while the other is outside the intention. Now moral acts receive their species according to that which is intended, but not from that which is outside the intention.
>
> (ST, IIa-IIae.64.7)

Aquinas is addressing the question of "Whether it is permitted for someone to kill someone else in defending themselves?" In the type of case in question, by performing an act of preserving one's own life, one brings about the aggressor's death. Stephen Brock summarizes Aquinas's position regarding this type of case:

> It is never licit for a private person to aim to kill someone, i.e. to act precisely in order to bring about a person's death, even as a way of defending himself against an attack. But in defending himself, it may be licit to use means which,

in addition to having the effect of conserving one's life by putting a stop to the attack, also have the effect of the aggressor's death. This is licit when the use of such means is "proportionate," or not more violent than is necessary to stop the attack.

(1998, p. 221; cf. Montaldi, 1986)

An added stricture is that death is unavoidably necessary in order to achieve the good of preserving one's life. Furthermore, Aquinas is referring to causing the death of an "aggressor" – that is, one from whom the threat to life directly comes. Cavanaugh and Matthews are correct in cautioning that Aquinas does not appear to offer an unqualified assertion of PDE, which can be immediately applied to cases outside of defending one's life against an aggressor.

Nevertheless, in addressing the specific case of self-preservation, Aquinas makes what seems to be a fairly generalizable assertion: "Nothing prohibits one act from having two effects, only one of which is in the intention, while the other is outside the intention" (ST, IIa-IIae.64.7). I will explore whether this assertion is indeed generalizable across other types of cases besides self-defense in a way that allows for such "double-effect" cases to be morally permissible.

Aquinas states that every human action can be considered as good or evil with respect to four different categories:

> In a human action a fourfold goodness can be considered. First, according to genus – viz., insofar as it is an act – because to the extent that it has being as an act, it has goodness…In another way according to species, which is received according to the appropriate object. Third, according to the circumstances, as if in accordance with certain accidents. Finally, fourth, according to the end, as if in accordance with the condition toward the cause of its goodness.
>
> (ST, Ia-IIae.18.4)

An action's genus is merely the action as such. Its species is the particular kind of action it is – the "form" or "object" of the action: "what is done." Circumstances, as Aquinas says, are the accidents attendant upon an action – for example, the place and time the action occurs, and any other quality that is not part of the action's definition as the kind of action it is. An action's end is its intended goal.

Two questions need to be answered. First, under which of the four categories does a foreseen negative consequence fall in double-effect cases? It is not the action as such or the object of the action. It is also not what is directly intended. The two remaining options are that it is either part of the end or an accidental circumstance attendant upon the action. The second question concerns how the fact that the negative consequence is somehow part of the action affects the action's goodness and moral permissibility.

An agent in a *bona fide* double-effect case does not directly intend the negative consequence of their action. It is a foreseen concomitant consequence of their directly intended action. Joseph Boyle claims that foreseen consequences of a directly intended action,

> which follow always or for the most part [i.e., are concomitant]...are not *per se* intended and thus can be called *praeter intentionem* [outside the agent's intention]...This is not to deny that in some sense it cannot be separated from the agent's intention, or that it is *per accidens* intended, or that it is in some sense willed by him.
>
> (Boyle, 1978, p. 660; cf. Boyle and Sullivan, 1977;
Boyle, 1980, 1989; Boyle et al., 2001)

Foreseen concomitant consequences are separated from an agent's intention, but not completely separated; they are still willed in some respect. Aquinas states, "What always or frequently is joined to an effect falls under the same intention. It is foolish to say that someone intends something and does not will that which is frequently or always joined to it" (In Ph, II.8; trans. Boyle); "If the evil is joined always or for the most part to the good which is intended *per se*, one is not excused from sin although he does not *per se* intend this evil" (QDM, I.3.ad 15; trans. Boyle). I will return to the issue of an agent's responsibility for consequences that they do not directly intend. The key point here is that the foreseen concomitant consequences of an agent's directly intended action are *praeter intentionem* – outside the agent's intention – and are thus *per accidens* – that is, they are "accidental" features of the directly intended action.

If an action's foreseen concomitant consequences are accidental circumstances, how do such circumstances affect the action's goodness, its moral permissibility, and the agent's culpability? Aquinas asserts, "The primary goodness of a moral action is considered from its suitable object" (ST, Ia-IIae.18.2). He also asserts that an action must be good not only in its object, but in all four of the above-named respects: "Yet an action is not good simply, unless all goods concur" (ST, Ia-IIae.18.4.ad 3) – that is, the action is good in its genus (of which the goodness is given), object, circumstances, and end. Aquinas specifically refers to the circumstances: "The plenitude of [an action's] goodness does not consist wholly in its species, but to some extent is added from what comes to it as certain accidents. And such are its due circumstances" (ST, Ia-IIae.18.3); "The circumstances of actions are considered in moral doctrine" (ST, Ia-IIae.18.3.ad 2). In double-effect cases, there is a defect in the goodness of the circumstances, due to the negative consequence. Hence, the action is not good "simply" (*simpliciter*); but this defect need not entail that the action is morally impermissible or that the agent has "sinned."

In ST, Ia-IIae.18.5, Aquinas argues that whether an action is good or evil is part of its species. For one considers an action's object as either good or evil – for example, if the object is to steal something, it is evil, whereas if the object is to help someone, it is good. In ST, Ia-IIae.18.10–11, Aquinas addresses the issue of whether an action's circumstances can change its species from good to evil. He answers that circumstances do not change an action's species, but they can make a good action better or an evil action worse (ST, Ia-IIae.18.11).

There is a caveat, though. Whenever a circumstance that "is considered as a principle condition of the object...is specially ordered to reason, either for or against, the circumstances must specify the moral act as either good or bad" (ST, Ia-IIae.18.10). By "principal condition of the object," Aquinas means that the circumstance is part of the object's definition. His example is stealing from a holy place as opposed to stealing merely someone else's possession. The circumstance of "place," in this case, defines the act as one of "sacrilege" and not merely "theft." It is thus a different kind of action. This example is one in which an already evil action – theft – is changed into another worse kind of evil action – sacrilege. Aquinas also states that the appropriation of property, which is *per se* morally permissible, becomes evil if the action includes the defining circumstance of the appropriated property being "another's" (ST, Ia-IIae.18.10). Here, a good action is changed to an evil action due to one of its circumstances.

In ST, Ia-IIae.20.5, Aquinas speaks directly about an action's consequences: "An event following [i.e., a consequence] does not make an act bad which was good or good which was bad" (ST, Ia-IIae.20.5). On the specific issue of an action's foreseen consequences, Aquinas states, "If it is foreseen, it is clear that it adds to the goodness or malice" (ST, Ia-IIae.20.5). Aquinas does not assert that foreseen consequences can change an action's specific nature from good to evil; but they can make a good action better or an evil action worse.[18]

One cannot ignore, however, the fact that such a defect in an action's attendant circumstances prevents the action from being good "simply" or having the "plenitude of goodness." Does this entail that the action is morally impermissible? Aquinas states:

> It must be said that evil is broader than sin, just as good is broader than right. For every privation of good in anything whatsoever designates the idea of evil; but sin properly consists of an act that is done for a certain end, where it does not have due order toward that end.
>
> (ST, Ia-IIae.21.1)

Although an action in a double-effect case lacks goodness in some respect, this lack does not entail that the agent has "sinned." In fact, it would seem that they have not sinned because their action was rightly ordered to a good end.

I now return to Boyle's contention that a particular concomitant consequence, which follows from a directly intended action, may be *per accidens* and thus *praeter intentionem*, but not completely separated from an agent's volition: "The unintended evil effect...is clearly imputable to the agent: he knowingly and willingly brings it about" (Boyle, 1980, p. 529); "What one intends and what one permits are both voluntarily brought about, and thus *both* are imputable" (Boyle, 1980, p. 530). Stephen Brock agrees that "Foreseen side-effects cannot be outside the agent's intention in such a way as to remove his responsibility for them or their imputability to him" (1998, p. 213). "Responsibility," here, refers to an agent being "answerable for [an action], able to be called to account, fit to be asked *why* he did it" (Brock 1998, p. 213).

An agent is not immediately morally culpable for the foreseen concomitant consequences of their intentional action. Rather, the agent is merely "responsible" as the one who brought about such consequences when they could have avoided them by not performing the directly intended action with which the consequences were concomitant. This requires the agent to give a justifying explanation for bringing about such consequences: "Thus if the agent is certain that he will bring about such an effect, he cannot reject the question 'Why?' as irrelevant. A *contravening reason* is required" (Sullivan, 2000, p. 447). The appropriate "contravening reason" by which an agent can exonerate themselves is the goodness of the directly intended object and end of their action.

Consider, for example, a case in which a pregnant woman discovers she has a form of cancer which, if left untreated by aggressive means, will be terminal. By undergoing radiation and chemotherapy, her unborn child may be harmed or aborted. Assuming that the values of both the mother's and the unborn child's lives are of equal value, it is morally permissible for her to undergo the aggressive treatment in order to preserve her life, even though it is foreseen to produce what would, under normal circumstances, be an impermissible consequence.[19]

By respectively administering and consenting to receive the aggressive treatment, both the physician and the mother cannot avoid being accused of performing an action that resulted in the harm or abortion. This action, however, may be justified by explaining that the child's deformation or death was not directly intended. Rather, the preservation of the mother's life was directly intended and the harm or abortion was a foreseen accidental consequence, which was unavoidably concomitant with the act of providing the treatment necessary to preserve the mother's life.

I thus conclude that Aquinas's account of intentional action and moral appraisal allows an agent to be morally justified in directly intending a good end while at the same time being responsible for any foreseen concomitant negative consequences. I will apply this conclusion to certain types of cases in Chapters 4 and 5.

Conclusion

Aquinas's accounts of human nature and morality have been foundational for the Roman Catholic and broader Christian approach to medical practice. Nevertheless, the wider community remains largely influenced by antithetical postmodern conceptions of human nature and morality. These include the metaphysical views that human beings are nothing but biological organisms, are simply brains in bodies, or are "persons" only insofar as they have a sufficiently rich mental life, as well as ethical theories such as utilitarianism, emotivism, relativism, or subjectivism. Advancing the Thomistic viewpoint in pluralistic, secular discussions of bioethical issues is a valuable and feasible pursuit because Aquinas's conception of human nature and his natural law ethic can be coherently formulated and understood without theological appeal. The former is grounded foremost in Aristotelian philosophy and human beings' phenomenological experience of their psychosomatic nature. The latter is founded upon a teleological understanding of human nature and not an arbitrary set of revealed divine commands

(Lisska, 1996, pp. 116–38). While Aquinas often refers to Judeo-Christian theological tenets and revealed Scripture in his philosophical writings, his purpose for such references is in many cases, as Norman Kretzmann points out in reference to Aquinas's *Summa contra gentiles*, to show "that what has just been achieved by unaided reason agrees with what he takes to be revealed truth" (Kretzmann, 1997, p. 7). Therefore, one does not have to be a Roman Catholic, a Christian, or even a theist to consider Aquinas's philosophical accounts of human nature and morality, and their relevance to certain bioethical issues at the margins of human life.

2   The beginning of a human person's life

Introduction

Bioethicists sometimes neglect or outright reject metaphysics as useless for offering conclusive arguments about the beginning and end of human life. Nevertheless, various positions regarding issues related to the limits of human life often presuppose some metaphysical understanding of human nature. Hence, there is at least a tacit need to adopt a metaphysical account of human nature for the sake of addressing certain types of bioethical issues. In this chapter and the following, I will provide Thomistic metaphysical conclusions to the questions of when a human person's life begins and ends. These conclusions provide a foundation for responding to issues such as embryonic stem cell research, abortion and the use of abortifacient contraceptives, cloning, care for patients who are in a persistent vegetative state or who are terminally ill, and organ procurement. Complete responses to these issues, though, require combining such metaphysical conclusions with a particular ethical theory and taking various values into account. I will accomplish this task in Chapters 4 and 5.

In addressing issues at the beginning of human life, one primary concern is to establish when a developing human embryo or fetus can be considered a "person"; for it is typically held that only persons are the subjects of rights, such as a "right to life." Aquinas argues that all human beings are persons (ST, IIIa.16.12.ad 1), but that an embryo or fetus is not a human being until its body is informed by a "rational soul." Aquinas's explicit account of human embryogenesis has been generally rejected by contemporary scholars due to its dependence upon medieval biological information, which has been far surpassed by current scientific research. A number of scholars, however, have attempted to combine Aquinas's basic metaphysical account of human nature with current embryological data to develop a contemporary Thomistic account of a human being's beginning.[1] The issue at hand in developing such an account is whether "hominization" is "immediate" – occurs when fertilization of an ovum by a sperm cell is complete[2] – or "delayed" – occurs sometime after fertilization. The term hominization refers to when a developing embryo first has a specifically "human" rational soul as its substantial form, or organizing principle. Scholars who argue for either immediate or delayed hominization debate the proper application of Aquinas's metaphysical principle that only an "appropriate" body may be informed by a rational soul to compose a human being.

Scholars who favor delayed hominization, such as Joseph Donceel (Donceel, 1970), Robert Pasnau (Pasnau, 2002), and Norman Ford (Ford, 1988), argue that an early embryo has certain intrinsic qualities which indicate that it is not "an individual substance of a rational nature"[3] until it reaches a certain point in its biological development. Those who favor immediate hominization, such as Benedict Ashley (Ashley, 1976), claim that there is nothing about a human embryo's biological nature, from the moment the process of fertilization is complete, that disallows its being informed by a rational soul. The question to be considered here regards the proper understanding of Aquinas's metaphysical principles and whether current embryological data support the interpretation offered by Donceel, Pasnau, Ford, or Ashley. First, though, I will elucidate Aquinas's explicit account of human embryogenesis.

Aquinas's account of human embryogenesis[4]

Aquinas understands a human being to be composed of a rational soul informing a material body.[5] In defining the necessary and sufficient conditions for something to be informed by a soul – which may be vegetative, sensitive, or rational[6] – Aquinas first notes Aristotle's definition of "soul" as "the actuality of a physical organic body having life potentially" (ST, Ia.76.4.ad 1; cf. Aristotle, 1984, 412a20–1). Aquinas explains this definition as follows:

> It is said that the soul is the actuality of a body, etc., because through the soul it is a body, is organic, and has life potentially. But the first actuality is said to be in potentiality with respect to the second actuality, which is the operation. For such a potentiality does not reject, that is, does not exclude the soul.
>
> (ST, Ia.76.4.ad 1; cf. In DA, II.2)

Aquinas holds that a soul's potentiality to perform its definitive operations – whether life, sensation, or rational thought – is necessary for it to exist (QDA, XII.ad 7). The actualization of such potentiality, however, is *accidental* to the soul's existence: "To be actually thinking or sensing is not substantial being, but accidental" (QDA, XII).

Of course, a developing human embryo or fetus, and even a newborn infant, does not actually exercise all the operations proper to a human being, including rational activity. Nonetheless, Aquinas denies that this lack implies that a rational soul does not inform a developing human embryo, fetus, or newborn infant. All that is required for a rational soul to be present, and thus for a human being to exist, is a human body with the potentiality for a rational soul's proper operations:

> If a human being derives his species by being rational and having an intellect, whoever is within the human species is rational and has an intellect. But a child, even before leaving the womb, is within the human species; although there are yet no phantasms in it which are actually intelligible.
>
> (SCG, II.59)

Concerning the question of when the potentiality for a rational soul's proper operations is first present in a developing human body, Aquinas asserts that a body must have the appropriate organic structure if it is to have a rational soul as its substantial form (QDP, III.12). The appropriate organs for a rational soul are those associated with sensation, because it is through sense-perceptions of particular things that the mind comes to possess intelligible forms, which are the natures of things understood as abstracted from any particular material conditions.[7] The abstraction of intelligible forms from the products of sensation – the "phantasms" referred to in the earlier passage from SCG – is the essence of rational thought as Aquinas defines it: "Therefore, the rational soul ought to be united to a body which may be a suitable organ of sensation" (ST, Ia.76.5; cf. ST, Ia.55.2). This understanding leads Aquinas to develop an account of successive ensoulment in a human embryo's formation. After conception occurs,[8] a material body exists that has a vegetative soul as its substantial form – that is, an entity that has life at its most basic level. As the early embryo develops and its organic structure increases in complexity to the point where it can support sensitive operations, the embryo's vegetative soul is annihilated and its matter is informed by a sensitive soul. Since, according to Aquinas, a thing's identity is determined by its having the same substantial form (Eberl, 2004, pp. 353–9), the early vegetative embryo has ceased to exist and a new embryo has come into existence that is an animal life form with the capacity for sensation.

The final stage of embryonic development occurs when the embryo has developed a sufficiently complex organic structure to allow for rational operations.[9] At this point, the sensitive soul is annihilated and the animal embryo ceases to exist as its matter becomes informed by a rational soul:

> And thus it must be said that the vegetative soul is first in the seed, but it is discarded in the generative process and another succeeds it that is not only vegetative but also sensitive, which, having been discarded, again another is added that at the same time is vegetative, sensitive, and rational.
>
> (QDA, XI.ad 1; cf. QDP, III.9.ad 9; ST, Ia.76.3.ad 3,
> Ia.118.2.ad 2; SCG, II.89; CT, 92;
> QDSC, III.ad 13)

Since Aquinas adopts Boethius's definition of a person as "an individual substance of a rational nature" and all human beings are persons, a developing embryo is neither a person nor a human being until its matter is informed by a rational soul. At this point, one may consider the possibility that a developing embryo, prior to rational ensoulment, is an individual human being, though it is not yet a person. In other words, perhaps you existed as the embryos informed by vegetative and sensitive souls prior to your matter being informed by a rational soul. This view, however, conflicts with Aquinas's understanding of what is essential to human nature. First, Aquinas asserts that every human being is a person (ST, IIIa.16.12.ad 1): personhood is *essential* to human nature. Furthermore, Aquinas's interpretation of the Boethian definition of personhood requires, at minimum, that a rational soul exists as the substantial form of an appropriate physical body. As Brian Leftow points out (Leftow, 2001, p. 129), Aquinas does not consider something "human" unless it is, or has been, "part of a whole, ensouled human body." A developing embryo with human DNA is not necessarily, just for that reason, a human being or part of a human being. Only matter informed by a rational soul fulfills the definition of a human being. Hence, Aquinas's explicit view of human embryogenesis entails that a human being does not exist prior to a rational soul informing a developing embryo.

The basic metaphysical principle Aquinas employs in his account of embryogenesis is that a rational soul does not inform a physical body unless the body is properly disposed for that type of soul. The requisite disposition is the body's having sense organs and a brain capable of imagination such that phantasms of sensible objects may be generated for the mind to abstract intelligible forms, which is the nature of rational thought. A body disposed in such a way does not seem to exist immediately after fertilization, but only after a vegetative embryo first, and then an animal embryo, have existed. Aquinas thus concludes that a living, sensitive, and rational human being does not begin to exist until some point well after conception:[10] "Therefore, it must be said that a rational soul, which at the same time is sensitive and nutritive, is created by God[11] at the end of human generation; the pre-existing forms having been corrupted" (ST, Ia.118.2.ad 2).[12]

Recent interpretations

As mentioned above, Aquinas's explicit account of human embryogenesis has been generally rejected because it is based on outdated biological information. Nevertheless, the basic metaphysical principles Aquinas employs remain sound and have inspired scholars to combine these principles with up-to-date biological data to develop a contemporary Thomistic account of human embryogenesis.

Donceel and Pasnau[13]

Joseph Donceel and Robert Pasnau both contend that a sufficiently organized body, capable of receiving a rational soul as its substantial form, does not exist until the cerebral cortex of the embryonic brain is formed. This conclusion is purported to follow from the fact that a functioning cerebral cortex is required for rational thought to occur because (1) it is the organ of a human being's sensitive and imaginative capacities, and (2) cerebral neural activity is correlated with rational activity.[14] Donceel thus argues:

> Man's higher, spiritual [i.e., rational] faculties have no organs of their own, since they are immaterial, intrinsically independent of matter. But they need, as necessary conditions of their activity, the cooperation of the highest sense powers, imagination, memory, what the Scholastics called the "cogitative power." Its activity presupposes that the brain be fully developed, that the

cortex be ready. Only then is the stage set for another ontological shift; matter now is highly enough organized to receive the highest substantial form, the spiritual, human soul, created by God.

(1970, p. 83)

Donceel refers in this passage to the necessity of neural development for the sake of rational "activity." It is important to recall here that Aquinas, in his account of embryogenesis, never asserts that a fetus must *actually* think rationally in order for it to be a human being. He contends that only the *potentiality* for rational thought must be present. Such potentiality is sufficient for a fetus to be informed by a rational soul. Donceel agrees and yet contends that the potentiality for rational thought is present only when a fetus has developed a functioning cerebral cortex: "The least we may ask before admitting the presence of a human soul is the availability of these organs: the senses, the nervous system, the brain, and especially the cortex" (Donceel, 1970, p. 101). Hence, we must consider carefully Aquinas's notion of "potentiality" and how it should be applied to determine when a human embryo or fetus first has the potentiality for rational thought.

In the passage quoted earlier in this chapter from ST, Ia.76.4.ad 1 and elsewhere, Aquinas distinguishes between a "first" and "second" actuality: "The first act is a thing's form and integrity, and the second act is its operation" (ST, Ia.48.5; cf. In DA, II.2; QDP, I.1). A first actuality is the "active potentiality" to perform some operation. The locus of a substance's set of first actualities, or active potentialities, is its substantial form, which, for a human being, is a rational soul. A second actuality is the operation of a first actuality brought about through some additional cause (QDV, V.8.ad 10). In contrast to an active potentiality, something has a "passive potentiality" if it can be the subject of externally directed change such that it can become what it is not already.

In addition to the difference between a first and a second actuality, it must be noted that the first actuality comes in two varieties. The first is what Pasnau refers to as a "capacity in hand" to perform an operation, which means that no further development or significant change is required for the potentiality to be actualized (Pasnau, 2002, p. 115). For example, I have, as a first actuality, the capacity to speak Spanish – having majored in it in college along with philosophy. It just happens to be the case at this moment that I am not using this capacity and so it is not in a state of second actuality, which it would be if I were actually speaking Spanish right now. It is apparent that Donceel has this construal of first actuality in mind when he asserts that the potentiality for rational thought is present only after cerebral development. The second is what Norman Kretzmann refers to as a substance's "natural potentiality" to develop a capacity to perform an operation (Kretzmann, 1999, p. 39). For example, before I learned to speak Spanish and thus developed a capacity to do so, I had a natural potentiality to develop this capacity. I have numerous other natural potentialities, some of which I have developed into capacities in hand, such as my capacity to play chess, and others which I have left undeveloped, such as my potentiality to learn to read Sanskrit.

In applying the concepts of first and second actuality to the presence of a rational soul, Aquinas contends that all that is required for a rational soul to inform a particular body is that the body has an active potentiality to perform the operations proper to a rational soul – vegetative, sensitive, and rational. The actual performance of these operations is accidental to the soul's existence (QDA, XII). Thus, since a rational soul is a human body's substantial form, the existence of a human body with active potentialities for life, sensation, and rational thought entails that it is informed by a rational soul. It is inconsequential whether such operations are actually exercised in a body for a rational soul to inform it: "A soul in first actuality *is* a *soul*: a sleeping animal continues to have an *actual* sensory soul, just not an *actually operating* sensory soul" (Kretzmann, 1999, p. 379, note 27; see ST, Ia.118.1.ad 4).

With respect to a human embryo, Aquinas asserts, "Just as the soul in an embryo is in act, but imperfectly, so also it operates, but imperfect operations" (QDA, XI.ad 9). By the soul being "in act," Aquinas refers to a soul being present in a human embryo as its first actuality. The soul being "imperfectly" in act refers to the fact that a human embryo does not yet exhibit all the soul's powers as second actualities. Aquinas concludes that a soul thus "operates" in a human embryo as its substantial form and in the actual exercise of at least vegetative, and possibly also sensitive, operations; but the soul performs "imperfect operations" in that it does not fully exercise all its proper operations until later in the embryo's development.

In contrast to a sleeping animal that is sensitive, because it has an active potentiality for sensation, sperm and ova do not have such an active potentiality. Rather, sperm and ova are best understood as having a passive potentiality to become a living, sensitive, and rational human being:

> [Things] are always in potentiality to actuality when they can be reduced to actuality by their proper active principle with nothing external hindering them. However, seed is not yet such. For it must be by many changes that an animal comes from it. But when by its proper active principle, namely, something actually existing, it can already become such, it is then already in potentiality.
>
> (In M, IX.6.1837)

The "seed" of a living animal – that is, a sperm cell or ovum – cannot be said to be a living animal, because it has merely a passive potentiality to become such. The seed must first undergo a change brought about by an extrinsic principle: sperm must be changed through union with an ovum and vice versa, which transforms them into a substance with active potentialities for a living animal's definitive operations. Once this "substantial change" occurs, a living animal exists even if it is not actually exercising all its definitive operations.

The change required for something to actualize an active or passive potentiality is brought about by its "proper active principle." An active principle is required because a potentiality can be actualized only by something that is already in a state of actuality. Something can be moved from a state of potentiality to a state of actuality only by some active principle that is either internal or external to it. A sufficient condition for something's having an active potentiality is if it can actualize the potentiality by some active principle *internal* to it. In his explicit account of embryogenesis, Aquinas does not recognize the presence of an active internal principle in a zygote – a fertilized ovum – or early embryo which indicates that it has an active potentiality to develop the proper organs required for rational thought. This lack of recognition, though, is due to Aquinas not being aware of how DNA functions in a zygote or early embryo to guide its natural development such that it comes to have the requisite organs. Aquinas postulates a "formative power" (*virtus formativa*), which is transmitted by the male semen and thereby is extrinsic to a zygote or early embryo, that guides its development (SCG, II.89).[15] The contemporary understanding of DNA, however, places the formative power in a zygote or early embryo itself. This fact would arguably motivate Aquinas to define a zygote or early embryo as having an active potentiality for rational operations, since it has an active internal principle guiding it to develop the requisite organs for such operations to occur (Wade, 1975; Reichlin, 1997).[16]

Donceel contends that only a functioning cerebral cortex provides the proper material organization for rational thought and thus is the only sufficient evidence that a fetus has of an active potentiality for such operations. But this contention overlooks the distinction between a natural potentiality and a capacity in hand. It must be noted that, from the moment the fertilization process is complete, a zygote has a complete human genome and other material factors that are *sufficient* – given a nutritive uterine environment – for it to develop a functioning cerebral cortex. From this fact, one can infer that a zygote or early embryo, before it forms a functioning cerebral cortex, has an active potentiality for rational thought insofar as it has a natural potentiality to develop a capacity in hand for such operations.

Pasnau argues that a zygote or early embryo does not have an active potentiality for rational thought by asserting that Aquinas defines an active potentiality as having a capacity in hand to perform some operation (Pasnau, 2002, p. 115). He thereby denies that a natural potentiality, as defined above by Kretzmann, is a type of active potentiality. Pasnau uses the distinction between an assembled hammer, which has a capacity in hand to drive nails, and unassembled pieces of metal and wood, which lack a capacity in hand to drive nails. In the first case, no further change is required to the hammer's constitution in order for it to drive nails; whereas, in the second case, an external agent must assemble the metal and wood pieces for them to have a capacity in hand to drive nails, and so they have merely a passive potentiality. Pasnau concludes that a zygote or early embryo is akin to the unassembled parts of a hammer. It has only a passive potentiality to develop into an organism with a capacity in hand for rational thought.

Pasnau is correct in holding that if the development of a zygote or early embryo depends upon the assembling powers of some external agent, then it does not have an active internal principle for developing into a being that actually thinks rationally. It thus would have merely a passive potentiality for rational thought, and would not be informed by a rational soul. Contemporary genetic understanding, however, indicates that a zygote or early embryo has an active internal principle guiding its development into a being that actually thinks rationally; it has an active potentiality for rational thought in the sense of a natural potentiality. A zygote or early embryo is not akin to the unassembled pieces of a hammer; while such pieces depend upon an external agent to assemble them in the proper fashion, a zygote or early embryo has no such need. Given a supportive environment – one that provides simply nutrition, oxygen, and protection from harmful external influences – a zygote or early embryo will develop into a being that has a capacity in hand for rational thought and that actually thinks rationally. That the actualization of this potentiality requires time and internal development does not count against its being an *active* potentiality.

A zygote or early embryo and a hammer differ greatly in that the former is a "natural substance," whereas the latter is an "artifact." Aquinas's Aristotelian understanding of the distinction between natural substances and artifacts leads to different conclusions about what is required for there to be an active potentiality in each type of thing. Pasnau correctly understands Aquinas's criterion for an artifact to have an active potentiality for performing its proper function and thus being the type of artifact it is. An assembled hammer requires no further change in its constitution in order to actualize its potentiality to drive nails; it thus has a hammer's definitive capacity as an active potentiality, and thereby *is* a hammer. The unassembled pieces of a hammer, on the other hand, require change in their constitution brought about by an external agent before being able to actualize a hammer's definitive capacity, and thus are not yet a hammer.

For a natural substance, though, its *ordered natural development*, the principle of which is active and internal to it, is sufficient for it to *be* that toward which it is developing. Though I have not found an explicit statement by Aquinas on this point, it is likely that he would follow Aristotle, who concludes in his *De generatione animalium*:

> When we are dealing with definite and ordered products of nature, we must not say each *is* of a certain quality because it *becomes* so, but rather that they *become* so and so because they *are* so and so, for the process of becoming attends upon being and is for the sake of being, not *vice versa*.
>
> (Aristotle, 1984, 778b2–6; see Reichlin, 1997, p. 15)

A key difference between a natural substance and an artifact is the location of their respective "formal causes."[17] When a builder is building a house, the formal cause of the house is the idea the builder has in their mind of how the house should appear – that is, what structure it is to have – once completed. Perhaps this idea has been materially instantiated in a blueprint. Once the house is completed to the builder's satisfaction, in accord with the mental or printed blueprint, the formal cause is now located in the house itself. The matter, having been assembled in the proper fashion, has taken on the form of the house which had previously been found only in the blueprint. The form of the house is not present in the matter composing it until the building process is complete.

For a natural substance, however, there is no analogue to the builder in whose mind the formal cause of the substance is located – putting aside the possibility that

God acts as such a builder. Rather, the formal cause must be located in the natural substance itself as it is developing toward its final appearance and structure. Its blueprint is internal to it in a way that a house's blueprint is not, since the latter has an *external* efficient cause that brings it from being potentially a house to being actually a house. A natural substance, which has an *internal* efficient cause of its development, must be guided in its development by the formal cause already instantiated in it as it moves from being, for example, a human being with the potential for rational thought to a human being who actually thinks rationally after having developed the requisite organic structure. A human being's form is thus present in the matter composing it from the moment its development begins.

I conclude that the interpretations offered by Donceel and Pasnau,[18] while they closely follow what Aquinas explicitly says concerning embryogenesis, do not correctly take account of the role Aquinas's nuanced concept of "active potentiality" plays in defining the nature of a zygote or early embryo in the light of contemporary genetic understanding. Evidence that a zygote or early embryo has an active internal principle guiding its ordered natural development into a being that actually thinks rationally is sufficient, I contend, to conclude that it is already a rational being. It has an active potentiality for rational thought and is thereby informed by a rational soul. Thus far, I have consistently referred to "a zygote or early embryo," because a contentious issue among interpreters of Aquinas concerns whether a one-celled zygote – the immediate product of conception – or an early embryo – formed approximately two weeks after conception – should be properly understood as informed by a rational soul. The remainder of this chapter offers an adjudication of this debate.

Ford

Norman Ford argues that neither an active potentiality for rational thought, nor an embryo's existence as an "individual substance," is possible until approximately fourteen days after fertilization is complete. At this time, the embryo implants on the wall of its mother's uterus and begins to form the "primitive streak," which is the "epigenetic primordium"[19] of the central nervous system: the brain and spinal cord. The primitive streak's formation indicates that an embryo is beginning to develop a cerebral cortex and thereby demonstrates its having an active potentiality to engage in rational operations. The occurrence of this event also signals an end to the possibility of twinning: an embryo's division into one or more genetically identical separate organisms. Ford contends that a preimplantation embryo's intrinsic capacity to twin indicates that it is not a unified, individual substance; rather, it is a conglomeration of individual cells.[20] Once twinning is no longer possible and an embryo's cells have begun to function collectively as one organism – evidenced by the loss of cellular totipotentiality[21] – there is sufficient evidence to warrant the assertion that the embryo is informed by a rational soul. Thus, Ford concludes, a human being begins to exist about two weeks after conception.

While the event of uterine implantation coincides with formation of the primitive streak, it is the latter that signals the beginning of a human being on this account (Smith, 1983, p. 206). Furthermore, while the primitive streak's appearance provides evidence that an implanted embryo has an active potentiality for rational thought, it is the impossibility of division into genetically identical twins, once the primitive streak appears, which signals the embryo's existence as a unified, individual substance and not a conglomeration of distinct substances. The key biological markers, according to Ford, which indicate an embryo's existence as "an individual substance of a rational nature," are the impossibility of twinning, the loss of cellular totipotentiality and the beginning of differentiation into embryonic and extraembryonic tissues, and the beginning of organized cellular functioning to sustain the life of *one* organism.

Ford begins his case by considering the possibility that an individual human being begins to exist at conception. He asserts that at the completion of fertilization, there exists something that has a unique genetic identity and a unique ontological identity *as a biological cell*. It does not, however, have a unique ontological identity *as a human being*. After the first mitotic event – the first division of a one-celled zygote – two cells exist which have the same *genetic* identity, but are *ontologically* distinct (Ford, 1988, p. 117, 2001, p. 160, 2002, p. 65). The same follows for every event of cellular mitosis until the point is reached when mitosis that results in ontologically distinct beings can no longer occur.

The ontological uniqueness of each cell in a preimplantation embryo is evidenced by the lack of differentiation among them. Cells remain undetermined for quite some time as to where they will go and what role they will play in the developing organism. The same indeterminism occurs in cases of twinning. A single cluster of cells is shared in the early developmental process by what will become two ontologically distinct organisms; to which organism each cell will ultimately go is largely undetermined (Ford, 1988, pp. 133–5).

Another implication of cellular indeterminacy in a preimplantation embryo is that a great number of cells, once they become differentiated from other cells, are used to form extraembryonic material: the trophoblast (Ford, 1988, p. 124). These cells do not contribute to the "embryo proper." Only the "inner cell mass" (ICM) is differentiated from the cells that form the trophoblast to form the embryo itself. Furthermore, there is no strict determiner for which cells will form the trophoblast versus the ICM. Ford points out that it is a matter of which cells are spatially located in relation to other cells and the outer membrane – *zona pellucida* – that places cells into the trophoblast or ICM. Carlos Bedate and Robert Cefalo also note the requirement of "positional information" for cellular differentiation and development in a preimplantation embryo. They argue that the requirement for such information, which is not coded in a preimplantation embryo's DNA but results from the interaction of embryonic molecules with maternal molecules, implies that "an individual zygote does not possess in itself all the necessary, and surely not sufficient, information to become a human person" (Bedate and Cefalo, 1989, p. 644). A zygote thus appears to have only a passive potentiality to become a human being, because it requires extrinsic information for its development.

Differentiation into the trophoblast and ICM occurs at the *morula* stage. Ford argues:

> At the morula stage, it is extremely difficult to establish the presence of the sort of unity that would be required for the cluster of cells to be an actual ontological individual. There does not appear to be any strict commitment or rigid predetermination in cells from the earliest cleavages to become the inner cells... The relatively independent behaviour of the individual cells, together with the indeterminate and uncommitted nature of their developmental potential within the cluster of cells as a whole, seems to be incompatible with the individuation of the morula itself as a distinct ontological individual.
>
> (1988, pp. 148–9)

Nevertheless, the question arises whether, once the cells have differentiated at the end of the morula stage, the ICM constitutes an ontologically unique individual. Ford states that there is still indeterminate differentiation that occurs as the embryo implants itself on the uterine wall (Ford, 1988, p. 161). Some of the ICM's cells, formed before implantation, will not in the end form part of the embryo proper, but will form extraembryonic material. Hence, there cannot be a unique individual entity until all the cells which will contribute to the formation of the embryo proper are determined to that end and no other. Prior to strict cell determination, there is more than one entity present – the embryo proper and extraembryonic material – and they cannot be completely differentiated from each other.

In addition to the possibility of an embryo having been constituted by different cells, due to the lack of differentiation in its preimplantation form, more than one ontologically unique organism may be formed out of the cluster of undifferentiated totipotent cells. At any time before the primitive streak is formed, one or more cells may separate from the others, divide through mitosis, and form a new cluster that may implant in the uterus and form another, genetically identical, organism. The possibility of such division is lost when the primitive streak is formed (Ford, 2002, pp. 66–7).

Ford thus concludes, based on the lack of cellular differentiation and the possibility of twinning, that a preimplantation embryo cannot be a person under the Boethian definition since it is not an "individual substance." The primitive streak's appearance, coincident with uterine implantation, indicates an embryo's existence as an ontologically unique organism informed by a rational soul:

> The appearance of the primitive streak is an important landmark, indicating the position of the embryo proper with the main features of the new individual's body plan. This appears to be the stage of development when the cells of the epiblast first become organized through this primitive streak into one whole multicellular individual living human being, possessing for the first time a body axis and bilateral symmetry. Its developing cells are now integrated and subordinated to form a single heterogeneous organic body that endures with

its own ontological as well as biological identity through all its subsequent stages of growth and development. A new human individual begins once the matter of the epiblastic cells become one living body, informed or actuated by a human form, life-principle or soul that arises through the creative power of God. The appearance of one primitive streak signals that only one embryo proper and human individual has been formed and begun to exist. Prior to this stage it would be pointless to speak about the presence of a true human being in an ontological sense. A human individual could scarcely exist before a definitive human body is formed. As mentioned earlier, the formation of an ontological individual with a truly human nature and rational ensoulment must coincide.

(Ford, 1988, pp. 171–2; cf. Smith, 1983; van Inwagen, 1990, pp. 152–4; Shannon and Wolter, 1990; McCormick, 1991; Olson, 1997, pp. 89–93; Eberl, 2000a)

Critics of Ford's position argue that cellular totipotentiality does not imply a lack of organic unity, since organized cellular functioning to sustain the life of a single organism begins when fertilization is complete, and the possibility of a preimplantation embryo dividing into genetically identical twins does not count against its existence as an individual substance. While I have previously advocated Ford's account (Eberl, 2000a) and continue to consider it a metaphysically coherent and plausible position, I agree with the critics who conclude that Ford does not offer a sufficiently compelling argument to deny that a preimplantation embryo may be an individual human organism informed by a rational soul.

"Organic" unity is often understood in this debate as a definitive sign of the "substantial" unity required in the Boethian definition of personhood Aquinas adopts. Since, however, Aquinas holds strict criteria for something to have substantial unity, it is necessary to see if the concept of organic unity satisfies the relevant criteria. Aquinas notes various ways in which something may be considered a "unity." For example, a heap of stones is a unity in terms of the constituent stones being spatially contiguous, a house is a unity in terms of its constituent parts being functionally organized in a certain fashion, and a mover and that which it moves are a unity in terms of their agent/patient relationship (QDA, X; SCG, II.57). None of these types of unity count as substantial unity, though. Aquinas defines a substance as *unum simpliciter* ("one unqualifiedly"). Examples of things that are *unum simpliciter* are elemental substances, certain mixtures of elemental substances, immaterial substances, and living organisms (Pasnau, 2002, p. 88). Aquinas understands living organisms "to have a unity fundamentally different from that of nonliving aggregates" (Pasnau, 2002, p. 93):

For since the body of a human being or any other animal is a natural whole, it will be called "one" insofar as it has one form; by which it is perfected [i.e., completed or made whole] not merely as an aggregate or an assemblage of parts, as in the case of a house and other things of this kind.

(QDA, X)

A living organism is *unum simpliciter*, because its heterogeneous parts do not each have their own substantial form. Rather, they are all informed by one substantial form by which each part has its own existence and specific nature (QDA, X; SCG, II.57; In DGC, I.xv.108). This unity among a living organism's parts is signified by their *interdependent* functioning. Mere "functional unity" is not sufficient for substantial unity. The bricks, roof tiles, wood beams, etc., that compose a house are functionally unified in that they must all be organized in a certain fashion relative to each other in order for the house to exist with its proper structural integrity; but a house is not *unum simpliciter*. A house's functional unity is distinguished from that of a living organism, because a living organism's parts depend upon their functional relationship to each other for their very existence as the types of things they are (QDA X.ad 15; SCG, II.57; see van Inwagen, 1990, pp. 81–97). A brick depends upon its functional relationship to the other parts of a house in order to exist "as a part of the house"; but it does not depend upon that relationship in order to exist "as a brick." An organ – for example, an eye – that composes an organism depends upon its functional relationship to the organism's other organs not only for its existence "as a part of the organism," but also for its existence "as an eye." Aquinas asserts that an eye which is functionally disconnected from a living organism can be called "an eye" only equivocally; it is no longer an eye in the proper sense of the term.

Hence, for Aquinas, a living organism's organic unity – defined in terms of the interdependent functional relationship among its parts (cells, tissues, organs, etc.) – is a paradigm example of substantial unity. In reviewing Ford's account, then, it is necessary to determine whether the cells composing a preimplantation embryo are functionally interdependent. Evidence of their functional interdependence would make it reasonable to assert, *contra* Ford's conclusion, that a preimplantation embryo has organic, and thus substantial, unity.

Therefore, the first criticism of Ford's position is that the evident totipotentiality of the cells constituting a preimplantation embryo does not indicate that the embryo lacks organic unity. Paul Flaman asserts, "The totipotentiality of cells or groups of cells does not mean that they can not be parts of one ontological individual, one living organism or one human being" (Flaman, 1991, p. 41; cf. Lee, 1996, pp. 94–5; Serra and Colombo, 1998, p. 172; Panicola, 2002, pp. 80–1). Flaman supports this contention by pointing out that "Even in the adult human being 'stem cells' in the bone marrow are pluripotent.[22] These cells which actualize a pluripotentiality are certainly parts of one ontological individual, living organism or human being" (Flaman, 1991, p. 41).

That cellular totipotentiality does not inhibit a preimplantation embryo's organic unity is evidenced by indications of an inchoate organization and inter-communication among the embryo's cells. Such organization and intercommuni-cation may also indicate functional interdependence among the cells. Evidence of an inchoate organization among a preimplantation embryo's cells is their coming together at implantation to form the primitive streak, as well as other embryonic and extraembryonic tissues shortly thereafter. Germain Grisez charges that "Ford has trouble explaining why a few thousand distinct individuals work together in embryogenesis to make themselves into one individual" (Grisez, 1989, p. 37; cf. Lee, 1996, p. 102). Flaman and others note that an embryo has an "identifiable body plan" before implantation and formation of the primitive streak (Fisher, 1991, p. 66; Flaman, 1991, p. 46; Serra and Colombo, 1998; Vial Correa and Dabike, 1998, pp. 317–28).

Furthermore, Ford acknowledges that there is some sort of "clock" mechanism programmed in a zygote's DNA that guides organic development and "continues through childhood for the growth of teeth, biological changes at puberty, adulthood etc. right through to old age" (Ford, 1988, p. 155, note 37). This clock "seems to be set from the time of fertilization, with each cell's 'clock' running in dependence on, and in co-ordination with, what is happening in its surrounding cells" (Ford, 1988, p. 155). Ford interprets this phenomenon as supporting his view that each cell constituting a preimplantation embryo is a distinct individual organism that has its own internal clock, which is synchronized with the clocks of the other cells. Grisez, though, considers such harmonious synchronization to be what one would expect if such cells "are, not a mass of distinct individuals, but integral parts of one developing *individual*" (Grisez, 1989, p. 38).

The fact that some of a preimplantation embryo's cells exercise their potentiality to become extraembryonic organs – for example, the placenta or umbilical cord – as opposed to constituting the ICM or embryo proper, is also not a threat to the embryo's organic unity. So-called "extraembryonic" organs may be understood rather as prenatal organs of the embryo itself. As Anthony Fisher contends:

> The biological evidence is clearly that these tissues are formed by the embryo, usually with its genetic constitution, and for its sole benefit and use, and are indeed its organs: they are clearly not the mother's organs, nor a tumor, nor some alien third organism living symbiotically with mother and embryo.
> (Fisher, 1991, p. 60; cf. Grisez, 1989, p. 38; Flaman, 1991, p. 44;
> Howsepian, 1997, p. 38; Finnis, 1999, p. 15)

On this construal, the placenta and umbilical cord are understood as parts of a developing fetus. When the fetus is born and no longer requires those parts, they are naturally shed or otherwise artificially removed. Once removed from the fetus, the placenta and umbilical cord are no longer parts of the fetus and may be disposed of or used for some other purpose – for example, the derivation of stem cells.

Ford's case against a preimplantation embryo's organic unity is supported by the contention that information not coded in its DNA, but which is from an extrinsic source – namely, maternal molecules that interact with the embryonic molecules – is required for the embryo to exercise its preimplantation development and implant upon the uterine wall (Bedate and Cefalo, 1989). By investigating the growth of ovarian teratomas,[23] however, Antoine Suarez concludes:

> The domain governed by embryonic information remains well separated from the domain governed by maternal information...The biological identity of

the human embryo is not determined by the influence of the maternal environment, but depends basically on the information capacity of the embryo itself...that the adult into which an embryo develops is a man and not a dog or a cat, depends on embryonic information alone.

(Suarez, 1990, p. 630; cf. Austriaco, 2002, p. 672)

Granting the claim, though, that a preimplantation embryo requires extrinsic information to execute its developmental plan toward implantation, Patrick Lee argues that this requirement does not count against the embryo being an organized individual:

> Even if it were true that some information is received from maternal molecules, this would not show that the preimplantation embryo was not a complete human individual. There is no reason to expect that *all* of the future features of the developing organism should be already determined by its internal genetic make-up...If informational factors are received from maternal molecules, still, how this information fits within the overall development of this organism is determined from within by the organism's own directed growth...primary organization comes from within the embryo itself.
>
> (1996, p. 101)

There is evidence that a preimplantation embryo, despite the totipotentiality of its constituent cells to form any embryonic or extraembryonic tissue, or even another embryo, has an intrinsic organization grounded in its unique genetic identity to grow by cellular mitosis, implant itself in its mother's uterus, and develop into a mature human being capable of rational thought. Evidence of a preimplantation embryo's organic unity provides a reasonable foundation for asserting the embryo's substantial unity, fulfilling Aquinas's requirement that something be *unum simpliciter* in order to count as a substance. The above responses to Ford's account show that his charge that cellular totipotentiality decisively precludes organic unity lacks a sufficient foundation to demonstrate that a preimplantation embryo cannot be an "individual substance."

The totipotentiality of a preimplantation embryo's constituent cells also allows for the embryo to potentially divide into genetically identical twins. It appears to be quite metaphysically problematic for one individual organism to give rise to two distinct organisms; especially if the substantial form of each organism in question is a rational soul.[24] This is Ford's most powerful means of arguing for his conclusion that rational ensoulment cannot occur before uterine implantation. Ford's interpretation of the twinning phenomenon, however, can be called into question and alternative interpretations offered.

Ford considers it problematic that an individual human organism informed by a rational soul could potentially divide into two or more human organisms. The following questions arise: Does the rational soul informing the first organism divide? Do all the organisms share the same rational soul with the original? Does the original organism cease to exist, its soul separating from its matter, and are two new rational souls created to inform the divided matter? There is also a fundamental issue concerning *identity*. That something is identical to itself is necessary, and the relation of identity is transitive. Hence, a zygote is identical to itself and, if a preimplantation embryo has the same rational soul as the zygote from which it developed, then the embryo is identical to the zygote. If the embryo divides into twins, it appears that each twin is identical to the original embryo and thus to the zygote. The twins are obviously not identical to each other, but they must be identical if they are both identical to the original embryo, since identity is transitive. Therefore, an incoherency seems to follow from the assertion that an embryo capable of dividing into twins is a substance identical with itself.

Against Ford's depiction of the twinning phenomenon, I propose that the best way to describe the phenomenon, which is both consistent with Aquinas's account of human nature and avoids the above identity issue, is that the original rationally ensouled embryo loses some of its matter and the matter becomes informed by a new rational soul. As George Klubertanz explains:

> It is quite probable that the human soul is created at the moment when the new individual is formed by the union of ovum and sperm. If this is what happens, then, in the division of the embryo by which identical twins are formed, the individual soul remains in one of the parts...Meanwhile, as soon as the other part is fully separated, and so removed from the information of the already created soul, a new soul is created for the second twin...the original human being does not cease to be, but loses half [or some percentage] of its matter; and in the new being thus formed by division a new soul is created.
>
> (1953, pp. 410–11)

On this construal of the twinning phenomenon, when one organism A divides into two organisms B and C, either B or C is identical to A,[25] because one of them has the same substantial form as A.[26] If, say, B is identical to A, then B's existence can be traced back to the one-celled zygote from which A developed before its division. In this case, C is not identical to A, because its substantial form is a new rational soul that was created at the moment of A's division (Suarez, 1990, p. 631; Fisher, 1991, pp. 61, 67; Flaman, 1991, p. 50; May, 1992, pp. 80–1; Crosby, 1993, pp. 410–11; Finnis, 1999, p. 15; Panicola, 2002, pp. 80–1). Therefore, since it is not the case that both B and C are identical to A, no incoherency follows from B and C not being identical to each other and A being a substance identical to itself.

Natural embryonic twinning is thus akin to the artificial production of a "clone" insofar as an external agent acts upon an organism to separate some of its matter from it and the matter comes to constitute a genetically identical organism with its own substantial form (Ashley and Moraczewski, 2001, pp. 195–8). While the biological process of twinning is not fully understood, it appears to be a random event, with no apparent internal genetic factor or any clear environmental factor that causes an embryo to twin (Piontelli, 2002, p. 19). To the best scientific understanding, it is as likely that twinning is caused by factors respective of the uterine environment acting upon weak intercellular bonds to cause the embryo to lose some of its cells as it is that an embryo is genetically "programmed" to divide. If there were a genetic determiner for twinning intrinsic to an embryo, then one could argue that this factor precludes an embryo that has it from being an individual substance prior to its division. There is, though, no conclusive evidence of an intrinsic genetic determiner for twinning (Ford, 1988, p. 119).

A preimplantation embryo and an adult human being have the same potentiality – that is, a passive potentiality which requires some external manipulation – for producing a genetically identical human organism. As Patrick Lee explains:

> Theoretically, any of our cells could be cloned; that is, a cell could be isolated and something done to the cell to activate it so that it began to replicate using the whole genetic code instead of the restricted part of it relevant to its specialty.[27] One could claim, then, that each cell of our body has the active potentiality, *given the right conditions*, to produce a distinct organism. But of course the right conditions referred to here include much more than just an appropriate environment. Something must be done positively to activate it. Similarly, the right conditions referred to by Ford, for the splitting of a two-, three-, four- or eight-celled embryo into twins, are more than just the appropriate environment.
>
> (Lee, 1996, p. 93; cf. Panicola, 2002, p. 81)

Ford's account faces a dilemma. If a preimplantation embryo has an active potentiality to divide into genetically identical twins – and the conclusion follows from this premise that the embryo cannot be an individual substance – then Ford must conclude that an adult human being – who has the same type of potentiality to produce a genetically identical clone – cannot be an individual substance as well. On the other hand, if a preimplantation embryo is best understood as having a passive potentiality for twinning (Grisez, 1989, p. 38; Flaman, 1991, p. 48; May, 1992, p. 80), because it requires more than merely its supportive environment for such an event to occur, then, since an adult human being is also best considered as having a passive potentiality to produce a clone, both embryo and adult exist as individual substances.

I propose that, when an embryo twins, it is not the case that it is "dividing," but that it loses some of its matter. Since the separated matter is totipotent – that is, it has an active potentiality to develop into a human being – it is immediately informed, once separated, by a rational soul. It is not necessary to accept Ford's conclusion that a preimplantation embryo's potentiality to divide is a threat to its previous substantial unity. Furthermore, the understanding of twinning as an event in which an embryo merely loses some of its matter allows for an embryo to maintain its substantial unity through the twinning process; and thereby one of the resultant twins is identical to the original embryo.

Having examined Ford's account of human embryogenesis from a Thomistic metaphysical perspective, I conclude that the possibility of a human embryo dividing into genetically identical twins does not preclude its being informed by a rational soul. Nevertheless, even if one grants that cellular totipotentiality and the possibility of twinning do not preclude a preimplantation embryo's existence as an individual substance with organic unity, more needs to be said to support the assertion that the embryo's substantial form is a rational soul, as opposed to a merely vegetative or sensitive soul; especially given that Aquinas explicitly holds that an embryo's first substantial form is a vegetative soul. Responding to this issue requires providing a reason to think that a preimplantation embryo has an active potentiality for rational thought. I will elucidate one attempt to provide such a reason.

Ashley

Benedict Ashley argues that a human zygote contains the epigenetic primordia of the biological structures proper to a human being. In place of the developed cerebral cortex (Donceel and Pasnau) and the primitive streak (Ford), Ashley points to a zygote's DNA-filled nucleus as the "control center" that regulates embryonic biological functioning, such that a zygote is a unified, individual substance from fertilization onward:

> From the moment of fertilization there already exists in the zygote (and this was probably already pre-determined in the ovum) a metabolic *polarity*, with the nucleus determining the upper pole of the metabolic gradient, and a *bilaterality* which will eventually be fundamental to the plan of the adult body. Consequently, as the first cell-divisions take place, there is already some differentiation in the cytoplasm of the daughter cells. They may be totipotential when separated, but as existing in the morula, they already constitute heterogeneous parts. At this stage it appears that the maternal RNA produced in the cytoplasm by the DNA of the nucleus of the original ovum plays a regulative role, and the nuclei, with their new unique DNA, are still relatively quiescent. Nevertheless, it was the nucleus of the zygote which initiated the whole process, and it will be the new nuclear DNA which finally takes over the regulation of the development from the blastula on. Thus, during this intermediate phase, it is still the nuclear DNA which has ultimate regulatory control, although it permits the maternal RNA to play its own role. We ought, therefore, to hold that, during this time, the primary organ are the daughter nuclei, which originated from the nucleus of the zygote. Since all are essentially similar, they can be said to act collectively, although it is probable that some of them, or even one, located at the superior pole of the organism, has the dominant effect, and can be identified as the primary organ of the whole.
>
> (Ashley, 1976, p. 123; cf. Ashley and Moraczewski, 2001, p. 197)

Various studies on the development of mouse embryos support Ashley's description of an inherent organizational structure in a zygote and its daughter cells that determines an embryo's future biological development (Gardner, 1997, 2001, 2002; Beddington and Robertson, 1999; Piotrowska and Zernicka-Goetz, 2001; Piotrowska *et al.*, 2001).

Ashley correctly understands Aquinas to hold that there is a "primary organ" by which a soul's power to move the other parts of its body is manifested (QDA IX.ad 13, X.ad 4, X.ad 11, XI.ad 16; In Sent, I.8.v.3.ad 3).[28] Aquinas asserts that the primary organ is the foundation of an animal's unity as an organic substance and thus indicates that the animal is ensouled. Hence, Ashley and Albert Moraczewski conclude:

> By "a body proportionate to ensoulment as a human person," Aquinas meant a body with a principal organ capable of being the efficient cause of the activities specific to a human person, given the organism's state of development. Present embryology shows that the zygote fulfills this requirement.
>
> (2001, p. 194)

In fact, all parties discussed in this debate recognize the need to define a primary organ in order to assert that a developing embryo has a rational soul. Donceel and Pasnau contend that the primary organ is the brain with a functioning cerebral cortex, because it is directly correlated with both rational operations and metabolic regulation. Ford argues that the primitive streak is the primary organ because it is the epigenetic primordium for the brain and nervous system. Ashley finds the zygotic nucleus to be the primary organ as it is the epigenetic primordium of the primitive streak, and thus of the brain and nervous system (Ashley, 1976, p. 124).

The zygotic nucleus not only functions as a preimplantation embryo's metabolic regulator, but is also the epigenetic primordium for the organ correlated with rational operations: the cerebral cortex formed out of the primitive streak. This supports the conclusion that a one-celled human zygote is informed by a rational soul:

> Thus the primary organ that is required in the fetus for its intellectual ensoulment is not the brain as such but a primary organ capable of producing a brain with the capacity for intellectual cognition in the body at some appropriate phase of the human life cycle. What is the primary organ that causes the human body to develop so as to be proportionate to ensoulment and human personhood? Modern embryology shows clearly that it is the nucleus of the zygote produced by the fertilization of a human ovum by a human sperm, since the nucleus 1) contains all the genome or *information* (formal cause) required to build the mature human body with its brain as its primary organ and the instrument of intellection; and 2) is the principal *efficient cause* proportionate to the task of the mature development of the human organism.
>
> (Ashley and Moraczewski, 2001, pp. 199–200)

It is not merely because of its unique genetic identity that a zygote is an individual human being. For its genetic identity will not remain unique if an identical twin or clone is formed, or be sufficient for a human being to develop if a hydatidiform mole is produced.[29] A zygote must also have a primary organ and any other intrinsic biological factors necessary for its unilateral development into an actually thinking rational human being.[30] In normal cases, a human zygote has an active potentiality to be an actually thinking rational human being, and this is sufficient to conclude that it is informed by a rational soul. By applying Aquinas's metaphysical principles to contemporary embryological data, I conclude that a human being begins to exist at conception.[31]

Conclusion

My goal in this chapter has been to develop a proper Thomistic understanding of the beginning of a human being's life, which involves determining when one can assert that a rational soul informs a human body. The evidence required to support such an assertion is a body's having, at minimum, active potentialities for vegetative, sensitive, and rational operations. I conclude in agreement with Ashley's contention that these active potentialities are present when an organism with human DNA comes into existence with some sort of primary organ through which integrative organic functioning is exercised; such functioning indicates the organism's substantial unity. At the very beginning of human life, the primary organ is the nucleus of a one-celled human zygote. A zygotic nucleus provides the epigenetic primordium of a human being's brain and nervous system. A human brain is the integrative foundation for a human being's sensitive and vegetative operations,[32] and is correlated with rational operations. The presence of the brain's epigenetic primordium is thus sufficient for a human zygote to have active potentialities for a rational soul's proper operations, since the zygote's ordered natural development will result in an actually thinking rational human being. Therefore, one can assert that a human zygote is informed by a rational soul and is thus a human being – a person.

3   The end of a human person's life[1]

Introduction

As with the beginning of a human being's life, formulating a proper Thomistic account of a human being's death, given current scientific data, is quite contentious. Experts in the fields of medicine, biology, philosophy, and theology center the debate on three proposed criteria for determining when death occurs.[2] The classical "circulatory/respiratory" criterion specifies death to occur when the intake, processing, and distribution of oxygen throughout the body – the body's most vital metabolic functions – irreversibly cease.[3] Without oxygen, all bodily systems begin to shut down and necrosis ensues. In 1968, with the published report of the Ad Hoc Committee of the Harvard Medical School (Ad Hoc Committee, 1968), many scholars and medical practitioners began to argue that, since the brain is the central organ which regulates the body's metabolic functions, irreversible cessation of the functioning of the brain "as a whole" – cerebral cortex, cerebellum, and brainstem – constitutes death. This "whole-brain" criterion of death is based on the understanding that a human organism cannot function *as a unified whole* without a functioning brain.[4]

The general acceptance of whole-brain death has led to the postulation that perhaps not every part of the brain must irreversibly cease functioning in order for death to occur. Some scholars emphasize that the so-called higher-brain functions of the cerebral cortex are responsible for the peculiarly human "personal" activities of conscious rational thought and volition. Hence, they argue that a human being's death, as a *person*, occurs when their cerebral cortex becomes irreversibly nonfunctional. This higher-brain concept of death is used as the basis to argue that patients in an irreversible persistent vegetative state (PVS) are no longer persons and thus should be considered dead.

In what follows, I will examine arguments for and against these various understandings of death from the standpoint of Aquinas's metaphysical account of human nature. I will begin with a brief review of what Aquinas explicitly states about death and then evaluate how his account best coheres with current biological data.

Aquinas's account of human death

Aquinas's account of a human being's death begins with his understanding of a rational soul as a human body's substantial form and its *unitive* function as such: "The body is united by the soul; a sign of which is that, when the soul departs, the body is dissolved" (SCG, II.58). As the substantial form of a human body, a rational soul is the principle of the body's (1) existence (*esse*), (2) unified organic functioning, and (3) specific nature as a "human" body.[5] Aquinas asserts (1) and (2) in the following passages:

> "To live" is said in two ways. In one way, it is the very existence of a living thing, which results from a soul united to a body as form. In the other way, "to live" stands for the operation of life.
>
> (QDV, XIII.4.ad 2)

> "To live" stands for the operation of the soul which it produces in the heart insofar as it is a mover . . . and it infuses this life first in the heart, and afterwards in all the other parts [of the body].[6]
>
> (In Sent, I.8.v.3.ad 3)

As noted in Chapter 2, Aquinas understands a rational soul to be the principle of a human body's organic functioning and to operate by means of a "primary organ." Following Aristotle, Aquinas identifies this primary organ as the heart; although contemporary science would identify it as the brain. Rendering a human body's primary organ as the brain, as opposed to Aquinas's explicit reference to the heart, is warranted by the criteria Aquinas gives for considering the heart as the primary organ. First, Aquinas describes the primary organ as that through which the soul "moves" or "operates" the body's other parts. Second, he describes the primary organ as the "ruler" of the body's other parts in the sense that it orders them as a ruler orders a city through laws (QDA, X.ad 4). Third, he cites the dependence of the body's other parts upon the primary organ (QDA, XI.ad 16). It is now known that the brain functions as the source of operation for a body's vital autonomic and voluntary functions, regulates such functions and orders them to support the body's holistic-level existence and activity, and is the critical organ upon which the body's other vital organs – including the heart and lungs – depend for their functioning. It is thus evident that the brain best satisfies Aquinas's description of the primary organ and thereby warrants substituting it for the heart in Aquinas's account.

Aquinas's two understandings of life entail two understandings of death:

> Since death is the loss of life, it must be similarly distinguished so that it designates at one time the loss of that union by which a soul is united to a body as form, and at another time the loss of the operation of life.
>
> (QDV, XIII.4.ad 2)

Though he separates two understandings of the term "death," Aquinas nevertheless considers them united in one and the same event. When the union of a rational soul and its body is dissolved, the dissolution of the body's unified organic functioning immediately follows: "If that which holds the individual contrary parts[7] together is removed, they tend toward what is fitting to them according to nature, and thus the dissolution of the body is brought about" (QDV, XXV.6).

Aquinas understands death to occur because a premortem human body is not perfectly informed by its rational soul. As a result, material defects can arise in the body that may make it unsuitable for being informed by a rational soul (QDA, VIII.ad 9, XIV.ad 13).[8] Such defects result in a body's unsuitability for having a rational soul as its substantial form, which occurs when it becomes unable to actualize the soul's vegetative capacities:

> Although the soul, which is the cause of life, is incorruptible, yet the body, which receives life from the soul, is subject to change; and through this it withdraws from the disposition according to which it is suited for the reception of life. And thus the corruption of a human being occurs.
>
> (QDA, XIV.ad 20)

> Just as form does not come into matter unless the matter is made proper through the requisite dispositions, so, with the cessation of the requisite dispositions, a form cannot remain in the matter. And in this way the union of soul[9] and body is dissolved; if natural heat and moisture and others factors of this sort [i.e., vital metabolic factors] are removed, insofar as by these a body is disposed toward reception of a soul.
>
> (QDA, IX.ad 16)

Aquinas thus defines a human being's death – the separation of their rational soul from their body – as occurring when the body is no longer able to actualize the soul's vegetative capacities. The clinical criterion for determining when this event occurs is the irreversible loss of vital metabolic functioning as evidenced by, according to Aquinas, the cessation of respiratory activity: "If breath is subtracted, the union of soul[10] to body fails; not because breath is the medium [of the union], but because the disposition is removed through which the body is disposed toward this union" (ST, Ia.76.7.ad 2).

Having reviewed Aquinas's explicit account of human death, I will proceed to outline the contemporary debate between the higher-brain, whole-brain, and circulatory/respiratory concepts and criteria of human death. Illuminating this debate is key because a properly Thomistic account of human death may end up differing from Aquinas's explicit account as contemporary biological understanding is taken into account to determine when a human being's rational soul separates from their material body and the body corrupts.

Recent interpretations

As with Aquinas's explicit account of human embryogenesis, some may reject or ignore his explicit account of human death because of the outdated biological information at his disposal. Aquinas's account, however, primarily concerns metaphysical principles and invokes biology only twice: when he asserts that the heart is the body's primary organ through which the soul moves the rest of the body's parts, and when he asserts that the cessation of respiratory functioning is the proper criterion for determining when death occurs. One can thus put aside those two specific biologically based assertions and instead apply Aquinas's metaphysical account of the soul–body relationship to the contemporary biological understanding of how and when death occurs.

Higher-brain concept of death

The higher-brain concept of death defines the end of a human being's biological existence in terms of the loss of "the capacity to think, feel, be conscious and aware of other people" (Veatch, 1988, p. 173). The criterion for establishing the loss of this capacity is the irreversible cessation of neocortical functioning. Robert Veatch thus concludes, "A person should be considered dead when there is an irreversible loss of higher brain functions" (Veatch, 1988, p. 173). Some scholars advocate higher-brain death as a direct interpretation of Aquinas's understanding of human nature. Their argument is based upon the Thomistic principle that one can assert that a specific type of form informs a particular material body only by observing the body performing the operations that are peculiar to that type of form, or its having the inherent capacity to perform such operations. Therefore, since the form of a human being is a rational soul, the capacity for conscious rational thought being peculiar to that type of soul, one can assert that a particular body is informed by a rational soul, and thus composes a human being, only by observing that it has at least the capacity for conscious rational thought.

As noted in Chapter 1, Aquinas claims that conscious rational thought does not occur by means of a bodily organ; as, say, sight occurs by means of the eyes and visual cortex. Aquinas's claim, however, does not preclude rational activity and neural activity being *correlated* with one another; as long as the correlation is not explained in terms of a relation of identity or reduction of the former to the latter. Allowing such a correlation makes plausible the coherence of Aquinas's account of human nature with contemporary neurobiological data. Given the evident correlation between rational operations and cerebral functioning, it seems reasonable to conclude that irreversible loss of cerebral functioning implies the loss of the capacity for rational operations while a human being remains embodied. Due to this implication, it appears to follow that one cannot assert that a rational soul informs the body of a PVS patient.

Hence, D. Alan Shewmon, arguing from a Thomistic standpoint, concludes that irreversible loss of cerebral functioning entails the loss of a rational soul as a body's substantial form (Shewmon, 1985).[11] This construal of death involves a reversal of the "succession of souls" Aquinas holds to occur in human embryogenesis.[12] A human being is informed by a rational soul until their body becomes structurally insufficient to support the soul's definitive capacity for rational thought. While Aquinas understands the mind not to function through a bodily organ, he nevertheless asserts that the operation of a rational soul's sensitive and imaginative capacities, which do function through bodily organs, is required to provide the mind with its proper object of thought while a human being is embodied.[13] Thus, the loss of higher-brain functioning, which neurobiological evidence indicates is required for imaginative operation and is correlated with rational activity, precludes rational activity while the soul informs a material body.[14] At the loss of higher-brain functioning, then, it appears that a "substantial change" occurs in which the rational soul separates from the body and a sensitive or vegetative soul is instantiated as the body's substantial form – depending upon whether any sensitive capacities remain in the still living body. The body is thereby no longer identical to the body that composed the human being because it has a different substantial form, and a substance's persistent identity requires that it be informed by the same substantial form (Eberl, 2004, pp. 353–9). The body will continue to be informed by at least a vegetative soul until it reaches a point of deterioration where it can no longer structurally support vital metabolic functions. At this point, the vegetative soul is annihilated, the body ceases to exist as an organic whole, and it is reduced to a mere collection of basic elements.

Shewmon thus concludes:

> The moment the brain cells in the hemispheres…become irreversibly damaged, the body is rendered incompatible with the human essence, forcing a substantial change. The [rational] soul departs and a vegetative soul is actualized, which had been virtually present all along in the vegetative aspects of the original human soul.
>
> (1985, p. 48)

> In summary, then, the minimum sufficient condition for the death of a person is the irreversible destruction of those parts of the brain necessary for the properly human functions of the [rational] soul, namely intellect and will.
>
> (1985, p. 61)

Accepting the higher-brain concept of death, from a Thomistic standpoint, requires one to argue that when a body is no longer able to provide the biological foundation necessary for conscious rational thought, a substantial change occurs in which the rational soul separates and the body becomes informed by either a sensitive or vegetative soul. If this is what indeed occurs in cases of PVS, then the body on the bed is a "humanoid animal" or perhaps a mere "vegetable" (Shewmon, 1985, p. 51).[15]

This purportedly Thomistic account suffers from three serious flaws. First, it is at odds with Aquinas's contention that a rational soul's separation from its body is signaled by the body's inability to actualize its *vegetative* capacities; a PVS patient retains the intrinsic activity of spontaneous respiration and other vital metabolic functions. The higher-brain concept of death involves an unwarranted separation of a soul's rational capacity from its sensitive and vegetative capacities.

In his explicit account of human embryogenesis, described in Chapter 2, Aquinas holds that a human being's proper capacities do not begin to exist in a developing human embryo at the same time; the vegetative capacities are actualized first, then the sensitive capacities, and finally the rational capacity which signals the existence of a human being. Nevertheless, once a rational soul informs a human body that has developed sufficiently, it alone possesses all of a human being's proper capacities: vegetative, sensitive, and rational. It is not the case that there are three souls informing a fully developed human body. Rather, the vegetative soul that first informs a living human embryo is annihilated once the embryo develops to the point where it has sense organs and sufficient neural development for sensitive operations; it is then informed by a sensitive soul that has both sensitive and vegetative capacities. The sensitive soul is annihilated once the point is reached where neural development is sufficient to support rational operations and the embryo becomes informed by a rational soul that has vegetative, sensitive, and rational capacities. Aquinas argues at great length that a human being's proper capacities have their source in *one* substantial form: a rational soul (ST, Ia.76.3–4; In DA, II.5; DUI, I).

Given Aquinas's strong contention of the *unicity* of a human being's substantial form, it is not surprising that he characterizes human death differently from the way he does human generation. Once a rational soul informs a properly disposed human body, the body must lose its disposition for *all* the soul's proper capacities in order for the separation of soul and body to occur. Accepting the higher-brain interpretation entails the following metaphysical description of how death occurs: there exists first a rational substance informed by a rational soul, and then possibly a nonrational animal substance informed by a sensitive soul, and finally a merely living substance informed by a vegetative soul before its final transformation into a lifeless corpse. This description violates the widely held principle of Ockham's Razor, which states that *ceteris paribus* the simplest explanation of a given phenomenon – that is, the explanation that is the least metaphysically complex by requiring the postulation of the least number of entities – is the explanation to which one ought to give assent.

Finally, aside from the metaphysical determination of when death occurs, the higher-brain concept is epistemologically problematic for two reasons. First, it is extremely difficult to determine accurately which structures of the brain are correlated with rational activity and when such structures become irreversibly nonfunctional. In fact, there are a number of cases in which PVS patients have been misdiagnosed (Steinbock, 1989; Childs *et al.*, 1993; Andrews *et al.*, 1996). A significant example is Patricia White Bull, a New Mexico woman who awoke from a sixteen-year coma after being diagnosed as "permanently vegetative."[16] Second, while Aquinas notes that one can determine the presence of a certain capacity based upon observation of its corresponding activity (ST, Ia.87.1; Pasnau, 2002, pp. 336–41), it does not follow that failure to observe an activity entails the lack of its corresponding capacity. Therefore, it is fallacious to infer that a PVS patient does not have the capacity for rational thought only on the basis of not having observed the performance of any rational activity or correlative neural activity.

A rational soul is not only the seat of a human being's rational capacity; it is also a human body's substantial form and is thereby the source of its sensitive and vegetative capacities. While PVS patients may no longer be able to actualize their rational or sensitive capacities, their souls remain embodied and active by reason of their vegetative capacities. Before death, a human being is composed of a rational soul informing an organic body, and is not identified with merely the exercise of their rational capacity (Smith, 1990a,b; Moreland, 1995; Moreland and Wallace, 1995; Moreland and Rae, 2000, pp. 316–37). Hence, we cannot be certain that a PVS patient is no longer a human being – a person – until there is incontrovertible evidence that their rational soul has altogether ceased to be active as their body's substantial form. Irreversible cessation of higher-brain functioning may serve as evidence that a soul's rational capacity can no longer be actualized while it remains embodied, and one may wish to infer from this evidence that the rational soul has ceased to inform that body. Such an inference, however, is invalid because a PVS patient's remaining vegetative operations serve as evidence that their rational soul remains active as their body's substantial form insofar as the soul's vegetative capacities are still actualized in that body.

Aquinas's explicit statements regarding a human being's death indicate that he takes the cessation of vital metabolic functioning to be the proper evidence that a rational soul has ceased to inform a particular body. As mentioned earlier, it may be the case that a proper Thomistic understanding of death, when viewed in the light of contemporary biological data, may end up differing from Aquinas's explicit account. Nevertheless, the argument supporting a higher-brain interpretation of Aquinas's account does not conclusively or persuasively demonstrate that this interpretation is a proper contemporary rendering of Aquinas's account. As I will show in what follows, defining death in terms of the irreversible loss of a human organism's vital metabolic functioning is the most plausible interpretation of Aquinas's view in light of the current biological understanding of death. Such an interpretation allows for a contemporary rendering of Aquinas's account without the radical departure from his explicit assertions required by the higher-brain interpretation. The fulcrum of the debate now shifts to the determination of whether the irreversible loss of vital metabolic functioning should be identified with the cessation of the brain's functioning as a human body's "central organizer" or with the cessation of the vital metabolic functions themselves: circulation and respiration.

Whole-brain criterion

Philip Smith (Smith, 1990a,b,c) and Benedict Ashley (Ashley and O'Rourke, 1997, pp. 316–37; Ashley, 2001) argue for the whole-brain criterion of death from a Thomistic perspective. For Ashley, this parallels his interpretation of Aquinas's account of human embryogenesis, described in Chapter 2, wherein he argues that the presence of a body's central organizer from the one-celled zygote onward indicates a rational soul's presence as the body's substantial form.

The whole-brain criterion has its roots in an understanding of death being related to an organism "as a whole." As James Bernat puts it:

> My colleagues and I have defined death as the permanent cessation of functioning of the organism as a whole. "The organism as a whole" is an old

biological concept [Loeb, 1916] that refers not to the whole organism (the sum of its parts) but to that *set of vital functions of integration, control, and behavior* that are greater than the sum of the parts of the organism, and that operate in response to demands from the organism's internal and external milieu to supports its life and to maintain its health. Implicit in the concept is the primacy of the *functional unity* of the organism.

(Bernat, 1998, p. 17, emphasis mine;
cf. Bernat, 2002)

Bernat defines the "critical functions" of an organism as a whole, the cessation of all of which is necessary and sufficient to constitute the loss of an organism's functional unity:

Critical functions of the organism as a whole comprise three distinct and complementary biological categories: 1) *vital functions* of spontaneous breathing and autonomic control of circulation; 2) *integrating functions* that assure homeostasis of the organism...and 3) *consciousness*...The critical functions in all three categories must be permanently lost for the organism to be dead. Correlatively, the presence of any of the three elements constitutes sufficient evidence for life.

(Bernat, 1998, p. 17, emphasis mine;
cf. Bernat, 1999)

I will show that Bernat's description of what is necessary and sufficient to constitute death is consonant with Aquinas's understanding of human nature.

Bernat's three categories of critical functions that define the existence of an organism as a whole can be collectively termed the organism's "integrative unity." From a Thomistic standpoint, a human being's integrative unified existence involves a human body informed by a soul that has rational, sensitive, and vegetative capacities. Clearly, a soul's rational and sensitive capacities correspond to Bernat's reference to consciousness. Furthermore, it is reasonable to correlate Bernat's vital and integrating functions with a soul's vegetative capacities. I thus propose, in agreement with Smith and Ashley, that the Thomistic concept of death involves the irreversible loss of a human being's rational, sensitive, *and* vegetative capacities: "A person is dead when there has been total and irreversible loss of all capacity for integrating and coordinating physical and mental functions of the body as a unit" (White *et al.*, 1992, p. 81).

The above reference to the loss of a human being's capacity for integrating and coordinating their physical and mental functions raises a key issue. Many of the cases that are considered in determining when a human being has died involve the utilization of various forms of life-support technology to assist or replace the vital metabolic operations of a patient who has suffered the loss of whole-brain functioning. Hence, we must consider to what degree the utilization of various forms of life-support technology impacts upon the Thomistic account of human nature and death.

Aquinas understands a human being to be composed of a living *biological* organism. Furthermore, Aquinas considers natural substances, such as biological organisms, and artifacts to be significantly distinct types of beings: "Natural bodies are substances more than artificial bodies; for they are substances not only due to their material part, but also due to their formal part" (In DA, II.1). A natural substance has intrinsic unity – that is, it is *unum simpliciter* ("one unqualifiedly")[17] – by having a single, unique substantial form informing the matter that composes it. An artifact, on the other hand, has unity in a merely "accidental" sense insofar as it is an aggregate of natural substances organized in a particular fashion to perform certain functions or instantiate certain properties.

This fundamental difference between natural substances and artifacts precludes an artifact becoming a "proper part" of a natural substance; an artifact cannot be informed by a natural substance's substantial form. An artifact is unsuitable for being informed by a natural substance's substantial form, because the artifact already has its own principle of organization – namely, the accidental form that results from the aggregate or functional unity of the artifact's constituents. Of course, simply having its own principle of organization is not sufficient to preclude something from becoming informed by a natural substance's substantial form. A banana has its own principle of organization, but it loses that principle through the process of digestion in which the banana is broken down into its constituent elements and those elements become part of the functional integrity of the organism that consumes it. A pacemaker, on the other hand, does not lose its principle of organization when it is placed inside a patient with bradycardia – an abnormally slow heart rate; it retains the integrity of the material constitution and programming that causes it to function properly in emitting weak electrical impulses to stimulate contraction of the heart muscle when it falls below a certain rate. While a pacemaker's functioning assists a patient's biological functioning, the pacemaker's function is not a function of the patient. There is no functional unity of the patient with the pacemaker, because the patient does not direct the pacemaker's functioning. The pacemaker functions due to its own internal constitution and programming; it is not "caught up in the life" of the patient (van Inwagen, 1990, p. 94).

Aquinas defines a human being's death in terms of their rational soul separating from their material body, which occurs when the body is no longer properly disposed to actualize the soul's vegetative capacities. The requisite disposition is lost when the body's vital metabolic functions cease. It is important to note that it is a body's loss of its soul's vegetative *capacities* that occasions the soul's separation. Hence, the criterion for a human being's death must be amended to refer to their body's loss of the capacity for vital metabolic functions, and not just the cessation of the functions themselves. A human being in cardiac arrest suffers the cessation of vital metabolic functions – circulation and respiration – and the loss of brain functioning quickly follows due to anoxia. But they may be able to have their vital metabolic functions restored through CPR. If the cessation of vital metabolic functions were sufficient for death, then a human being resuscitated by CPR would be considered as having died – their soul having separated from their body – and then coming back to life – their soul reinforming their body. While reports of "near-death experiences" may corroborate this interpretation, it is more plausible, I contend, to consider them as having ceased to actualize their soul's vegetative capacities and then actualizing those capacities once again with the external assistance provided by someone performing CPR on them.

One can cease to actualize one's capacity for vital metabolic functions and then actualize that capacity once again with external aid. Being dependent upon external aid to support the actualization of one's capacity for vital metabolic functions thus seems consistent with a body's continuing to be informed by a rational soul. The external aid provided by CPR or a pacemaker, however, is not constitutive of a human being's vital metabolic functions. CPR simply "jump-starts" such functions and a pacemaker helps to regulate them; neither actually performs those functions. A mechanical ventilator, on the other hand, does perform a vital metabolic function: it forces air into the lungs, which in turn stimulates cardiac activity. If cardiac arrhythmia or asystole develops, which usually occurs, then additional artificial support must be provided for cardiac functioning to continue. Patients who suffer the cessation of whole-brain functioning require mechanical ventilation and other artificial life-support measures to maintain both respiratory and cardiac activity (Field *et al.*, 1988, pp. 818–19).

There is an important distinction between having one's vital metabolic functions "jump-started" or regulated by external aid and having such functions "taken over" by external artificial support. The distinction is in terms of a human being having *control* over such functions. An artifact cannot be informed by a natural substance's substantial form due to the artifact having its own principle of organization, which precludes its being under the natural substance's functional control. A human being having control over their vital metabolic functions is arguably a necessary criterion for them to have the functional integrity one would expect of an organic substance that is *unum simpliciter*. I thereby propose that a human being remains alive – that is, their vegetative capacities are intact – only if they have the capacity to *coordinate* their vital metabolic functions. The persistence of uncoordinated metabolic functions – vital or otherwise – is not sufficient to constitute a human being's substantial vegetative activities. It is not merely the persistence of vital metabolic functions that suffices for a human body – and hence the human being it composes – to be alive and have integrative unity. Rather, a human being must have an "active potentiality"[18] to exercise such functions. If a human being cannot actually perform their vital metabolic functions, then they are dead. If a mechanical ventilator or cardiopulmonary bypass machine actually performs a human being's vital metabolic functions, then such functions and the capacity for performing them are no longer attributable to the patient dependent upon such a device; unless the patient's dependence on artificial life support is temporary and their inability to actually perform their vital metabolic functions is reversible – for example, a patient who is put on cardiopulmonary bypass while undergoing an open-heart procedure. A patient who is permanently dependent upon artificial lifesupport has only a "passive potentiality" to receive the benefits – that is, oxygenated air being introduced and circulated throughout their body – which such support can provide.[19] I thus conclude that a human body loses integrative unity when it no longer has the active potentiality to coordinate the vital metabolic functions of circulation and respiration, and such functions can be maintained only by external artificial means. The clinical sign of this capacity being lost is the irreversible cessation of *spontaneous* heartbeat and respiration.

When integrative unity has been irreversibly lost, a body is no longer "proportionate" for rational ensoulment; it can no longer materially support a soul's proper capacities in a *unified* substance:

> As the source of life and the single organizing principle of the body, the soul not only enables the person to breath, circulate blood, think, choose, etc., but it also unifies these diverse activities into an integrated whole or system. When the soul separates from the body at death, the remaining organism is deprived of its internal unity and its radical capacity for human actions. Thus, human death . . . [is equated] with the death of the organism as a whole.
>
> (Smith, 1990c, pp. 24–5; cf. Smith, 1990a, pp. 54–5; Ashley, 2001, p. 8)

Advocates of the whole-brain criterion and those of the circulatory/respiratory criterion agree that the loss of a body's integrative unity is the proper concept of death. The difference between the two positions regards whether the cessation of whole-brain functioning is sufficient to constitute the loss of integrative unity.

Ashley argues that the cessation of whole-brain functioning constitutes death, from a Thomistic perspective, based upon the principle – utilized in his account of a human zygote's ensoulment – that a rational soul "moves" the heterogeneous parts of its body through a primary organ: "Physical life can exist only when the principal part of the total organism maintains its integrative unity by providing its highest and most specific function, both exists and operates at least minimally" (Ashley, 2001, pp. 7–8).

An additional reason for holding the whole-brain criterion is that it defines death in terms of the one organ that is directly correlated with *all* of a human being's proper capacities: vegetative, sensitive, and rational. Shewmon, in advocating whole-brain death before adopting his current criterion (see below), asserts:

> The vast literature on "brain death" reveals two basic schools of thought regarding the essence of human death: loss of integrative unity of the body and loss of specifically human properties [i.e., the capacity for conscious rational thought and volition]. If the intellectual soul is indeed the substantial form of the body, these two aspects ought to converge to one and the same patho-physiological event. I take this conceptual unity to be as fundamental an axiom as either separate notion, so that convergence of the two approaches could be used as a kind of litmus test for formulations of death.
>
> (1992, p. 31)

Despite Shewmon's later denial of this "fundamental axiom," I consider it to have value because it disallows the distinction favored by some scholars – namely, advocates of the higher-brain concept of death – between "personal death" and "biological death" (Rachels, 1986, pp. 5–6, 24–7). Ashley also adopts this axiom as it serves to define the loss of all of a human being's proper capacities as coinciding in a single, empirically verifiable event: the cessation of whole-brain functioning (Ashley, 2001, p. 8).

Whole-brain death consists of the cessation of all three sets of critical functions Bernat defines as individually sufficient for a living human organism to exist (Bernat, 1998, p. 18). Furthermore, since these critical functions correspond to the Thomistic understanding of a rational soul's vegetative, sensitive, and rational capacities, I conclude that the irreversible cessation of whole-brain functioning[20] constitutes a human being's death from a Thomistic standpoint. Whole-brain death is *the* event which indicates a rational soul's separation from its body (Smith, 1990a, p. 55; Manni, 1999, p. 106; Ashley, 2001, p. 9).

Circulatory/respiratory criterion

In a reversal of his previous positions, Shewmon rejects the whole-brain criterion after examining cases in which a human body appears to maintain its integrative unity after whole-brain functioning has ceased. Such cases lead Shewmon to conclude that the brain does not function as the body's central organizer. Rather, Shewmon argues that the brain "fine-tunes" the vital metabolic functions that the body itself exercises as an integrated whole (Shewmon, 1997, 1998a, 2001). If, as Shewmon argues, a body can maintain its integrative unity without any brain functioning, then whole-brain death cannot be equated with a human organism's death. Shewmon thus advocates a return to the circulatory/respiratory criterion for determining when death occurs.

Shewmon's argument that the cessation of whole-brain functioning does not entail the loss of integrated somatic functioning can be formalized as follows:

(1) Somatic integrative unity does not entirely depend on whole-brain functioning – i.e., such unity can be maintained despite the loss of whole-brain functioning.

(2) The brain's role is more modulatory of an already unified living organism, than constitutive of that organism's present unity; somatically integrative functions are all the more effective when modulated by the brain, but they do not entirely vanish without the brain.

(3) Therefore, loss of somatic integrative unity is not a physiologically tenable rationale for equating whole-brain death with death of an organism as a whole.

(2001)

Shewmon purports that a human organism, without a functioning brain, can have "at least one emergent, holistic-level property" and that the existence of any such property is sufficient for an organism to have integrative unity (Shewmon, 2001,

p. 460). To demonstrate that the requisite holistic-level property exists, Shewmon provides what he terms a "litany of non-brain-mediated somatically integrative functions" that have been observed to persist in the body of a whole-brain dead patient. Such functions include homeostasis of various mutually interacting chemicals, cellular waste handling, energy balance, maintenance of body temperature, wound healing, infection fighting, stress responses, proportional growth, and even sexual maturation (Shewmon, 2001, p. 467–8).[21]

Shewmon appeals to a number of cases in which a whole-brain dead patient appears to exhibit integrative somatic functioning. One set of cases involves whole-brain dead pregnant women who are able, with artificial life support and pharmacotherapy, to maintain a nutritive uterine environment until the fetus can survive on its own (Dillon *et al.*, 1982; Field *et al.*, 1988; Bernstein *et al.*, 1989). Corrado Manni describes such women as "biological incubators" whose ability to provide a supportive uterine environment does not count against their being declared dead, because they lack *intrinsic* integrative somatic unity since their prolonged somatic survival requires at minimum mechanical ventilation and some degree of pharmacotherapy (Manni, 1999, p. 115). Shewmon counters that such a description "does injustice to the complex, teleological, organism-level, physiological changes of pregnancy (weight gain, internal redistribution of blood flow favoring the uterus, immunologic tolerance toward the fetus, etc.), which occur despite the absence of brain function" (Shewmon, 2001, p. 469; cf. Siegler and Wikler, 1982, pp. 1101–2; Lütz, 1999, p. 120; Potts, 2001, pp. 484–5).

The second type of case to which Shewmon appeals involves patients who are properly diagnosed as whole-brain dead and yet survive for extended periods of time with very little life-support technology. The most extreme case is that of a 19-year-old boy who was declared whole-brain dead at age four and, at the time of Shewmon's article, "remains on a ventilator, assimilates food placed in his stomach by tube, urinates spontaneously, and requires little more than nursing care. While 'brain dead' he has grown, overcome infections, and healed wounds." Shewmon concludes, "There is no question that he became 'brain dead' at age four; neither is there any question that he is still alive at age nineteen" (Shewmon, 1998a, p. 136; cf. Lütz, 1999, p. 121; Jones, 2000, p. 98; McMahan, 2002, p. 430).

Despite the absence of spontaneous heartbeat and the requirement of mechanical ventilation for respiration to occur, Shewmon contends that these patients exhibit somatic integrative unity by virtue of exercising somatic functions such as digestion, waste excretion, infection resistance, wound healing, chemical and cardiovascular homeostasis, growth, and development associated with the beginning of puberty. Shewmon thus concludes that these patients cannot be considered dead, even though they lack whole-brain functioning.

A third type of case supporting Shewmon's denial of whole-brain death involves patients whose brains are "functionally disconnected" from the rest of their body and yet maintain clear evidence of somatic integrative unity – as with Guillain-Barré Syndrome (GBS) (Shewmon, 1997, pp. 65–6) – and may even be conscious – as in cases of high cervical cord transection (Youngner and Bartlett, 1983; Shewmon, 1998a, pp. 140–1, 1999). Referring to such cases, Shewmon contends,

"If the body's integrative unity depended on brain functioning, then the body should fall apart just as surely from functional disconnection from the brain as from destruction of the brain" (Shewmon, 1998a, p. 140).

Guillain-Barré Syndrome is a condition in which patients present with varying degrees of neuropathy. In its most severe form, GBS clinically resembles whole-brain death, with cerebral activity detectable by electroencephalogram being the only means of distinguishing GBS from whole-brain death (Langendorf *et al.*, 1986; Drury *et al.*, 1987; Coad and Byrne, 1990; Hassan and Mumford, 1991; Marti-Masso *et al.*, 1993; Stojkovic *et al.*, 2001). GBS patients initially require life support in the form of mechanical ventilation, nutrition and hydration, and pharmacotherapy; over time, however, they usually recover neural functioning and life support can cease as they regain the ability to respire spontaneously, among other functions (Coad and Byrne, 1990; Stojkovic *et al.*, 2001, p. 431). While GBS resembles whole-brain death, it is not equivalent to whole-brain death, because the loss of neural function is reversible and there is persistent electrical activity in the cerebral cortex.

High cervical cord transection involves a structural "break" between the upper vertebrae and the brainstem, as in the injury suffered by Christopher Reeve when he was thrown from a horse (Reeve and Rosenblatt, 1998). This structural separation results in there being no electrical communication between the brainstem and the rest of the body. Patients in this condition are conscious and able to control those parts of their body that remain neurally connected to the brain above the transection – for example, facial muscles, eyes, and mouth – but they cannot spontaneously respire and must be connected to a mechanical ventilator.

Patients with GBS or high cervical cord transection are not dead, for GBS is reversible and high cervical cord transection does not preclude consciousness. Hence, such patients are rationally ensouled, which is sufficient for their bodies to have integrative unity. If, however, GBS and high cervical cord transection are functionally equivalent to whole-brain death, insofar as all three conditions involve the loss – regardless of reversibility – of electrical communication between the brainstem and the rest of the body, the bodies of patients in these conditions should not have integrative unity. This conclusion contradicts what follows from these patients being rationally ensouled.

As a result of this contradiction, Shewmon concludes that the notion of whole-brain death being sufficient for the loss of integrative unity should be abandoned (Shewmon, 1997, p. 66). Physiological data do not support the equivalence of whole-brain death with a human organism's death:

> The integrative functions of the brain, important as they are for health and mental activity, are not strictly necessary for, much less constitute, the life of the organism as a whole. Somatic integration is not localized to any single "critical" organ but is a holistic phenomenon involving mutual interaction of all the parts. Under ordinary circumstances the brain participates intimately and importantly in this mutual interaction, but it is not a *sine qua*

non; the body without brain function is surely very sick and disabled, but not dead.

(Shewmon, 2001, p. 473; see Truog, 1997; Byrne and
Rinkowski, 1999; Lütz 1999; Jones 2000;
Austriaco *et al.*, 2001; Potts 2001)

According to the Thomistic understanding of human nature, a rational soul's separation from its body occurs when the body can no longer support the soul's rational, sensitive, and vegetative capacities. If, as Shewmon maintains, integrative vegetative operations can remain in a whole-brain dead human body, one ought to conclude that a rational soul continues to inform such a body until it ceases its vital metabolic functions of circulation and respiration (Seifert, 1992, 1993, 2000; Jones, 2000, p. 109).

Does this conclusion require abandoning the Thomistic understanding of human death in terms of whole-brain death? Not necessarily. There are several issues that can be raised about the cases Shewmon uses to support his conclusion and the inferences he draws.

First, in the cases of pregnant women who were kept alive to carry their fetuses to term, "a great deal of effort had to be taken to keep their bodies alive" (Potts, 2001, p. 489; cf. Manni, 1999, p. 115). David Field and his colleagues list the measures required to maintain the body of a 27-year-old pregnant woman for nine weeks so that she could successfully gestate a healthy fetus: mechanical ventilation, vasopressors to treat fluid-resistant hypotension, warming or cooling blankets to treat temperature lability, nutritional support, replacement hormones to treat endocrine abnormalities, aggressive surveillance for and treatment of infections, and heparin prophylaxis (Field *et al.*, 1988, p. 818). Field notes that "maximum effort was directed at treating the severe hypotension, temperature fluctuations, diabetes insipidus, hypothyroidism, and cortisol deficiency that were thought to be the result of the autoregulatory function of the brain" (Field *et al.*, 1988, pp. 816–17). The requirement of *extensive* technological and pharmacological support – far beyond the "little more than nursing care" required in Shewmon's case of the 19-year-old whole-brain dead boy – indicates that the source of such patients' vegetative operations is not something intrinsic to them, but rather is from an extrinsic source. If so, then there are no grounds for asserting that these patients have active potentialities for vegetative, sensitive, and rational operations and are thereby informed by rational souls.

Second, Shewmon describes a human brain as more a "regulator" or "fine-tuner" of a body's vital metabolic functions, rather than being constitutive of them. It does not seem, however, that this distinction makes a real difference in criticizing the whole-brain criterion. While brainstem functioning is certainly not solely responsible for the vital metabolic functions of circulation and respiration, a human body cannot carry out such functions on its own in the absence of brainstem functioning. The assumption of such functions by life-support machinery indicates that the body has lost the capacity to perform them under its own control. These functions are no longer part of the body's "integrative" organic life, since, according to Aquinas, artifacts cannot be integrated into the substantial unity of a natural substance such as a biological organism. Hence, integrative unity has been lost in such cases.

Third, one may question the validity of the inference Shewmon makes based on his contention that certain holistic-level functions can be carried out in the absence of whole-brain functioning, and that an organism's possession of "at least one emergent, holistic-level property" (Shewmon, 2001, p. 460) is sufficient for it to have integrative unity. Shewmon's conclusion that certain functions – for example, homeostasis, energy balance, wound healing, stress responses, sexual maturation, and proportional growth (Shewmon, 2001, pp. 467–8) – are "integrative" just because they are holistic does not follow. Such functions can be understood as emerging from the interaction of a body's organ systems without entailing that the body has the integrative unity required for it to compose an individual substance that is *unum simpliciter* with a single substantial form. As Nicholas Tonti-Filippini contends:

> There is, however, a difference between the dynamic interactions of matter and form which is a living human individual, and the human organism whose organs keep functioning and interacting in a merely systemic way without the dynamic and ongoing integration of some form of control of the system as a whole. The essential dynamic organization and integration which constitute a living human body are far more than the bio-mechanical interaction of organs within the body.
>
> (1991, p. 33)

A human body's having control over its vital metabolic functions is a necessary criterion, I contend, for it to have integrative unity. Furthermore, such control must be exercised over the specific activities of circulation and respiration, which have long been understood as *the* fundamental metabolic functions necessary for somatic integrative unity. Without circulation and respiration, all other holistic-level somatic functions rapidly cease. Shewmon's case for abandoning the whole-brain criterion depends upon there being cases in which spontaneous heartbeat and respiration occur in the absence of whole-brain functioning. Shewmon has not presented any such case.

While Shewmon has not presented any case involving spontaneous heartbeat and respiration in the absence of whole-brain functioning, he nevertheless purports that, in the cases he does present, patients who have survived for years without whole-brain functioning have somatic integrative unity and thus are not dead. These cases, though, fail to be conclusive for two reasons. First, all of the patients require mechanical ventilation; none are capable of spontaneous respiration as well as other metabolic activities: "Immediate intervention is needed for the brain dead individual to survive, which includes the ventilator, but also includes pharmacological intervention (epinephrine, vasopressin, careful maintenance of electrolyte and water balance)" (Potts, 2001, p. 489).

Second, as Michael Potts notes, "Shewmon's examples of multi-year survivors of whole brain death suffered their injuries as young children, whose systemic plasticity is greater than that of adults" (Potts, 2001, p. 489).[22] Given the cases that Shewmon cites – the oldest patient being 14 years old and prepubescent when he suffered whole-brain death – it appears that the organic systems of young children, possibly up to some point just prior to the onset of puberty, are more "plastic" than those of more mature human beings. Shewmon admits that an "age factor" was present among the cases he analyzed (Shewmon, 1998b, p. 1543). Perhaps the integrative functions normally carried out by the brainstem in mature human beings can be taken on by other neural structures in young children; although not the most vital functions of heartbeat and respiration. Nevertheless, it may be the case that the bodies of such patients ought to be considered as rationally informed until death is declared using the traditional criterion.[23]

Finally, I wish to address the cases Shewmon uses of GBS patients and those who suffer high cervical cord transection. Although GBS patients cease to exercise their vital metabolic functions and thereby require artificial life support, they retain the capacity to perform such functions due to the reversibility of their condition; this is sufficient to assert that they remain informed by a rational soul. Once the conditions associated with GBS are alleviated, a patient's capacity to perform vital metabolic functions will be actualizable once again.

Cases of patients with high cervical cord transection are more difficult to contend with. Given that life-support machinery cannot become a proper part of a human body's substantial unity and that a body dependent on artificial support for its vital metabolic functions cannot have integrative unity, it follows that the body of a patient with high cervical cord transection is no longer informed by their rational soul below the point of the transection. The patient remains conscious and able to control their body above the level of the transection, which indicates that they are alive and informed by their rational soul; but their soul now informs only their head and those parts of their body which their brain can still control. The rest of their body, though still structurally joined to them, is no longer a proper part of them, because it no longer participates in their integrative organic functioning. With the help of artificial life support, the rest of the body continues to circulate oxygenated blood to the brain, which allows it to continue functioning and the patient to remain conscious. This relationship, though, of bodytobrain is no different than if the patient's head were severed and connected to an external mechanical pump; neither the pump nor the body are proper parts of the patient. This conclusion is quite counterintuitive and Shewmon exploits this feature of it:

> Is such a body an implacably disintegrating "collection of organs," or a live "organism as a whole" that happens to be severely disabled and dependent on medical technology? If the former, then we would have the bizarre anomaly of a "conscious corpse"; if the latter, then the [brain dead] body must equally be an "organism as a whole" despite *its* severe disability and technological dependence.
>
> (1999, p. 320)

Shewmon presents a false dilemma, because the above account does not entail the "bizarre anomaly" of a "conscious corpse" for two reasons. First, it is not the body – the so-called corpse – which is conscious, but the human being now composed of only a head. Second, the part of the body that no longer composes the human being is a "corpse" only in the technical sense of not being informed by a rational soul; but this does not imply that there is no life in the body. The cells and independent organ systems maintained with artificial assistance are each alive, each informed by a vegetative soul; they just no longer constitute the human being's life – that is, their vegetative capacities are no longer those of the patient's rational soul. If a patient with high cervical cord transection regains functional unity of their brainstem with the body connected to them – by having new neural tissue or an artificial electrical conductor[24] grafted onto the spinal cord to eliminate the transection – then their rational soul would reinform the body owing to their brainstem's control over the body's vital metabolic functions being regained.

I thus offer the following conclusion regarding the proper Thomistic concept and criterion of death. A human being's death, which consists of their rational soul separating from its body, occurs with the irreversible cessation of the body's integrative unity. The loss of somatic integrative unity is normally associated with the cessation of whole-brain functioning, in agreement with Aquinas's understanding of how a rational soul moves the various parts of its body through a primary organ. In cases of young children, however, who suffer the cessation of whole-brain functioning, an alternative primary organ may assume some of the associated integrative functions. Thus, while the concept of human death is univocally understood as the loss of somatic integrative unity in all cases, the criteria for determining when such loss has occurred may differ depending on what primary organ fulfills the requisite integrative functioning. In most cases, the whole-brain criterion is appropriate; but, in cases of young children, the circulatory/respiratory criterion may be most appropriate for a proper diagnosis of death.

Conclusion

My aim in this chapter has been to develop a proper Thomistic understanding of the end of a human being's embodied existence – the possibility of postmortem bodily existence aside (Eberl, 2000b). As with the beginning of human life, such an understanding involves determining when a rational soul can be asserted as the substantial form of a particular human body. The evidence supporting this assertion is the body's having at least active potentialities for vegetative, sensitive, and rational operations. I conclude that, parallel to the conclusion arrived at in Chapter 2, the presence of a primary organ through which integrative vegetative functioning is exercised, and thus a human body's organic/substantial unity is achieved, signals that the body is informed by a rational soul. Evidence that the brain typically functions as the integrative foundation for its body's vegetative and sensitive operations, as well as being correlated with rational operations, indicates that it is a fetal, infant, and adult human body's primary organ in most cases. Therefore, the cessation of *both* a brain's rationally correlated and biologically integrative functioning indicates that a particular human body is no longer informed by a rational soul. With the possible exception of young children, the whole-brain criterion is sufficient for determining when a human being has died.

4 Issues at the beginning of human life

Abortion, embryonic stem cell research, and cloning

Introduction

Three issues that dominate current bioethical discussions regarding the beginning of human life – and which have polarized debate in scientific, social, and political arenas – are abortion, human embryonic stem cell (ESC) research, and human cloning. The first has been a significant point of public debate since the US Supreme Court's *Roe v. Wade* and *Doe v. Bolton* decisions in 1973. The latter two issues garnered national and international attention beginning in 1998 and 1997, respectively, and the recent reports of the President's Council on Bioethics (PCB), *Human Cloning and Human Dignity* (2002) and *Monitoring Stem Cell Research* (2004), demonstrate that debate on these issues is not likely to end anytime in the near future. Having argued for a Thomistic account of when a human being begins to exist in Chapter 2 and elucidated Aquinas's natural law ethic in Chapter 1, I will now apply these metaphysical and moral positions to these issues of contemporary societal concern.

Abortion and abortifacient contraceptives

The term "abortion" refers to the termination of a pregnancy, which results in a human embryo or fetus's death. Such a death is always intrinsically bad from a Thomistic perspective, because, as I concluded in Chapter 2, the proper contemporary interpretation of Aquinas's view of when a human being begins to exist is when fertilization is complete. Hence, any abortion involves the death of a human being – a person.[1] In the following section regarding ESC research, I will articulate this view more fully, as well as Aquinas's understanding of the fundamental, intrinsic value of a human being's existence. Despite the inherent negativity of any abortion, the question remains whether some forms of abortion may be morally permissible or occur without anyone being morally responsible. We must, therefore, consider four distinct types of abortion:

1   spontaneous abortion, also know as "miscarriage;"
2   directly intended abortion;
3   indirectly intended abortion;
4   abortion by means of an abortifacient contraceptive.

A spontaneous abortion is the only form of abortion for which nobody may be morally responsible. It is typically caused by some natural factor that is not under anyone's control which results in either an embryo failing to implant in the uterus or a fetus dislodging from the uterus sometime after implantation. In some cases, though, a spontaneous abortion may be caused, or its likelihood increased, by some behavior on the mother's part or an environmental condition for which certain individuals, institutions, or societies may be responsible. All other forms of abortion entail some measure of moral responsibility insofar as they involve human intervention in the natural process of a pregnancy.

Directly intended abortion occurs when a woman or some other agent desires to end a pregnancy and does so through either a surgical procedure or a chemical inducement, such as RU-486. In most cases, it is a pregnant woman herself who seeks an abortion with the surgical procedure performed by someone else; though, in some cases, an abortion is caused by someone else who seeks to end a pregnancy against the woman's own wishes. The moral impermissibility of directly intended abortion is clearly stated by Aquinas when he asserts, "It is by no means permissible to kill the innocent" (ST, IIa-IIae.64.6; cf. Kavanaugh, 2001, pp. 125–32; Gómez-Lobo, 2002, p. 85). Aquinas also refers specifically to causing an unborn fetus's death in the case of someone who strikes a pregnant woman: "If the death of either the woman or the animated fetus results, he will not avoid the crime of homicide" (ST, IIa-IIae.64.8.ad 2; cf. CDP, VII).

Indirectly intended abortion occurs when a medically necessary procedure must be performed to save a pregnant woman's life which has the foreseen side-effect of bringing about the embryo or fetus's death. Examples of such procedures include removing a pregnant woman's uterus with a malignant tumor, removing the pathological section of a fallopian tube in the case of an ectopic pregnancy where the embryo has implanted in the tube, or a pregnant woman receiving radiation and chemotherapy to remit a malignant cancer. These procedures are morally permissible insofar as they are justified by the Principle of Double Effect (PDE), which I argued in Chapter 1 that Aquinas holds. PDE states that an action taken to produce some consequence, that is "good" *per se*, may be permissible even if it produces a foreseen negative consequence, that is *per se* morally impermissible, provided that the relative value of the negative consequence does not outweigh that of the good consequence, and the production of the negative consequence is not *directly intended* as an end or the means by which the good consequence is brought about. The above procedures all count as indirectly intended abortions and are thereby justified by appeal to PDE (Irving, 2000; Gómez-Lobo, 2002, p. 95). The directly intended end of each action is a "good" *per se* – namely, saving the mother's life. The foreseen abortion is not a directly intended end – that is, continuation of the pregnancy would be desired in the absence of the maleficent conditions. Abortion is not the means by which the mother's life is saved; if in the first case, for example, the fetus had developed to the point of extra-uterine viability and could survive on its own, its survival once the cancerous uterus was removed would have no effect on whether the mother's life was saved. Finally, the embryo or fetus's death does not outweigh the good of the mother's life being saved insofar as all human beings have an equal fundamental value.

Other forms of abortion, however, done for various apparently good intentions, fail to be justified by PDE. Perhaps a woman seeks an abortion to avoid the severe economic, emotional, or physical burdens that may befall her because of her low socio-economic status, lack of access to adequate health care, or absence of paternal and familial support. While avoiding such burdens, especially if the circumstances of her life make them particularly acute, is certainly a good worth pursuing, utilizing abortion as a means to achieve this good does not meet the conditions of PDE. Alfonso Gómez-Lobo notes that, in such cases:

> The death of the fetus is the means to the attainment of the good end, not a mere accidental consequence. It is intended because it is the main immediate goal of the procedure or, if not, it surely is the standard consequence thereof. Finally, if anything less that the protection of life is the intended good effect, there will be a significant disproportion between the two consequences of the action.
>
> (2002, pp. 95–6)

Since the pregnancy's termination and the embryo or fetus's consequent death is directly intended as the means whereby the woman avoids the anticipated burdens, and the good effect of avoiding those burdens is disproportionate to a human being's death, an abortion sought for this reason is not justifiable by appeal to PDE.

What about abortion in cases of rape? In such cases, an abortion may occur in one of two ways: (1) a surgical abortion procedure that occurs sometime after implantation when the victim knows she is pregnant; (2) use of an "emergency contraceptive pill" (ECP) that prevents implantation by altering the uterus's lining such that the embryo will not implant. (1) is judged morally impermissible for the same reasons given above with respect to a woman's desire to avoid the anticipated burdens of pregnancy, birth, and child-rearing. Although the emotional burdens associated with carrying and potentially raising – if adoption is not utilized – the child of her rapist are certainly the most severe any woman may ever have to experience, the good of avoiding such burdens does not outweigh the fundamental goodness of a human being's life and the abortion would be directly intended in this case.

(2) presents a quite different sort of case, however. ECPs, as mentioned above, may function as an "abortifacient" by preventing an embryo's implantation in the uterus. The use of any postcoital drug or contraceptive device that functions as an abortifacient, such as an IUD, would be morally impermissible insofar as it directly causes an embryo to abort (Ford, 2002, p. 92). An ECP, though, may also function as simply a "contraceptive" by preventing ovulation or fertilization,[2] or not function at all given the uncertainty that a rape victim was in her fertile period at the time of the attack (Ford, 2002, p. 94).

Norman Ford analyzes statistical data regarding the frequency of pregnancies after rape and the various potential causes of some of those pregnancies failing naturally, as opposed to being caused by ECPs. He concludes, "Conservatively, one could assume that the risk to the life of an embryo [by utilizing an ECP after rape] would be about 8 percent or less" (Ford, 2002, p. 94). In the absence of confirmatory evidence that fertilization has occurred in a woman who has been raped, the "risk" that using an ECP would cause an embryo to abort is sufficiently low to justify its use in the case of rape by appeal to PDE:[3]

> It would seem to be ethically permissible to administer ECPs as soon as possible within 72 hours of rape to prevent conception if, after inquiry, there were no reasonable grounds to believe an embryo had been already conceived. In this case a risk of loss of an embryo due to the medication would not be more than about 8 percent, not disproportionate or significant after rape…But an ECP could not ethically be taken if a test showed conception had, or most likely had, occurred.
>
> (Ford, 2002, pp. 94–5; cf. Finnis, 1999, p. 17)

One cannot directly intend that an embryo be aborted if chances are that there is no embryo present in the first place. What is directly intended, by administering an ECP, is the prevention of ovulation or fertilization, which is a morally acceptable good worth pursuing in comparison to the overwhelming emotional burden – along with other potential burdens – a rape victim who finds herself pregnant may face. If, however, there is certainty or a high probability that an embryo already exists, then the use of an ECP becomes an abortifacient and the abortion is directly intended as the means by which the rape victim avoids the anticipated burdens resulting from her pregnancy.

Any form of directly intended abortion is morally impermissible from a Thomistic perspective. Nevertheless, bringing about an embryo or fetus's death as the result of a necessary life-saving medical procedure may be permissible if the conditions of PDE are satisfied. An embryo or fetus's death may also be *risked* – given a sufficiently low probability of its existence – in order for a rape victim to avoid the burdens associated with pregnancy in such a tragic situation. I will now consider two more recently debated issues that involve the death of human embryos or fetuses, among other effects that will be discussed: ESC research and cloning.

Human embryonic stem cell research

The first successful derivation of stem cells from human embryos was reported by James Thomson and his colleagues in 1998 (Thomson *et al.*, 1998). ESCs are self-renewable and "pluripotent," which means they can generate various types of cells, tissues, and perhaps even organs. ESC research thus has the potential to produce significant therapeutic benefits insofar as stem cells could be cultured and developed into such things as blood cells, cardiac muscle, bone marrow to treat leukemia, and insulin-producing pancreatic cells to treat diabetes. Stem cells may even be developed into neural tissue to treat victims of Alzheimer's, Parkinson's, or stroke (Kondziolka *et al.*, 2000).

The moral controversy surrounding ESC research concerns the process by which ESCs are derived. ESCs are found in the inner cell mass (ICM) of a blastocyst – the ball of cells that constitutes a human embryo prior to its implantation in the uterus – and must be "isolated" by removing the entire ICM and placing it in an appropriate culture medium.[4] Without the ICM, the remaining components of the blastocyst cannot develop into a fetus or child. Deriving ESCs from the ICM thus disrupts the biological integrity of the blastocyst and the embryo becomes nonviable; it is no longer capable of developing into a fetus. Hence, those who consider a human being to exist from the zygote stage onward argue that ESC research is morally impermissible, for it involves the destruction of a human being who has a strong right to life. Those who argue in favor of continued ESC research contend either that a blastocyst is not a human being, but merely a ball of cells with human DNA, or that a blastocyst may be a human being, but its right to life is outweighed by the enormous therapeutic benefits which may result from ESC research. The current policy in the United States permits ESC research and provides federal funding for research conducted on ESC lines[5] created before August 9, 2001. On that date, President George W. Bush announced that no further research on human embryos for the purpose of deriving ESCs will be supported by federal funding (Bush, 2001). A revision of this federal policy is under debate in the US Congress as of this writing.

In order to determine whether ESC research is morally permissible, several questions must be answered. First, what is the *metaphysical* status of a human blastocyst? Is it merely a ball of cells with human DNA or is it a human being? Second, what is the *moral* status of a human blastocyst? Does it have a strong – or perhaps inviolable – right to life, or can it be destroyed for the sake of the therapeutic benefits that might result from ESC research? Third, if ESC research is morally impermissible, what moral limits does this impose on reaping the benefits of such research, given that the research will no doubt continue despite any moral sanctions? Finally, what morally permissible alternatives might there be to ESC research that have the potential to provide similar therapeutic benefits?

Metaphysical status of a human blastocyst

A key first step in addressing the moral permissibility of ESC research is to establish the metaphysical nature of a human blastocyst. Is it a human being or is it merely a ball of cells with human DNA? Arguments for the latter position consist of claims that a blastocyst is a "potential" human being in this respect: although it is not yet a human being, if placed in a uterus and not disturbed, it will develop into such a being. Joseph Donceel, Robert Pasnau, and Norman Ford defend this view from a Thomistic perspective.[6] Prior to uterine implantation or the formation of the cerebral cortex, according to these authors, a human being does not exist because the embryo is not informed by a rational soul. By contrast, Benedict Ashley's account entails that a human blastocyst is a human being because it requires only a supportive uterine environment to develop into an actually thinking rational being. It is already informed by a rational soul that is the metaphysical blueprint for such development. I concluded in Chapter 2 that a human zygote is a rationally ensouled human being and that embryonic development is an extended process of actualizing that human being's vegetative, sensitive, and rational capacities. Therefore, the destruction of a human blastocyst that occurs in the derivation of ESCs constitutes a human being's death.

Aside from arguments put forth from a Thomistic perspective, Ronald Green argues against the claim that a human being begins to exist as a zygote by pointing out that the fertilization process from which a zygote results is precisely that – a *process*. It is therefore quite difficult, and probably arbitrary, to pinpoint exactly when rational ensoulment occurs and a human being begins to exist (Green, 2002, p. 21). Robert Orr counters that Green overlooks the relevance of the fact that the process is occurring in the first place and asserts that "the beginning of life is at the beginning of the beginning of the process, not the end of the beginning" (Orr, 2002, p. 58). A remaining question, however, is what event the "beginning of the beginning of the process" denotes. Perhaps we should not be concerned with identifying the event it denotes, since the concern here is not with the process of fertilization, but with the embryonic development that follows. Even so, there is a good candidate for the event that signals the end of two substances – sperm and ovum – and the beginning of a new substance – the zygote. This event is "syngamy," which is when the twenty-three maternal chromosomes line up with the twenty-three paternal chromosomes. Green admits:

> In biological terms, if we think of a new individual as coming into being with the appearance of a cell having a new "diploid" genome, a full complement of forty-six chromosomes, syngamy would seem to be a good candidate for a starting point. This is the moment that the "zygote" is said to come into being.
> (2002, p. 21)

Though Green does not challenge the idea that syngamy constitutes the "moment" at which a zygote comes into being, he raises further challenges to the claim that a zygote or early embryo is an individual human being. He does so by appealing to Ford's argument based on twinning and cellular totipotentiality. Having addressed Ford's argument in Chapter 2, I contend that there is nothing implausible about taking syngamy as *the* event which signals the "beginning of the beginning" of the process of a human being's life.

Once ESCs are derived from the ICM, however, we are no longer dealing with an ensouled human being. While ESCs have the potential to give rise to many different cells, tissues, and even organs, they cannot develop into a whole organism:

> It should be clear, however, that ES cells are not themselves embryos because, although they are *pluripotent* in that they could develop into any cell or tissue of the body, they are not *totipotent*. They are not capable of forming a new individual, as a fertilized egg or single cell taken from a four cell embryo might if cultured in vitro and placed in a uterus. Culture of ES cells followed by placement in the uterus would not result in the implantation of an embryo and eventual birth of a child.
> (Robertson, 1999, p. 111;
> cf. Maienschein, 2002, p. 18)

Ted Peters challenges this view by noting that a human ESC "contains all the same genetic material as the early embryo from which it is derived. It lacks only the environmental structure (trophoblast, etc.) to permit it to become an embryo" (Peters, 2001, p. 132). Peters raises this challenge in an effort to show that the potentiality of a human ESC is no different from that of any cell of an adult human body, which requires only a bit of genetic reprogramming and a suitable environment to develop into a "cloned" human being. This comparison calls into question the importance of an early embryo's potentiality with respect to its status as a human being, if such potentiality is had by not only the ESCs derived from it, but also any cell of a developed human body.

Peters fails to note, though, that there are two relevant types of potentiality – "active" and "passive," as defined in Chapter 2 – and an early embryo's potentiality to become an actualized human being differs in type from the potentiality an ESC or a somatic cell has to become such a being. An early embryo needs only a suitable uterine environment to continue its development and has within itself everything needed to form the tissues and organs required for the vegetative, sensitive, and rational operations definitive of a human being. A somatic cell from which a human being may be cloned does not have this sort of potentiality. In the cloning process a somatic cell's biological integrity is violated in that its nucleus is removed and implanted in an enucleated ovum, which is then induced to divide and thereby reproduce partheno-genetically. An ESC's potentiality is more like that of a somatic cell than an early embryo. Peters attempts to equate an ESC with an early embryo by stating that the former requires simply "environmental" factors, such as a trophoblast – the layer of cells that attaches the blastocyst to the uterus and out of which is formed the placenta and umbilical cord – to develop into a human being. This attempt fails because a tro-phoblast is not an "environmental" factor, but a biological component of an embryo in the blastocyst stage, one that the embryo requires for its continued development; the fallopian tube and uterus are the relevant environmental factors. Hence, an ESC, lacking a trophoblast and the other biological components required for its develop-ment into a human being – that is, lacking those things that are an early embryo's *proper parts* – does not have the inherent active potentiality that an early embryo has. Its potentiality is merely passive insofar as the requisite parts must be added to it.[7]

Thus, there clearly is nothing morally wrong – at least, there clearly is no mistreatment of a human being – involved in the manipulation of ESCs to grow cells, tissues, and organs with human DNA. The case is not so clear, however, when it comes to destroying early human embryos to derive ESCs from the ICM. Whether this practice is morally permissible is the issue on which the morality of ESC research hinges.

Moral status of an early human embryo and the ethics of ESC research

Embryos used for ESC research are typically surplus embryos which were produced as part of an *in vitro* fertilization (IVF) procedure, but then, rather than being implanted, were cryogenically preserved – "frozen." Embryos can also be created directly for the purpose of stem cell derivation through IVF or cloning. In addition to the ICM of early embryos, pluripotent stem cells may be derived from the germ cells of aborted fetuses (Shamblott *et al.*, 1998). Consequently, fetal germ cell (FGC) research holds similar therapeutic promise as ESC research, yet it does not require the destruction of an embryo in the process of stem cell derivation. In this section, I will address the moral status of embryos produced through IVF and the permissibility of using such embryos for ESC research. I will also consider the permissibility of deriving stem cells from the FGCs of aborted fetuses. Later, I will consider the moral permissibility of creating embryos directly for ESC research through cloning.

In a typical IVF procedure, anywhere between five and twelve zygotes are created and cultured to divide up to the four- or eight-cell stage, at which point some of them are transferred into a woman's uterus in the hope that at least one or two will implant and develop into a viable fetus. The remaining embryos are either immediately destroyed or, in most cases, cryogenically preserved for possible future use if the initial procedure fails to result in a pregnancy. If the initial procedure is successful, though, and the parents no longer require the frozen embryos and do not wish to donate them to another infertile couple, they will eventually be destroyed.

Another option for parents who have used IVF is to donate their surplus frozen embryos for ESC research. There are two arguments for the moral permissibility of using surplus embryos from IVF for research that will involve their destruction. First, such embryos are not human beings and thus have no right to life that is violated by their destruction. Second, although they may be human beings, such embryos are destined for destruction anyway and it is preferable that they be destroyed in a way that may yield significant therapeutic benefits.

Moral status of surplus embryos from IVF

I have argued earlier and in Chapter 2 that an early human embryo is a human being and that it remains one even if it is frozen, or in a petri dish, or in a woman's reproductive tract. Peter Singer and Karen Dawson believe otherwise. They contend that, if one argues for the personhood of an early embryo based on its potentiality to develop into a fully actualized human being, such potentiality is not present in a laboratory-produced, unimplanted embryo as robustly as it is in an embryo already present in woman's natural reproductive environment (Singer and Dawson, 1990). Their contention is based on the lower probability that an embryo existing in a laboratory or in a frozen state will develop into a human being, and the fact that human intervention is required to actualize such an embryo's potentiality – just as human intervention is required to bring sperm and ovum together to form a zygote. Singer and Dawson conclude that a laboratory-produced, unimplanted embryo's potentiality for personhood is a passive potentiality akin to that of a sperm or ovum, rather than the active potentiality of an embryo already in an environment conducive to its natural development:

> Whereas the embryo inside the female body has some definite chance of developing into a child unless a deliberate human act interrupts its growth, the egg and sperm can only develop into a child if there is a deliberate human act. In this respect the embryo in the laboratory is like the egg and sperm, and not like the embryo in the human body.
>
> (1990, p. 87)

Singer and Dawson mischaracterize the potentiality of a laboratory-produced, unimplanted embryo in two ways. First, the probability that a potentiality will be actualized is irrelevant to whether or not the potentiality is present in a substance. As long as the substance has within itself everything required for it to attain the actualized state, aside from a supportive environment, then it does not matter if it is deprived of the requisite environment for its development. There is nothing internally distinct between an embryo in a fallopian tube traveling toward the uterus for implantation, an embryo in a petri dish waiting to be transferred to a uterus for implantation, and a frozen embryo waiting to be thawed and then transferred for uterine implantation. The only difference is the lack of a supportive environment in the latter two cases, but this difference has no bearing on whether the embryo has an *intrinsic* potentiality to develop into a fully actualized human being.

Second, the need for human intervention to actualize a laboratory-produced, unimplanted embryo's intrinsic potentiality also makes no difference to whether the embryo has a natural tendency to develop, given a supportive environment, into an actually living, sentient, and rational being. The difference in potentiality between sperm and ovum, and an embryo in a fallopian tube, lies not in the fact that the former require human intervention whereas the latter does not, but in the fact that the former must cease to exist by combining together to form a new substance. No substantial change results from the human act of transferring an embryo from a petri dish to a woman's reproductive tract. There is no metaphysical change in the nature of the embryo itself, as there is in the case of sperm and ovum forming a zygote.

It is not sufficient, however, simply to establish that an early embryo which is the product of IVF is a human being. An argument for its strong moral status must also be provided. Typically, when one claims that something is a human being or a person, it is assumed that it has a "right to life" or that it cannot be treated as a mere means, rather than as an end in itself (Kant, 1785, ch. 2). Aquinas, though, never defines a human being's moral status in terms of its having a "right" or in terms of its being "an end in itself." Rather, he defines a thing's moral status solely in terms of its intrinsic *goodness*. Whatever "rights" it may have are derived from its inherent value and the natural law mandate to pursue the good in all its forms while avoiding evil. Thus, for example, a nonhuman animal has a measure of goodness insofar as it is a living, sentient being. The value of its nature as such ought to be respected unless it would interfere with respecting the value of a being with a greater degree of intrinsic goodness, such as a living, sentient, and rational being. Aquinas's natural law ethic thus recommends – although Aquinas himself does not explicitly endorse – some form of "animal rights" in cases where respect for animals' intrinsic goodness does not detract from the pursuit of essential human goods (Barad, 1988).[8]

A human being's intrinsic goodness is based on their nature as a living, sentient, and rational substance – a person. Rationality, in Aquinas's view, is the highest capacity found among natural substances because it enables a person to come to know universal conceptual truths and to determine their own actions (ST, Ia.29.1). Hence, he says, the term "person" is attributed to rational beings insofar as they have a special dignity – that is, a particularly high degree of intrinsic goodness among natural substances (ST, Ia.29.3).

Peters contends, against Aquinas, that "dignity is a relational concept that begins first with the external conferral of dignity before it is claimed by a person as something intrinsic" (Peters, 2001, p. 128). This contention would perhaps be true if a thing's goodness were solely a matter of convention, or existed only in view of its usefulness or desirability for those rational beings with the capacity to confer dignity upon it. For Aquinas, though, the goodness which makes something desirable in the first place must be found in the thing itself. There would be no starting point for, say, my desire to own a bird unless there was something intrinsically good about the bird. One could counter that whatever feature of the bird that makes ownership of it desirable, that feature makes such ownership desirable only *to me* – subjectively – and not desirable *in itself* – objectively. The denial of any objective intrinsic goodness in the bird requires the denial that the bird has a place in the natural order and that its existence, with all the capacities appropriate to its avian nature, is beneficial to the world whether or not any rational being considers it desirable. Space does not permit me to argue here against such a denial, but I raise this point to show what Peters is committed to if he holds that human beings or other things do not have intrinsic dignity in some measure.

From a Thomistic perspective, an early embryo is a human being and thereby has an intrinsic dignity – an inherent goodness that must be promoted. Life, Aquinas asserts in formulating his natural law ethic, is a fundamental good for human beings (ST, Ia-IIae.94.2; Finnis, 1980, p. 86). Without life, none of a human being's other inherently valuable capacities – including rationality – can be actualized in the service of contributing to the overall goodness of the natural world in which human beings exist and flourish. To act against the existence and flourishing of a human being – in this case, an early embryo – constitutes a morally impermissible act that must be avoided due to the natural law mandate to promote life as a fundamental good.

Some supporters of ESC research admit that an early embryo is a human being whose life is intrinsically valuable to a certain degree, but argue that its value is not significantly strong and ought to be weighed against the value of reduced human suffering from diseases such as leukemia, Alzheimer's, and Parkinson's, the remedy of which is the promise of ESC research. Karen Lebacqz and the members of the Geron Ethics Advisory Board[9] maintain that an early human embryo's intrinsic goodness should be respected in ESC research "by ensuring that it is used with care only in research that incorporates substantive values such as reduction of human suffering" (Geron Ethics Advisory Board, 1999, p. 33). This conclusion, which results from weighing the value of an early embryo against the value of reduced human suffering, conflicts with the implications of Aquinas's method of moral reasoning.

Aquinas holds that certain goods may be violated for the sake of a greater good; for example, the goodness of plant life may be violated insofar as it is necessary to promote the greater good of animal and human life (ST, IIa-IIae.64.1). Human life, in fact, may not be an absolutely inviolable good if what is at stake is the promotion of other human lives or other greater goods. As Gómez-Lobo notes in interpreting Aquinas's natural law ethic:

> At times it may seem as if the grounding good – life itself – should *always* take precedence over everything else. Indeed, it is so basic that in most cases it is clear that aiming at other goods at the cost of life would be irrational. Yet there may be circumstances in which not even life should be preserved at all costs. It may be rational to give up one's life (which is not the same as *taking* one's life) so that others may live.
>
> (2002, p. 40)

Aquinas recognizes, for example, that it is virtuous for a human being to sacrifice their life for the greater good of bearing witness to the Christian faith (ST, IIa-IIae.124.3–4). He even asserts that it may be lawful for the state to *take* the life of a wrongdoer who may be a source of corruption, and thus the wrongdoer's life is sacrificed for the sake of the common good (ST, IIa-IIae.64.3–4).

Nevertheless, when Aquinas turns to the question whether it is lawful to kill an *innocent* human being, he unequivocally asserts that such killing is never permissible (ST, IIa-IIae.64.6). It is interesting to note that the primary reason Aquinas gives for this prohibition is that an innocent human being's life "preserves and advances" the common good insofar as each human being is unavoidably a member of a community and one's existence is inherently beneficial to one's community so long as it does not become a corrupting influence. The Geron Ethics Advisory Board holds that it may be "respectful" to an early embryo to sacrifice its life for the sake of the common good because ESC research has the potential to reduce human suffering. Aquinas, though, would counter that the embryo's very existence already contributes to the common good even if its contribution is not readily apparent or must await the embryo's further development. Destroying an embryo for ESC research thus fails to promote not only the goodness of the embryo's life, but also the goodness of the community to which the embryo unavoidably belongs and for which it may provide significant material contributions once it develops to the point where it may actualize its rational capacity.

Using embryos that are destined for destruction

Many early embryos produced by IVF are not allowed to develop to the point where they may make a material contribution to the common good. They are destined for destruction because they are no longer needed for future IVF attempts. Although some people have attempted to adopt frozen surplus embryos to give the embryos at least a chance of implantation and development into fully actualized human beings, this approach is legally complicated and has not caught on with any fervor (Watt, 1999, 2001; Davidson, 2001; Iozzio, 2002; Berkman, 2003; Tonti-Filippini, 2003). This raises the question whether it would be wrong to substitute, for the usual manner in which these embryos are destroyed, one that may produce significant therapeutic benefits; instead of the embryos' lives simply being "wasted" in a process that destroys them but yields no further good.

President Clinton's National Bioethics Advisory Commission (NBAC) concluded that the destruction of surplus embryos from IVF for ESC research would not be wrong since they "have no prospect for survival even if they are not used in deriving ES cells." They have no such prospect because their destruction is accepted as part of the routine course of IVF: "If embryo destruction is permissible, then it certainly should be permissible to destroy them in a way that would generate stem cells for bona fide research" (NBAC, 1999, p. 53). Françoise Baylis points out, however, that this way of arguing for the permissibility of ESC research *presumes* the moral permissibility of destroying surplus embryos from IVF (Baylis, 2001, pp. 54–5). Although the destruction of surplus embryos is legally accepted and widely practiced in the United States and in other nations, its moral status remains controversial and hence furnishes poor support for the claim that because surplus embryos are destined for destruction anyway, it is morally permissible to destroy them for ESC research. Since a human embryo's destruction *simpliciter* is morally impermissible according to Aquinas's natural law ethic, neither the destruction of surplus embryos from IVF nor their destruction for the sake of ESC research is justifiable.

Fetal germ cells as a source for deriving stem cells

Surplus embryos produced by IVF are not the only source of pluripotent stem cells. They may also be derived from FGCs of human fetuses that have already been destroyed through procured abortion. As shown earlier, directly intended abortion is clearly morally impermissible according to Aquinas. The question here is whether, given that abortion is morally impermissible, one may use aborted fetal tissue for the purpose of obtaining FGCs in order to derive stem cells. On the one hand, there appears to be no moral quandary, because the abortion and the obtaining of FGCs are two separate actions and the latter is morally neutral. As long as abortion is not performed *for the intended purpose* of obtaining FGCs for research, it seems that obtaining FGCs from aborted fetal tissue is morally permissible insofar as it is disconnected from the act of abortion. On the other hand, obtaining and using FGCs from aborted fetal tissue to derive stem cells may involve "complicity" in the immoral act of abortion. This issue of complicity with an immoral action also bears on whether it is permissible either to benefit from ESC research if the promised potential for significant therapeutic breakthroughs is realized, or to conduct research using ESC lines derived and cultured by someone else.

John Robertson argues that there is no moral complicity in any of these cases, given certain conditions:

> If the original immoral derivation of ES cells occurred with the intent to make later ES cell research possible, then it is reasonable to view the later researchers as complicit in the original derivation, on the causative theory that the derivation would not have occurred if the later use had not been contemplated. Complicity based on causation, however, would not exist if the original immoral derivation of cells would have occurred regardless of the activities of any particular later researcher. Once the ES cells have been derived for particular kinds of research or for particular researchers, they exist and could be used by other researchers. Under a causative theory of complicity, making the ES cells available to later researchers would not make those researchers complicit in the immoral derivation of the ES cells if their research plans or actions had no effect on whether the original immoral derivation occurred.
>
> (1999, p. 113)

> Under a causative theory of complicity, neither derivation nor later use of ES cells from abortions that would otherwise have occurred would make one morally complicit in the abortion itself because there is no reasonable basis for thinking that donation of tissue for research after the decision to abort has been made would have caused or brought about the abortion. Thus persons who think that induced abortion is immoral could support the use of fetal tissue or ES cells derived from abortions as long as the derivation or later research or therapy had no reasonable prospect of bringing about abortion, just as they could support organ donation from homicide victims without approving of the homicide that made the organs available. To do so, however, such individuals would have to be convinced that research uses of fetal tissue from abortions otherwise occurring would not bring about future abortions or in some way make abortion appear to be a positive, praiseworthy act.
>
> (1999, p. 114)

Moral complicity, Robertson contends, involves having a "causative" role in the occurrence of some action. So long as one's research using ESCs derived from embryos which are destroyed in the process – or one's derivation and use of stem cells derived from aborted fetal tissue – does not in any way cause either the embryo's destruction or the abortion when it would not have occurred otherwise, then that act is justified. One would also be justified in being the beneficiary of such research (Cataldo, 2002; Green, 2002).

The question remains, however, whether one's use or benefit from stem cell research, though not causally related to the *past* destruction of an embryo or fetus, may encourage *future* embryonic or fetal destruction. Albert Moraczewski asks:

> Would the destroyer of the embryo benefit financially – directly or indirectly – from the use of stem cell lines? Most likely. Would not such persons be encouraged to destroy additional embryos for the sake of obtaining stem cells,

especially since there is already a call from more stem cell lines in order to have a wider genetic representation? And if it turns out that the use of stem cells actually proves to be clinically successful in the treatment of one or more serious medical conditions, the demand for additional stem cells will increase enormously. Thus the use of stem cell lines obtained from the destruction of human embryos rewards the original evil doer and encourages him to repeat performance. Is this not scandal in its strict sense?

(2002, p. 45)

James Bopp, Jr raises the concern that any research utilizing fetal products, such as tissue for transplantation or FGCs, "will add one more reason for women to have an abortion" (Bopp, 1994, p. 72).

The issue, as Moraczewski notes, has to do with the concept of "scandal," which Aquinas defines as "something said or done less rightly, causing another's [moral] ruin" and occurs when "someone by his admonition, inducement, or example leads another to sin" (ST, IIa-IIae.43.1). Aquinas further specifies two types of scandal: active and passive. Active scandal occurs

when someone by his evil word or deed intends to induce another to sin; or, if he does not so intend, when the deed is such that by its nature it is an inducement to sin; for example, someone publicly commits a sin or something that has a resemblance to sin.

(ST, IIa-IIae.43.1.ad 4)

Passive scandal, on the other hand, occurs "when it is outside of the agent's intention, and outside the nature of the action, and yet someone who is disposed toward evil is induced to sin" (ST, IIa-IIae.43.1.ad 4). Aquinas contends that active scandal is always an occasion of moral wrongdoing on the part of the agent who scandalizes another, while passive scandal may not entail moral wrongdoing on the part of the agent so long as the word or action which led to the other's moral downfall was good in itself (ST, IIa-IIae.43.2). Peter Cataldo correctly notes that scandal, thus understood, is irrelevant to the question of complicity with an immoral action that has already occurred (Cataldo, 2002, p. 36). Nevertheless, the concern remains that using or benefiting from the derivation of stem cells from early embryos or FGCs of aborted fetuses may "scandalize" others in the future to destroy more embryos or abort more fetuses for research purposes.

Consider the case of someone with Parkinson's disease who may benefit from therapeutic treatment developed from ESCs that have been cultured to give rise to neural tissue. Does this person's willingness to benefit from the treatment for their disease lead in some fashion to the moral downfall of a researcher who will destroy more embryos in the future to derive ESCs? In order to count as a case of active scandal, the person would have to either (1) do an evil action with the intention of leading the researcher to destroy more embryos, or (2) do an action which is of such a nature that it leads the researcher to destroy more embryos – even if they did not intend to induce the researcher to perform such an act – by (3) publicly doing an evil action or by (4) giving the appearance of doing an evil action that leads the researcher to destroy more embryos. If the person who suffers from Parkinson's directly supports embryo destruction for ESC research or otherwise publicly expresses their desire to benefit from the research for the intended purpose of inciting the progress of such research and the further destruction of embryos, then they may be involved in active scandal under condition (1). This is because the moral wrongness of embryo destruction has been independently established above and it is morally wrong in itself to encourage another to do an immoral action. If, however, they have not explicitly supported or called for further ESC research in this manner, but commit only the act of willfully receiving therapy that results from ESC research, it is not at all apparent that they are guilty of active scandal. It is not apparent because condition (2) – in the form of either (3) or (4) – requires that the agent commit an *evil* action or give the appearance of doing so. Receiving therapy which is beneficial to one's health does not in itself constitute an evil action. To contend otherwise would beg the question whether receiving such therapy is a case of active scandal.

If any scandal occurs merely because someone willfully receives therapy that results from ESC research, that scandal can at most be passive scandal. It will constitute such scandal if the researcher whose intentional act is to derive ESCs by destroying an embryo is already disposed toward doing this action whether or not any particular person willfully elects to receive the resulting benefits. The same conclusion applies to a researcher, other than the one who destroys the embryo, who uses a cultured ESC line to develop beneficial therapies. This is so unless the researcher explicitly requests further ESCs to assist their research and thereby intentionally encourages another to destroy more embryos. The case is similar with the use of FGCs from aborted fetuses to derive stem cells and develop beneficial therapies. So long as a researcher who utilizes FGCs or derived stem cell lines, or a person who willingly receives whatever therapy may be developed, does not directly intentionally encourage further abortions for the sake of providing more FGCs, they are morally justified in their own action.

It could be objected that there may be some researchers who are not already disposed to destroying embryos to derive ESCs, but would become so disposed, and very likely engage in acts of embryo destruction, given further demand for ESCs. Thus, since the researcher who uses derived ESCs or the sufferer of Parkinson's who reaps the benefits of such research contributes to that demand, they are both contributing to the likely increase of an immoral practice. Would this not constitute some form of scandal?[10] This objection is *consequentialist* in nature, which is inimical to Aquinas's natural law ethic. Whereas Aquinas is concerned with the nature of a moral act, consequentialists are concerned only with what results from a moral act. Furthermore, consequentialism does not take into account whether the positive or negative effects of one's act involve the act of another moral agent.[11] Nonconsequentialist theories, such as Aquinas's, do not require that one moral agent be responsible for the acts of another moral agent, except in special circumstances such as those which define scandal.

Hence, merely increasing the demand for ESCs may constitute morally illicit scandal from a consequentialist perspective, if ESC derivation is itself judged to be morally illicit from the same perspective, because those whose acts result in the increased demand are to some degree responsible for what others do to meet that demand. For Aquinas, however, a prerequisite for scandal is an agent's performance of an inherently "evil" act, which thereby influences another agent to perform their own evil act. Benefiting from medical research or using derived ESCs to develop beneficial therapies are not inherently evil acts. Furthermore, while it could be argued that generating a demand for ESCs "by its nature is an inducement to sin," no particular person is the target of such inducement and the demand for ESCs may go unmet. It is up to the conscience of each person who has the resources to engage in ESC derivation to weigh the demand for ESCs against the moral illicitness of embryo destruction. That someone elects to respond to the demand and engage in acts of embryo destruction is not the responsibility of those who generated the demand *indirectly* through their development or use of therapies that result from ESC derivation; although the beneficiary's moral responsibility would be different if they *explicitly* lobbied for further ESC derivation.

Consider the following analogy. As Robertson notes, benefiting from organs donated by homicide victims does not entail approval of the act of homicide which made the organs available for transplant. But a physician who is not typically inclined toward homicide may judge that it would help meet the extensive demand for vital organs for transplant if they began secretly euthanizing homeless patients whose deaths would be of no negative consequence to society, or so they convinces themselves.[12] Does it constitute scandal for those who benefit from organ transplant to have created the demand whereby this physician was motivated to begin killing innocent people to meet it? A potentially disanalogous feature is that increasing the supply of vital organs for transplant can be accomplished in other, morally licit, ways, such as participating in a public awareness campaign or better counseling of families of deceased or dying patients about organ donation. Thus, the burden of moral responsibility for the homeless persons' deaths falls squarely on the shoulders of the physician who neglected to pursue these alternative means to meet this demand. As will be shown in the next section, however, there are morally licit alternatives to ESC research to meet the demand for beneficial therapies for diseases such as Parkinson's. Hence, the burden of moral responsibility for the act of embryo destruction to derive ESCs likewise falls squarely on the shoulders of the researcher who neglects to pursue these alternative avenues of research.

Alternatives to ESC research

Given the conclusion that the intentional destruction of human embryos for ESC research is intrinsically morally wrong, it is important to point out some of the viable alternatives to ESC research that may produce similar therapeutic benefits. The first is research on adult stem cells (ASCs). ASCs function similarly to ESCs, but are not as pluripotent; they can generate more cells of the same kind or, with coaxing, produce one or two other types of cells. ASCs have been identified in the pancreas, in bone marrow, and even in the brain, as well as in many other parts of the body. Hence, although ASCs are more limited than ESCs, they can neverthe-less be potentially cultured to produce some of the key cells and tissues sought by proponents of ESC research: insulin-producing pancreatic cells to treat diabetes, bone marrow to treat leukemia, and even neural tissue (Juengst and Fossel, 2000; Ahmann, 2001, p. 148; Coors, 2002, p. 306; Ford, 2002, p. 60; Doerflinger, 2003, p. 785, n. 51; Prentice, 2003; PCB, 2004, pp. 121–6; Prentice in PCB, 2004, pp. 309–46). Stem cells may also be derived from neonatal products such as umbilical cord blood, fetuses that have spontaneously miscarried (Michejda, 2002), perhaps even from unfertilized ova:

> Experiments are now being conducted that show "that monkey eggs can be chemically treated and modified to the point where they begin behaving enough like embryos to generate stem cells – all without the addition of sperm normally required for embryogenesis, and without any capacity to grow into a baby monkey." If research using parthenogenesis in humans could produce pluripotent stem cells directly, and not totipotent embryonic stem cells first, there would be little ethical debate since at no time would a developing embryo be formed. This could be the source of stem cells that have all the potentially good qualities of embryonic stem cells and the ethical advantage of not having been derived from an embryonic cell mass.
>
> (McCartney, 2002, p. 616;
> see Mitalipov *et al.*, 2001)

In conclusion, there are various, morally unproblematic, potential sources for both ESCs and other types of stem cells that may fulfill most, if not all, of the therapeutic promise of ESCs derived directly from human embryos. Human embryos have an active potentiality to develop into fully actualized living, sentient, and rational human beings and are thereby already human beings – *persons* – themselves. They thus possess a level of intrinsic goodness and an inherent dignity that merits robust respect and rules out the kind of instrumentalization that entails their destruction.

Therapeutic and reproductive human cloning

Closely related to ESC research is the possibility of creating human organisms that are genetically identical to already existing human organisms: cloning. The two issues are closely related in that cloning may be a means of creating human embryos in order to derive ESCs for research purposes: "therapeutic" cloning. Cloning may also be used to create human embryos which subsequently are implanted into a woman's uterus in order to gestate and eventually give rise to a live birth: "reproductive" cloning.

Cloning occurs in two ways: "blastomere separation" and "somatic cell nuclear transfer" (SCNT). Blastomere separation involves splitting a two-, four-, or eight-celled embryo and is basically a form of induced twinning. The first successful case of blastomere separation involving human embryos was reported in 1993 by Jerry Hall and his colleagues at George Washington University (Hall *et al.*, 1993). SCNT is a much more complicated process in which the nucleus of an adult somatic cell is isolated and inserted into an enucleated ovum. The ovum is then induced to replicate itself and thereby reproduce parthenogenetically. SCNT was first successfully used to clone a mammal by Ian Wilmut and his colleagues at the Roslin Institute. In 1996, they announced that "Dolly" – a cloned sheep – had been born on July 5 of that year (Wilmut *et al.*, 1997). In 2001, Advanced Cell Technology announced that it had successfully cloned human embryos for nonreproductive research purposes (Cibelli *et al.*, 2001, 2002).[13] To date, no scientifically confirmed case involving the live birth of a human clone from SCNT has been reported.

Therapeutic and reproductive cloning,[14] using either blastomere separation or SCNT, differ from one another with respect to the intended end of the process. Reproductive cloning aims at the live birth of a child, whereas therapeutic cloning aims at the creation of an embryo from which ESCs may be derived, or on which research can be done to further our understanding of early human development. A number of reasons have been given for allowing cloning to go forward. On the reproductive side, cloning may (1) allow infertile couples to produce biologically related children, (2) prevent inheritable genetic diseases from being passed on from a particular parent, (3) provide for "rejection-proof" transplants, and (4) allow for the "replication" either of loved ones who have died or of individuals of great genius, talent, or beauty (PCB, 2002, pp. 79–80).[15] Cloning by means of blastomere separation as part of an IVF procedure adds further potential applications: (5) improving the chances of a successful pregnancy for those who produce only a limited number of embryos, (6) allowing preimplantation genetic diagnosis of one of the twin embryos before the other is implanted, (7) retaining a genetically identical embryo to serve as a potential replacement or as an organ/tissue donor for the implanted embryo, and (8) producing embryos for donation or sale to others (National Advisory Board on Ethics in Reproduction, 1994, p. 254).

The rationale for conducting therapeutic cloning is the same as the rationale for supporting ESC research: it results in the production of undifferentiated ESCs which then can be used to grow specialized cells, tissues, and organs to treat or cure diseases such as Parkinson's, Alzheimer's, diabetes, and leukemia, as well as spinal cord injury. Therapeutic cloning may be more advantageous than ESC research involving spare embryos from IVF or tissue from aborted fetuses insofar as the cells, tissues, and organs developed from the latter sources will not be a perfect genetic match with any potential recipient, and thus rejection by the recipient's immune system will remain a risk and require further treatment to nullify. Cells, tissues, and organs developed from ESC lines derived from a clone of the recipient, however, will be free from the risk of rejection. Experiments with mouse ESCs support the potential success of therapeutic cloning in this regard (Munsie *et al.*, 2000).

As many reasons have been given to restrict or ban cloning as have been given to go forward with it. With respect to reproductive cloning, concerns stem from (1) the possibility of psychological harm to the clone resulting from their perception of themselves as an individual with no unique identity, (2) the nature of cloning as the "manufacture" of human beings, (3) the possibility that cloning will lead to eugenic selection, (4) the confused family relations a clone may have with their progenitor as well as with their progenitor's children, siblings, and parents, and (5) the effect cloning may have on society's view of children and on the control one generation may have over the next (PCB, 2002, pp. xxviii–ix). An additional concern regards potential physical harm to the clone resulting from the fact that SCNT is a novel and imperfect process. When Wilmut *et al.* created Dolly, they began with 434 ova, 277 of which were successfully infused with DNA from somatic – mammary epithelium – cells. Of those 277 ova with a complete genome, only 29 formed a blastocyst. Out of 29, 13 were implanted in ewes, and only one of those thirteen resulted in a viable pregnancy that gave birth to Dolly (Wilmut *et al.*, 1997, table 1). Clearly, more work is required before SCNT can be considered a safe and reliable process; especially considering the fact that Dolly developed premature arthritis, showed signs of advanced cellular aging, and survived only half the normal life-span of a sheep of her breed (Ross, 2003). John Haldane notes a further risk to a clone's health:

> In the course of time, due to ultraviolet radiation and chemical contamination, body cells are liable to be damaged. In itself this may not matter if the process of replacement proceeds normally. However, cloning from adult body cells carries the risk of creating an embryo out of mutant genetic material. The resulting clone would then have a greater chance of developing cancer and could also be expected to have below average life-expectancy.
>
> (2000, p. 200)

Reasons given against therapeutic cloning echo those given against ESC research in general. At the forefront are three contentions: that early embryos have the moral status of persons; that research on embryos – cloned or not – wrongfully exploits developing human life; and that such exploitation is wrong in the further sense that it may harm the moral fabric of society (PCB, 2002, pp. xxxiii–iv). Much of the above discussion regarding the moral permissibility of ESC research will apply to therapeutic cloning as well. At this point, it is important to consider the metaphysical nature of clones – created for either reproductive or therapeutic purposes – as a basis for determining their moral status.

Metaphysical status of a human clone

The first obvious question in considering the metaphysical status of a clone is "What is a clone?" According to the PCB:

> A "clone" (noun, from the Greek *klon*, "twig") refers to a *group* of genetically identical molecules, cells, or organisms descended from a single common ancestor, as well as to *any one* of the one or more individual organisms that have descended asexually from a common ancestor.
>
> (2002, p. 42)

Next, it is appropriate to ask "When does a clone come into existence, biologically speaking?" And this should be followed by "When does a clone begin to exist as a *person?*"

Clones produced by means of blastomere separation come into existence in the same way naturally occurring identical twins do. Once a group of cells has been separated from a blastocyst, it constitutes a distinct blastocyst which has the same potential to develop into a fully actualized human organism. Hence, the biological and metaphysical status of a clone produced in this way will be the same as any genetically identical twin.[16]

Clones produced through SCNT are not akin to identical twins with respect to their initial formation. Rather, they resemble zygotes formed naturally through fertilization of an ovum. As the PCB correctly observes:

> The initial product of SCNT is a single cell, but it is no ordinary cell. It is also an "egg" and a "reconstituted egg." But even that is not the whole story. The "reconstituted" egg is *more* than reconstituted; it has been capacitated for development. Because the egg now has a diploid nucleus, it has become something beyond what it was before: it now contains in a single nucleus the full complement of genetic material necessary for producing a new organism. And being an *egg* cell, it uniquely offers the cytoplasmic environment that can support this development. The product of SCNT thus resembles and can be made to act like a fertilized egg, a cell that not only has the full complement of chromosomes but also is capable (in animals) or may be capable (in humans) of developing into a new organism. In other words, in terms of its future prospects, it is a "zygote-like entity" or a (cloned) "zygote equivalent."
>
> (2002, p. 47)

Julian Savulescu disagrees with this point, maintaining that nuclear transfer should not be understood as equivalent to natural conception:

> Conception involves the unification of two different entities, the sperm and the egg, to form a new entity, the totipotent stem cell. In the case of cloning, there is identity between the cell before and after nuclear transfer – it is the same cell.
>
> (2001, p. 219)

There is no doubt that conception involves two distinct entities combining to form a new entity in a process where each of the original two entities ceases to exist. Savulescu denies that the same type of metaphysical event happens in SCNT, because the ovum which is enucleated remains the same ovum once the nucleus of the progenitor's somatic cell is infused within it.

It is evident that most of what constitutes an ovum's biological integrity remains unchanged throughout the SCNT process. It has the same amount of cytoplasm and the same organelles bound by the same transparent membrane; only its nucleus has been "swapped." An ovum fertilized by a sperm cell, though, retains an even greater degree of its biological integrity throughout the fertilization process; it loses nothing, but only gains additional genetic material. A fertilized ovum, therefore, appears to be a stronger candidate for being "the same cell" as it was before fertilization than does an ovum that has lost its central biological component and has had it replaced by a component from a different cell. Savulescu describes SCNT as "a process of turning on some switches in an already existing cell" (Savulescu, 2001, p. 219). But this description does not do justice to the significant change in an ovum's biological integrity that occurs when it loses its nucleus and gains another. An ovum's having "some switches" turned on is a more apt description of what happens when an ovum is penetrated by a sperm cell, thereby receiving additional genetic information, than it is when an ovum undergoes nuclear substitution. If one holds, as Savulescu does, that when fertilization of an ovum occurs, the resulting cell is not diachronically identical to the one that existed before the event, one should also hold that when an ovum undergoes nuclear substitution, the resulting cell is diachronically nonidentical to the original.

With respect to the question "When does a clone first begin to exist as a *person* – that is, as a human being with full moral status?" there are three main responses that require discussion. First, a clone becomes a person when it develops beyond the fourteen-day mark, for it is at that time that its division into identical twins is no longer possible and it is successfully implanted in a supportive uterine environment (PCB, 2002, p. 136). Second, a clone becomes a person when it is "conceived" through either blastomere separation or SCNT (George and Gómez-Lobo in PCB, 2002, p. 258). Third, an implanted clone becomes a person when it develops a brain with the capacity to support consciousness (McMahan, 1999, p. 83).

The first response is based on Ford's argument that it is problematic to regard an embryo that is capable of dividing into two distinct embryos as an individual organism, yet a prerequisite for personhood is that a thing qualifies as an individual organism (Ford, 1988). I have addressed Ford's argument in Chapter 2 and concluded that an embryo's ability to produce a genetically identical twin does not preclude its existence as an individual organism prior to the twinning event. Furthermore, nothing prevents the embryo from being identical to one of the resultant twins; though there is no epistemic criterion for determining *which* of the two is the twin to which it is identical. Hence, the argument from twinning does not sufficiently demonstrate that it is metaphysically or biologically problematic to regard a cloned embryo in the first fourteen days of its existence as an individual organism, and thus a human being (PCB, 2002, pp. 154–5; George and Gómez-Lobo in PCB, 2002, pp. 262–4).

The second response comports with the conclusion arrived at in Chapter 2 regarding when a human being begins to exist. So long as a cloned embryo has everything *in itself*, other than a supportive environment, required to develop into a being that actually thinks rationally, it is correctly regarded as informed by a rational soul insofar as it has an active potentiality for rational thought. There is no reason to deny that a cloned embryo fulfills this criterion for rational ensoulment once it is "conceived" through either blastomere separation or SCNT.

The conclusion, however, that a cloned embryo has enough potentiality for rational thought that it qualifies as a human being from the moment of its existence is controversial, leading some to opt for the third response above.

Jeff McMahan, for example, assumes for the sake of argument that human beings are essentially souls and draws out a negative implication of the view that souls are first present at conception or the completion of nuclear transfer:

> And if [the soul] is present at either event, it seems that the soul can exist with-out the capacity for consciousness, for there appears to be nothing present in the womb in the early stages of pregnancy that has the capacity for consciousness. The soul, it seems, must await the development of the brain in order for consciousness to become possible.
>
> (1999, p. 79)

McMahan argues that if the soul depends on the brain to have the capacity for consciousness, then it cannot have such a capacity when it is separated from the body after death; human beings would thus spend the afterlife in an unconscious state. He then considers the Thomistic position for which I argued in Chapter 2 – namely, that "we begin to exist at conception and have the capacity for consciousness at that point, but cannot exercise our capacity" (McMahan, 1999, p. 79). He argues that this view has the same unfortunate implication regarding the afterlife:

> If the explanation of why the soul is unable to exercise its capacity for consciousness in the period following conception is related to the absence of brain function, then we should expect that the soul will also be unable to exercise that capacity in the afterlife, when brain functions have ceased.
>
> (1999, p. 79)

The subject of McMahan's discussion, as he describes it, is not precisely Aquinas's position. As noted in Chapter 1, Aquinas denies that human beings are *essentially* souls. Rather, we are essentially "rational animals": composites of soul and body. This construal of human nature allows for a human rational soul to persist beyond the death of its body, and thereby for a human being's continued existence insofar as their rational soul is the "blueprint" for their material body and has all the capac-ities specific to their nature as a living, sensitive, and rational being (Eberl, 2000b, 2004). This mode of postmortem existence, however, is "unnatural" and "incom-plete" (QDA, I; QDSC, II; Eberl, 2000b, pp. 215–16). Though a human being may exist as composed of their soul alone, they will not be able to exercise all their proper capacities without their body (ST, Ia.77.8). In particular, since Aquinas asserts that a human mind requires the bodily activities of sensation and imagination to engage in conscious rational thought (ST, Ia.84.6–8), a separated soul on its own will not be an actually conscious thinking thing:

> The disembodied soul after death is consequently something like the mirror image of a human being who is in a persistent vegetative state…When the soul of a person is separated from the body, Aquinas thinks, the cognitive powers that person had are curtailed and restricted.
>
> (Stump, 2003, p. 211)

This conclusion agrees with McMahan's, but unlike McMahan, Aquinas does not consider it absurd or problematic. He argues that a separated soul is an actually conscious thinking thing insofar as God is able to infuse objects of thought, which are normally derived from sensation, directly into the mind (ST, Ia.89.1). He also argues that a separated soul retains the objects of thought – universal, intelligible forms – it had previously derived from sensation while embodied in its "intellectual memory" (ST, Ia.79.6), and can thus consciously reflect on such objects while disembodied (ST, Ia.89.5–6). This response may strike one as *ad hoc* and so it may seem as if the soul should be understood as perpetually unconscious when it is without its body. If so, then the hope for a consciously experienced afterlife is nonetheless preserved in Aquinas's account of a separated soul's reunion with its "resurrected" body (Eberl, 2000b). At worst, then, human beings may exist for a time – between death and bodily resurrection – as unconscious entities, but will consciously experience the afterlife once their souls inform their resurrected bodies. Therefore, the Thomistic view that a rational soul informs a human body from conception – or nuclear transfer – onward does not have the problematic implication about the afterlife that McMahan supposes it to have.

The debate regarding a cloned embryo's potentiality does not end here. Some scholars argue that, though a cloned embryo is a potential human being, its potential is not sufficient for it to already be a human being:

> But the *potential* to become something (or someone) is hardly the same as *being* something (or someone), any more than a pile of building materials is the same as a house. A cloned embryo's potential to become a human person can be realized, if at all, only by the further human act of implanting the cloned blastocyst into the uterus of a woman.
>
> (PCB, 2002, p. 48)

This assessment of a cloned embryo's potentiality fails to consider Aquinas's distinction, described in Chapter 2, between active and passive potentiality. A cloned embryo has an active potentiality to be an actually thinking rational human being, because it has everything internally required for its *ordered natural development* toward such a state of actuality. A cloned embryo's potentiality is not akin to the potentiality of a pile of building materials to be a house. Such materials have merely a passive potentiality to be a house, because they require an external agent to organize them into the structure of a house. A cloned embryo with a complete human genome directs its own organized development from a single-celled zygote into a fully developed human being who actually thinks rationally.

A cloned embryo in a petri dish, though, does require external aid if its development is to continue beyond the earliest stages; it must be implanted in a supportive uterine environment. R. Alta Charo thus asserts:

> A fertilized egg or early embryo in a petri dish most certainly has an intrinsic tendency to continue growing and dividing. Without the provision of an artificial culture medium, however, it will never grow and divide more than about 1 week. If the provision of such a medium is considered a form of external

assistance akin to that at issue in passive potentiality, then the fertilized egg is a potential week-old embryo, not a potential baby.

(2001, p. 86)

The provision of a uterus or artificial culture medium is not "a form of external assistance akin to that at issue in passive potentiality." Though obviously a form of external assistance, it is merely a supportive environment for the cloned embryo to exercise its own developmental capacity. Uterine implantation or placement into a culture medium does not alter the intrinsic nature of the embryo itself or bestow upon it more inherent potentialities than it already possesses.

The form of external assistance in question is akin to an astronaut's spacesuit or an underwater explorer's submarine. Each provides what the astronaut or underwater explorer need to exercise their vital metabolic capacities, but the lack of such support does not entail that they lack those capacities. If an astronaut's spacesuit malfunctions and stops supplying oxygen, their vital metabolic functions will cease shortly thereafter. If, however, a fellow astronaut fixes their suit in a timely fashion and restores the flow of oxygen, their vital metabolic functions will resume. This indicates that the astronaut's intrinsic capacity for such functions remained despite the loss of the requisite supportive environment. Does their dependence on their fellow astronaut's assistance in restoring their supportive environment entail that their potentiality for being alive is merely passive? It does not because the assistance provided does nothing to alter or replace the astronaut's organic structure by which they are able to breathe in and circulate oxygen, and it is this intrinsic capacity which distinguishes living from nonliving organisms. Another example of external assistance that provides merely a supportive environment is the incubator most premature babies require to continue their postnatal development. Although such babies will surely die without the assistance provided by the incubator, their dependence on it does not entail that their potentiality for full development is merely passive and not self-directed.

I thus conclude that a cloned embryo's potentiality for development into an actually thinking rational human being does not preclude its existence as a human being already. This is because the potentiality at issue is an *active* potentiality, a potentiality that is part of the embryo's intrinsic nature, defined by its being informed by a rational soul:

> An embryo is, by definition and by its nature, potentially a fully developed human person; its potential for maturation is a characteristic it *actually* has, and from the start. The fact that embryos have been created outside their natural environment – which is to say, outside the woman's body – and are therefore limited in their ability to realize their natural capacities, does not affect either the potential or the moral status of the beings themselves. A bird forced to live in a cage its entire life may never learn to fly. But this does not mean it is less of a bird, or that it lacks the immanent potentiality to fly on feathered wings. It means only that a caged bird – like an in vitro human embryo – has been deprived of its proper environment.

(PCB, 2002, p. 156)

A further criticism of the argument from potentiality for the view that a cloned embryo is an actual human being is that the argument proves too much. For example, Savulescu asserts that since a human being can be cloned from a somatic cell, any such cell that currently constitutes my body is potentially a human being (Savulescu, 2001, p. 220; cf. PCB, 2002, pp. 148–9). But here again we have an assertion that ignores the active/passive potentiality distinction. Many changes, requiring the activity of an external agent, must accrue to a somatic cell before it can, in the relevant sense, have the potential to become a fully actualized human being. A somatic cell requires reorganization of its internal structure in order for it to develop into a human being, and this fact prevents it from having an *active* potentiality for such development:

> In general, it is reasonable to say that in order for an entity to be an embryonic animal, the entity must be able, given a favorable environment (of the sort natural to the species in question), *but without prior reorganization*, to undergo embryological development, that is, to commence or continue developing into a mature animal.
>
> (Burke, 1996, p. 509, emphasis mine)

Furthermore, as Michael Burke points out, to countenance the possibility that a somatic cell has the same potentiality as an embryo to become a fully actualized human being is to presume that it is *already* a human being. This presumption is implausible because a somatic cell that is *part* of a human being cannot itself be a human being:

> Like many of our concepts, *human* is "maximal," meaning that a proper part of a human, be it a small part (such as a cell) or large part (including, say, all of the human *except* a cell) is not itself a human.
>
> (1996, p. 510)

In Thomistic terms, when a rational soul informs a human body, it informs the body *as a whole*, every part of it (ST, Ia.76.8). Therefore, all parts of a human being's body are proper parts of them and not substances in their own right – unless they become separated from the body.[17] Since a somatic cell is not a substance itself, but only part of a substance, it cannot be a human being; nor can it have its own rational soul informing it and thereby giving it an active potentiality for further self-directed development into a fully actualized human being. A cloned embryo, on the other hand, is not a proper part of a human being – particularly since it is produced *in vitro* – and thus nothing precludes it from having its own rational soul such that it is an actual human being with an active potentiality for further development as such a being. To compare a cloned embryo's potentiality to that of a somatic cell is illegitimate insofar as there are metaphysical reasons why a somatic cell, unlike a cloned embryo, lacks an active potentiality to develop into a fully actualized human being.

Moral status of a human clone and the ethics of cloning

A number of arguments against the permissibility of human cloning invoke the fact that it is an "unnatural" form of reproduction and, as mentioned above, involves the "manufacture" of human beings. Many scholars take this view to represent a "natural law" approach to cloning. Peters, for example, contends that this approach

> betrays a veiled naturalism, a variant of the alleged "thou shalt not play God" commandment. It seems to presuppose that what nature bequeaths us prior to human choice has a higher moral status than what happens when we influence nature through technological intervention.
>
> (1997, p. 20)

Kathinka Evers thinks that to assess cloning on the basis of natural law is to come up with no clear or definitive answer as to whether cloning is morally permissible:

> Consequently, if the objection is to carry any weight we must assume the third interpretation, by which cloning should fail to conform to some natural moral law. But this is a notoriously opaque argument: the existence and contents of such an alleged law would have to be established. Its existence is not self-evident, and *prima facie* cloning could just as well agree with as violate a natural moral law. In other words, cloning could be *either* natural *or* unnatural by conforming (or failing to conform) to some natural moral law, the existence of which remains to be proven.
>
> (1999, p. 74)

In answer to Peters and Evers, I maintain that Aquinas's account of natural law, as described in Chapter 1, neither results in the "opaque argument" Evers describes nor places a higher value on "what nature bequeaths us" than on the ways in which human beings may influence nature through the proper exercise of reason. For example, Aquinas provides sound argumentation for the self-evidence of natural law – even if some human beings fail to acknowledge its self-evident truth (ST, Ia.94.4, 6) – and shows that the contents of natural law are suitably derived from an analysis of human natural inclinations (ST, Ia.94.2). Therefore, a clear, determinate assessment of cloning based on natural law is possible.

Certain scholars invoke natural law principles, either implicitly or explicitly, to defend the permissibility of cloning. Some members of the PCB, for example, contend that concerns about possible harms to a cloned child – whether psychological harm from being a "duplicate" of someone else or physical harm from being produced through an imperfect process – are ill placed next to the inherent goodness of existence itself (PCB, 2002, pp. 81–2): Better to exist with some psychological or physical disadvantages than not to exist at all. Furthermore, Joseph Fletcher argues in favor of cloning's progression on the basis of the inherent goodness of humanity's rational capacity and its use: "Man is a maker and a selector and a designer, and the more rationally contrived and deliberate anything is, the more human it is" (1971, p. 779).

Neither of these arguments is compelling from a Thomistic natural law perspective. The first argument fails because, as other members of the PCB point out, although existence itself is indeed an important good, other important goods – such as a child's psychological and physical well-being – must also be promoted. Far from being promoted, they may be violated through the deliberate creation of a child through cloning (PCB, 2002, p. 84). One cannot deliberately intend something that is morally impermissible – for example, psychological or physical harm to a child – in order to achieve something good, such as existence (ST, IIa-IIae.64.5.ad 3; In Rom, III.1).

Fletcher's argument fails because it attributes an overriding value to any use of human reason, while neglecting the distinction between proper and improper uses of reason. Aquinas understands reason, in part, as a human being's ability to perceive the inherent goodness in things they may pursue or in actions they may do. But anything may be considered good in some respect; for example, a shoplifter may consider their act of stealing to be good insofar as it fulfills their desire for a diamond necklace. A human being may rationally tend toward something or intend to perform some action that is less good than something else they are capable of pursuing or doing. Aquinas thus exhorts "prudence" as a virtue necessary for the development of "rightly ordered reason" (ST, Ia-IIae.57.5; Nelson, 1992). "Rightly ordered reason" properly perceives the inherent goodness in things and in potential actions, and weighs various goods according to their conformity with, or capacity to promote, the flourishing of human nature. Therefore, not just any exercise, but only the *prudent* exercise of human reason is morally good. Hence, one must investigate whether cloning – in either its therapeutic or reproductive forms – is a prudent application of human reason and scientific ingenuity, and not simply presume that it is good because it follows from reason and human design.

A third, and arguably the most persuasive, implicit use of natural law to support cloning – in particular, to support therapeutic cloning – cites the ways in which cloning can promote human health. Health is certainly a fundamental good for human nature. It is essential to each human being's existence, as well as to their ability to exercise various capacities: "Health indeed is esteemed as a kind of virtue" (ST, Ia-IIae.71.1.ad 3). The PCB notes several uses of therapeutic cloning that can promote human health. Cloning can be used to improve understanding of human disease, to devise new treatments for human diseases, to produce immune-compatible tissues for transplantation, and to assist in gene therapy (PCB, 2002, pp. 130–3).

As compelling as this third defense of continued progress in therapeutic cloning may be, there are other goods that must be taken into account in an ethical evaluation of cloning. In what follows, I will first cite concerns about therapeutic cloning with respect to its intended end compared with a human embryo's inherent goodness. I will then examine the moral permissibility of reproductive cloning in light of the inherent goodness of the natural social structure of human families.

Therapeutic cloning

Therapeutic cloning, like ESC research, has as its most proximate intended end the derivation of ESCs, the achievement of which clearly and unavoidably involves an embryo's destruction. The more remote intended end of therapeutic cloning is the set of human health benefits mentioned earlier. Some scholars argue that the goodness of the remote end is what is primarily intended by medical researchers involved in therapeutic cloning. They claim that the unavoidable destruction of human embryos is an unintended "side-effect" of the purpose for which they are created:

> Thus, in the case of cloning-for-biomedical-research, it is wrong to argue, as some do, that embryos are being "created for destruction." Certainly, their destruction is a known and unavoidable effect, but the embryos are ultimately created for research in the service of life and medicine.
>
> (PCB, 2002, pp. 141–2)

This argument invokes the PDE, described in Chapter 1, as a means of justifying therapeutic cloning, as well as ESC research. It purports to succeed even if embryo destruction is *prima facie* morally impermissible.

In order for PDE to be applicable in this case, the following conditions must hold: first, the negative value of the impermissible consequence – in this case, the destruction of human embryos – does not outweigh the positive value of the good consequence – the health benefits mentioned earlier. Second, the production of the impermissible consequence is not *directly intended* as an end or the means by which the good consequence is achieved. That the first condition holds in this case is plausible, for it may indeed be the case that the potential health benefits from therapeutic cloning at least equal the inherent goodness of a cloned embryo's existence. But even if the first condition is satisfied, the second is not. This is because therapeutic cloning involves the creation of embryos *with the purpose of destroying them*. As William FitzPatrick notes, ESC derivation from a cloned embryo is "constitutive" of its destruction and not merely causally related to it:

> The means we here aim at and employ in pursuit of curing disease involves isolating the inner cell mass of a five-day-old embryo by "removing" the trophectoderm (the rest of the blastocyst), which is done by cutting it away with microsurgery or breaking it down through immunosurgery . . . this pro- cedure does not merely *cause* some distinct harm but *constitutes* the destruction of the embryo. We therefore cannot say that we're aiming at the embryo's being disaggregated but not at its being destroyed, or that its destruction is merely a foreseen but unintended side effect of our action . . . we cannot avoid the conclusion that [therapeutic] cloning involves creating an embryo with the intent of destroying it.
>
> (FitzPatrick, 2003, pp. 33–4;
> cf. Haldane, 2000, pp. 192–4)

FitzPatrick goes on to argue that, despite the inapplicability of PDE to therapeutic cloning, the moral worries about such cloning are not sufficiently compelling to "ultimately lead us to oppose it, at least until we have clear evidence of less problematic, equally effective, and comparably accessible alternatives" (FitzPatrick, 2003, p. 36). *Pace* FitzPatrick, the inherent goodness of a human embryo's existence, insofar as it has an active potentiality to develop into an actually thinking rational human being, indeed warrants opposition to therapeutic cloning just as it warrants opposition to ESC research in general, as I argued above.

Reproductive cloning

Reproductive cloning raises a different set of moral concerns, and the opinions about its moral permissibility often differ from those about therapeutic cloning. For instance, both the majority and minority recommendations of the PCB call for a ban on reproductive cloning, whereas the PCB recommends that therapeutic cloning be subjected to a four-year moratorium (majority) or be allowed to go forward, subject to regulation (minority) (PCB, 2002, pp. xxxv–ix). Two members of the PCB, however, both of whom are natural law theorists who support the majority recommendation, claim that therapeutic cloning is more morally problematic than reproductive cloning. "It is our considered judgment that cloning-for-biomedical-research, inasmuch as it involves the deliberate destruction of embryos, is morally worse than cloning-to-produce-children" (George and Gómez-Lobo in PCB, 2002, p. 266).

These theorists nonetheless have sufficient moral worries about reproductive cloning to call for a ban on it in addition to at least a moratorium on therapeutic cloning; though they would prefer a total ban on both forms of cloning.

What is morally problematic about reproductive cloning from a Thomistic natural law perspective? A primary issue stems from the social disruption in which human cloning may result, which would be at odds with the natural law mandate to maintain a harmonious social order insofar as human beings are by nature "social animals" (In NE, I.9). As noted in Chapter 1, Aquinas explicitly cites the education of offspring as following from the first principle of natural law together with the social aspect of human nature (ST, Ia-IIae.94.2, IIa-IIae.57.4). He further contends that determinate parentage is fundamentally necessary for a child's optimal upbringing:

> We see in all animals in which the education of offspring requires the care of male and female, that there is not indeterminate sexual intercourse, but the male with a certain female…Hence, it is contrary to human nature that indeterminate sexual intercourse occur, but the male ought to be with a determinate female…It is thus natural for the male[18] in the human species to be concerned for the certainty of offspring, because on him rests the education of offspring. This certainty, however, would be lifted if sexual intercourse were indeterminate.
>
> (ST, IIa-IIae.154.2; cf. SCG, III.122–3)

Aquinas's reference to a human male's "natural concern for the certainty of offspring" implies a natural bond or affinity between parents and their biologically related offspring that arises once their biological relationship is known

(ST, IIa-IIae.26.9). The responsibilities that naturally follow from this bond, such as education and general upbringing, generate a desire to know exactly to whom one is related as a parent. Ronald Cole-Turner elucidates the nature of this bond:

> Furthermore, as creatures became more complex and needed parents to rear them, sexual reproduction assured that both parents have a genetic interest in their offspring, so sexual reproduction can be seen as ultimately encouraging the care of offspring by two parents. For human beings, this parental invest-ment must be substantial if the child is to thrive. Sexual reproduction creates a genetic bond between both parents and the child.
>
> (1997, p. 127)

Parents are naturally driven to care for their genetically related offspring; though this does not preclude them from caring equally for offspring to whom they are not genetically related. Nevertheless, to maximize the likelihood that children receive their proper upbringing in an optimal fashion, they should be related to those responsible for their upbringing in such a way that the latter have a natural inclination to fulfill their parental obligations.

These remarks about the value of the natural bond between parents and their genetically related offspring bear on the moral permissibility of reproductive cloning. They do so because such cloning disrupts the natural order of procreation through which this bond is generated. The result is that parents of a cloned child may not experience as strong a natural inclination to care for the child, even if the child is genetically related to one of them. This is because the child is genetically unrelated to at least one of the parents – if not both in the case of donated genetic material – and the child's relationship to its parents is the result of choice, selection, and artifice, rather than openness to whatever sort of child may result from natural procreative activity. Paul Conner exploits this negative feature of reproductive cloning:

> Clones would not be related to others in society in any way more profound than by human desire and by technology that has no flesh or soul and that always introduces human limitations, if not errors. For example, those who produce or pay for a clone would not be responsible for his or her upbring-ing in the same way as true parents, who are the cause of a child's conception (origin) and contribute equally to his or her real make-up (nature). Cloners would be responsible only by desire and choice. Should any undesired limita-tions develop in their clone, their original choice would be sorely tested. Moreover, their parental instincts would not be fulfilled primarily on a level of human nature but on a level of personal preference. Hence, much shallower roots than natural ones would bind clones to their originals, to their designers and makers, and to their purchasers.
>
> (2002, p. 654)

Reproductive cloning does not provide as strong a bond between parent and child as natural procreation. As a result, proper care and upbringing may not necessarily be provided, particularly in cases where a "defective product" is created. The "natural and social affinity" at the foundation of familial relationships and the family's nature "as a place of unconditional belonging" may thus be compromised (Waters, 1997, pp. 84–5).

Not only may a cloned child's upbringing be potentially threatened by the weak parental bonds generated through reproductive cloning, but societal relationships in general are at risk: "Familial relationships are the foundations for fulfilling the social dimension of human nature" (Conner, 2002, p. 653). A child who does not have properly structured familial relationships, particularly with its parents, may have difficulty in its future social engagements. Lisa Sowle Cahill voices this concern in her testimony before the NBAC during its 1997 hearings on human cloning:

> Cloning violates "the essential reality of human family and . . . the nature of the socially related individual within it. We all take part of our identity, both material or biological, and social, from combined ancestral kinship networks . . . Whether socially recognized or not, this kind of ancestry is an important part of the human sense of self (as witnessed by searches for 'biological' parents and families), as well as a foundation of important human relationships." Cloning to create children, Cahill concludes, would constitute an "unprecedented rupture in those biological dimensions of embodied humanity which have been most important for social cooperation."
>
> (p. 53)

Cahill emphasizes the "biological dimensions of embodied humanity" and cites their importance in defining a human being's individual and social identity. This emphasis echoes Aquinas's own emphasis, elucidated in Chapter 1, on a human being's essential "animality." It also echoes his definition of human nature not simply as an immaterial soul – a purely psychological entity – but as a soul–body composite – a psychobiological entity. This emphasis is supported by Cahill's point that adopted children, even those who are raised in the most nurturing and loving of adoptive families, are naturally inclined to seek out their biological parents. The PCB also notes this phenomenon in voicing its concerns about reproductive cloning that uses donated genetic material – material that belongs to neither of the parents by whom the cloned child will be raised:

> A desire to seek out connection with the "original" could complicate his or her relation to the rearing family, as would living consciously "under the *reason*" for this extra-familial choice of progenitor. Though many people make light of the importance of biological kinship (compared to the bonds formed though rearing and experienced family life), many adopted children and children conceived by artificial insemination or IVF using donor sperm show by their actions that they do not agree. They make great efforts to locate their "biological parents," even where paternity consists of nothing more than the donation of sperm. Where the progenitor is a genetic near-twin, surely the urge of the cloned child to connect with the unknown "parent" would be still greater.
>
> (2002, pp. 111–12)

This argument could be criticized on the grounds that it ignores or devalues alternative family structures that are prevalent in contemporary society and among various cultures (de Melo-Martín, 2002, pp. 251–2). This criticism is certainly worth noting, for it is indeed true that children are in many cases raised successfully by parents or guardians who are not genetically related to them; and in many cases children suffer abuse or neglect at the hands of parents who are their genetic progenitors.

The first set of cases, though – that is, those of successful parenting by people who are genetically unrelated to their children – reveals only that the natural bond between parent and offspring, and the moral responsibility for education and upbringing attached to that bond, may be assumed by other human beings through intentional choice. The above assertions about the nature of familial bonds and natural responsibility in genetic parent–child relationships do not discount either the fact that strong bonds may exist in alternative family structures or the fact that commensurate responsibility may be assumed by others – for example, heterosexual and homosexual couples who adopt children. The creation of such bonds, however, through intentional choice is not optimal and is employed only as a means of rearing children when the creation of natural bonds through genetic relatedness is not possible. In cases where such relatedness is possible, nongenetic parent–child relationships are typically not sought. This is evidenced by the great lengths some couples go through in using IVF to have genetically related offspring when they cannot do so otherwise, and do not choose to adopt a nongenetically related child. But reproductive cloning is a means of creating children whose genetic relationship to at least one parent is nonexistent. It also involves intentional choice and human artifice where they are not necessary. Other means already exist to allow those incapable of having genetically related children to become parents.

The second set of cases – those in which children are neglected or abused by parents to whom they are genetically related – shows, at most, that the natural bond between parent and offspring may be mitigated by human intention and that behavior contrary to natural law can commonly occur. Human beings, according to Aquinas, have an innate awareness of natural law (ST, Ia.79.12, Ia-IIae.94.1.ad 2), but it is not equally known by every human being (ST, Ia-IIae.94.4). Aquinas notes that various factors, such as "passion, evil habit, or an evil natural disposition" may pervert one's reason and thus diminish the ability to properly understand and apply the principles of natural law. As a result, some parents may eschew the responsibility they naturally possess for their genetically related offspring. But such behavior is the result of intentional choice influenced by a perversion of reason; it does not demonstrate that in some cases a natural bond and commensurate responsibility is lacking between genetically related parent and child.

Conclusion

Based on the metaphysical conclusion I reached in Chapter 2, I have argued in this chapter that a human embryo enjoys the full moral status that a fully actualized human being is recognized to possess. It does so because a human embryo, from conception onward, has an active potentiality to become an actually thinking rational human being – a person. Consequently, directly intended abortion and the use of abortifacient contraceptives are morally impermissible. Furthermore, despite the potentially significant therapeutic benefits of ESC research and therapeutic cloning, each is morally impermissible because it unavoidably involves the directly intended destruction of human embryos. ASC research, often derided by proponents of ESC research or therapeutic cloning, holds a significant degree of promise for the treatment or cure of numerous human diseases. It also has a record of success in converting certain types of differentiated cells into largely undifferentiated stem cells.[19] Another potential alternative to ESC research involves the creation of "nonviable embryo-like artifacts" that lack the biological status of an organism – and hence the moral status of a human being – but nevertheless provide a source for deriving functional ESCs (Hurlbut in PCB, 2002, pp. 274–6; PCB, 2004, pp. 90–3). While the creation of such "pseudo-embryos" can be construed as "unnatural," it would not necessarily constitute a violation of the natural law so long as what is created is truly a mere biological entity that lacks an active potentiality for developing into an actually thinking rational human being if only provided a suitable nutritive environment. Though such an entity would be alive and thereby have a degree of intrinsic goodness akin to other living beings, its goodness would nonetheless be of a significantly lesser degree than that of the human beings who may benefit from the therapeutic research conducted utilizing the ESCs derived from them.

Finally, reproductive cloning is morally problematic, because it severs the natural bond that exists between genetically related parents and offspring. Though reproductive cloning may assist those for whom it is not feasible to have genetically related children naturally – for example, infertile heterosexual couples or homosexual couples – other avenues are open to them if they want to raise children, such as adoption, which does not entail the birth of a child who is entirely the product of human artifice, design, and choice.

5 Issues at the end of human life

PVS patients, euthanasia, and organ donation

Introduction

In Chapter 3, I argued that Aquinas's metaphysical understanding of human nature entails that a human being's death occurs when they suffer the irreversible cessation of whole-brain functioning. This conclusion, along with Aquinas's view of the inherent goodness of human life, has clear implications for how we should treat patients in a "persistent vegetative state" (PVS). Furthermore, Aquinas's natural law ethic requires that we treat not only PVS patients, but any terminally ill or dying persons, in a fashion that safeguards their life while avoiding undue prolongation of their pain and suffering. In this chapter, I will first address the metaphysical and moral status of PVS patients and then follow with an ethical assessment of various means by which we may strive to alleviate the pain and suffering experienced by the terminally ill or dying. Such means include active euthanasia, palliative treatment that may hasten death, the nonutilization of life-sustaining treatment, and terminal sedation. Finally, I will discuss the practice of organ donation, which involves, among other issues, the question of how and when a patient should be declared dead.

Metaphysical and moral status of PVS patients

From 2003 to 2005, when she died, the case of Terri Schiavo (Krueger, 2003) – a PVS patient – brought national attention to the question of whether someone who shows no neurological or clinical signs of conscious awareness is still a "person," or, regardless of this daunting metaphysical question, whether life in such a state is sufficiently valuable to warrant keeping the patient alive by artificial means such as tube-feeding and hydration. It is important to differentiate PVS from the more commonly known term "coma." A comatose patient may be either temporarily or irreversibly so, and their coma may be either pharmacologically induced – as in the case of terminal sedation which will be discussed below – or caused by neurological trauma. Comas caused by neurological trauma may include either damage to the cerebral hemispheres themselves, which are correlated with conscious rational activity, or damage to the brain's reticular formation, which is the "on-off switch" for wakefulness. A PVS patient shows no neurological or clinical signs of conscious awareness or rational activity, despite the fact that their eyes are open and they may exhibit certain reflexive behaviors – such as tracking a moving object in front of them – that mimic purposeful conscious activity (Jennett and Plum, 1972). PVS is understood to be *irreversible* in all correctly diagnosed cases, though there have been exceptions indicating that misdiagnosis occurs a significant number of times (Mappes, 2003, pp. 122–5).

The ethical treatment of PVS patients can be addressed in two basic ways: (1) Is a PVS patient still a person, or has the person died leaving merely a living human organism? (2) Even if a PVS patient is still a person, what value does their continued existence have without the possibility of consciousness? The "higher-brain" concept of death described in Chapter 3 entails that a person dies when they falls into a PVS. If the neurological structures necessary to support conscious rational thought are irreversibly nonfunctional, there is no basis for asserting that the patient has a rational soul or is a person. Jeff McMahan thus asserts:

> Recognition that we are embodied minds distinct from our organisms allows us to embrace the intuition behind the revisionist higher-brain proposals – namely, that we cease to exist when we irreversibly lose the capacity for consciousness – while at the same time recognizing that an organism that has suffered neocortical or cerebral death is nevertheless a living organism. For if we are not identical with our organisms, one of us can cease to exist even if his or her organism remains in existence and, indeed, even if it remains alive.
>
> (2002, p. 424)

McMahan further contends, regarding the moral status of a PVS patient:

> I propose that we should assign the living organism in a PVS much the same status we now assign a dead human organism...a living organism in a PVS is, in relevant respects, just like a dead body: they are both instances of the physical remains a person leaves when he or she ceases to exist.
>
> (2002, p. 447)

McMahan's metaphysical view of human persons is that we are essentially "embodied minds" – that is, a person exists and persists only insofar as their brain functions sufficiently to generate consciousness or mental activity (McMahan, 2002, p. 68). This view is quite distinct from the Thomistic account of human nature described in Chapter 1. For Aquinas, a person exists (premortem) so long as their body is informed by their rational soul, and the soul informs the body until the body can no longer support the soul's *vegetative* capacities. Rational *activity* is not required to contend that a rational human being continues to exist:

> It is irrelevant that the ability[1] to express [conscious rational] functions is permanently lost due to the PVS, since function does not determine personhood; personhood is determined by essence. The proper functions of a human

person are grounded in the essence of human personhood, and they cannot stand alone apart from a human nature in which these critical functions are grounded. Losing the essence of personhood does not follow from having lost the functions one deems critical to being a person.

(Moreland and Rae, 2000, p. 332)

The "essence of human personhood" is a human being's "nature," defined by Aquinas as the composite unity of a rational soul and a material body such that a human being has the capacities for life, sensation, and conscious rational thought. So long as a rational soul continues to inform its body, the two compose a human being[2] regardless of whether any of the soul's definitive capacities – other than its basic vegetative capacities – are presently actualizable in that body. A PVS patient is a human being because their body remains informed by their rational soul. This is due to the soul's basic vegetative capacities still being actualized in their body, which is exemplified by spontaneous respiration and heartbeat, as well as the ability to metabolize food and water if provided.

Even if a PVS patient is a human being and not merely a vegetative "corpse," the question remains whether such a person's life is sufficiently valuable to warrant being maintained through artificial nutrition and hydration or other means. Grant Gillett argues that "nothing matters" to a creature – person or animal – who is without consciousness:

> In order for something to matter to an individual, he must have or be able to form an attitude or preference about that thing – it must figure in his thought in some salient or significant way. That is what it is to care about something.
>
> (1990, p. 196)

While benefits and harms may still be visited upon someone who is unconscious – for example, the benefit of honoring their requests stated in a will or the harm, as depicted in Quentin Tarantino's film *Kill Bill, Vol. 1* (2003), of sexually violating their body – Gillett contends that such benefits or harms do not *matter* to the person if they are unable to ever be consciously aware of them. The question thus arises whether continued life matters to a PVS patient and it would seem that it does not: "Therefore, where the neocortex is destroyed or permanently nonfunctional, our rational moral commitment to preserving life can be withdrawn in the case of an individual who has suffered this tragedy" (Gillett, 1990, p. 197).

But is a PVS patient's continued biological life truly valueless because it does not matter to them? From a Thomistic perspective, goodness is inherent in all forms of existence, though the level of goodness is relative to the different levels of being Aquinas defines – inanimate, vegetative, sensitive, and rational[3] – as well as to the degree that an individual being's definitive capacities are actualized. One could thus argue that a PVS patient's existence is not "as good" as when they were a more fully actualized human being. Nevertheless, the inherent fundamental goodness of their basic existence as a rational being and a living organism persists even when they are unable to actualize their rational and sensitive capacities.

Holmes Rolston III calls attention to the inherent value of a human being's biological existence, even when it no longer subserves conscious rational activity:

> After the struggle for personal self-possession has been lost, one ought further to respect, albeit in a different ethical relationship, the continuing struggle for biological self-possession. This is not a self-deceived rationalizing about crude vitalistic processes. It is rather the recognition of dignity across the whole of life...whatever is biologically *vital* also carries ethical *value*. When the subjective life is gone, the remaining objective life is admittedly incomplete, but does it follow that it is valueless? When the patient was yet self-aware, he counted these biological processes among his goods and interests...Now exactly the same kind of natural good here continues, diminished in degree in his debilitated condition. Somatically, objectively, he still fights for life and health. From the patient's perspective, if we can still judge such a thing on the basis of his continuing life efforts, the former goodness has not been neutralized by no longer having a subjective owner. So then we who care for him have to ask ourselves what duty is still owed to this objective side of life.
>
> (1982, p. 342)

Rolston here reflects the Thomistic view that not only does vegetative existence have a certain degree of goodness in itself, but also the persistent vegetative existence of a human being has a sufficient degree of goodness to warrant being supported within reasonable limits. The primary concern now is what constitutes the reasonable limits of support and care to be provided to a PVS patient, or to a fully conscious terminally ill patient who has reached the end of what medicine can do to cure them or alleviate the debilitating symptoms of their condition. In what follows, I will discuss the relevant limits and various forms of support and care.

Euthanasia[4]

The topic of euthanasia includes several dimensions. The most controversial is what is termed "active euthanasia," which includes both the outright killing of a patient and the acts of "physician-assisted suicide" performed by Dr Jack Kevorkian. More accepted, but not without its own issues, is "passive euthanasia," which includes various acts such as the nonutilization of life-sustaining treatment, administration of palliative treatment that may hasten a patient's death, and terminal sedation. Though some philosophers and bioethicists have disputed it (Rachels, 1975; Kuhse, 1998), the American Medical Association's (AMA) Council on Ethical and Judicial Affairs affirms the moral distinction between the two forms of euthanasia: active euthanasia is contrary to the ethical practice of medicine, whereas the nonutilization of life-sustaining treatment or palliative treatment that may hasten death are permissible within medical practice (AMA, 1992). I will argue that the Thomistic ethical perspective agrees with the AMA's assessment.

Active euthanasia

The term "active euthanasia" refers to several forms of so-called "mercy killing": suicide, assisted suicide, and homicide.[5] Since each form of active euthanasia involves suicide in some analogous sense of the term – that is, all such actions begin with a patient's expressed or presumed wish to die – what Aquinas says regarding suicide in general will apply to all forms of active euthanasia, except those in which a patient is killed against their wish to live and thereby this constitutes murder. Aquinas states that "one sins more gravely who kills himself, than who kills another" (ST, Ia-IIae.73.9.ad 2) and gives a "triple indictment" against suicide (ST, IIa-IIae.64.5). I will consider here only two of Aquinas's indictments which are based on natural law.[6]

Natural inclination to live

Aquinas begins by stating, "Everything naturally loves itself," and asserts that suicide violates the natural law because "everything [which loves itself] naturally conserves itself in being and resists corruptions so far as it can" (ST, IIa-IIae.64.5). Since everything naturally seeks to maintain its own existence and avoid any type of corruption, suicide violates that principle of natural law, for it is the termination of a human being's natural mode of existence.[7]

A human being's "love" for themselves involves the fulfillment of their natural inclinations shared with all other human beings. Human beings are biological organisms. As noted in Chapter 1, Aquinas does not hold a form of Platonic substance dualism, in which a human being is identified with an immaterial soul that merely uses a body as its instrument. Rather, Aquinas holds that human beings are substances composed of both physical matter and an immaterial soul that organizes the matter into an individual living organism of the genus "animal" and the species "human."

This account of human nature directly impacts Aquinas's natural law ethic and his understanding of human natural desire. Aquinas holds that the first, fundamental precept of natural law is that "good is to be done and pursued, and evil avoided" (ST, Ia-IIae.94.2). He characterizes the "good" as whatever is fulfilling to a being's nature insofar as it satisfies its natural inclinations. Since part of what constitutes human nature is to be a *living* biological organism, life is a "good" and interference with a human being's life would be an "evil." Therefore, suicide, which interferes with one's nature as a living biological organism, violates the first principle of natural law. This conclusion is not merely a moral injunction, but also reflects a fundamental anthropological fact: human beings, as living organisms, have a natural inclination to live.

David Novak, in elucidating Aquinas's indictment of suicide, considers the objection that the evident desire of some persons to cease living indicates that Aquinas is mistaken in asserting that all human beings have a natural inclination to live. Novak counters this objection by first showing the *objective* nature of Aquinas's account of natural law and how Aquinas's assertion that life is a fundamental good is derived from his understanding of human nature, as described earlier. Novak then contends, "The suicidal person is not suicidal because *his* natural inclination is *not* to persist in being, rather, he is suicidal because he has circumvented *the* natural inclination already present" (Novak, 1975, p. 49). A suicidal person does not fail to have a natural inclination to live, but has a competing desire to end their present state of suffering. Death is not desired by a suicidal person for its own sake, but as a means to end their suffering: "One who contemplates suicide does not will non-existence or evil but only the termination of his troubled existence; what is the real object of his natural appetite is a good – untroubled existence" (Gustafson, 1944, p. 25). For many persons, though, especially the terminally ill, "untroubled existence" is not an attainable goal. As a result, they must choose between troubled existence and death. For Aquinas, human life is an inherent fundamental good; a person's troubled existence retains its value even when tainted by suffering.

Lisa Sowle Cahill argues, however, that the inherent goodness of a human being's life is but one of many goods that constitute the fulfillment of human nature, and notes Aquinas's recognition that certain specific goods must be violated "to respect and safeguard the integrity and welfare of the whole human being" (Cahill, 1977, p. 49). The subordination of the goodness of a human being's parts to the overall goodness of the whole person is known as the "principle of totality," which I will discuss in more detail below with respect to organ donation. Aquinas states:

> Now every part is directed toward the whole as imperfect toward perfect. And thus every part is naturally for the sake of the whole. And on account of this we see that if cutting off some member provides for the health of the whole human body, because it is rotten and corruptive to the other members, it is laudable and healthy to have it cut off.
>
> (ST, IIa-IIae.64.2; cf. ST, IIa-IIae.65.1; SCG, III.112)

Cahill argues:

> Since the distinctive and controlling element of human nature is the personal self or spirit [i.e., rational soul], then according to the principle of totality, the body which is a "part" may in some cases be sacrificed for the good of the "whole" body-soul entity.
>
> (1977, p. 61)

> The prolonged and meaningless physical deterioration of a permanently comatose individual can be construed as an insult to his or her total personhood. In such a case, as well as that of the dying person, [active] euthanasia may be present as a viable moral option. Once a patient is in the terminal stage of a fatal illness or is permanently comatose, it may become evident that his or her life is past the point of possible restoration to a quality which would support significant pursuit of the highest human values.
>
> (1977, p. 59)

Cahill's rationale for supporting active euthanasia as "a viable moral option" is echoed by almost every advocate of euthanasia whose primary concern is the "quality of life" a terminally ill or comatose patient may experience.

Cahill purports that her case is presented from a Thomistic perspective, so it is appropriate to evaluate her argument from the same viewpoint. While Aquinas does indeed hold the principle of totality, the example he gives to elucidate the principle in the preceeding passage is not analogous to a case of "cutting off" a human being's ill body to fulfill some higher rational or spiritual good or to safeguard their the human being's overall personal integrity. Aquinas asserts that it is wrong for one to mutilate their body for the sake of their spiritual well-being (ST, IIa-IIae.65.1.ad 3) or to commit suicide to avoid sin (ST, IIa-IIae.64.5.ad 3; Colbert, 1978, p. 191). Furthermore, the two cases are not analogous because the example Aquinas gives is of a human being's "integral" part being removed for the sake of preserving the whole body; integral parts are "components that add to the quantity of the material whole they compose, in the way that a roof is part of a house and a head is part of a body" (Stump, 2003, p. 209). A human body, on the other hand, is not an integral part of a human being, but a "metaphysical" part that is fundamentally constitutive of a human being's substantial nature along with their rational soul (Stump, 2003, p. 42). As William E. May contends, "Bodily life is, in fact, intrinsic to the human person and not merely a possession of the person" (May, 1998, p. 48).

It is thus a mischaracterization to construe euthanasia as merely the "cutting off" of one's body as one would sever a gangrenous limb to preserve one's overall health and well-being. Without their bodies, though human beings may continue to exist composed of their souls alone, their existence will be quite deficient because many of their capacities – vegetative and sensitive – will not be actualizable and they will not be able to gain knowledge in the natural way through sensation (Eberl, 2000b, 2004).

Cahill argues that the goodness of a human being's bodily life may be sacrificed to prevent "an insult to his or her total personhood." John Kavanaugh counters this "admission that human vulnerability, our very condition as embodied, is degraded and undignified":

> The response of an individual or a community that values the intrinsic dignity of persons, however, is not to kill the sufferer or eliminate the wounded but to alleviate the suffering and affirm the sufferer's goodness, regardless of the deprivation, the loss, or the presumed shame of human frailty... What is required of us is to live and act in a way that entails acknowledging that no pain or dying or "degenerate" condition robs us of our intrinsic dignity. The direct choice to kill damaged persons betrays that truth.
>
> (2001, p. 137)

A human being's intrinsic goodness persists despite whatever condition their body or soul may be in. Hence, the goodness of "the whole human being" is in fact violated through active euthanasia: "Thus an attack on the body and bodily life of a human person is an attack on the person" (May, 1998, p. 48).

Communitarianism and suicide

Aquinas's second injunction against suicide is derived from his intellectual ancestor, Aristotle: "Every part, as such, is of the whole. Now every human being is part of the community; and so, as such, is of the community. Hence, in the case that he kills himself, he causes injury to the community" (ST, IIa-IIae.64.5).[8] All human beings are interrelated in variously defined political communities. We also belong to one overall *human* community, which transcends nation, race, and gender boundaries. As a result of this conception of human nature as essentially "communitarian," Aquinas holds that each individual human being is responsible not only to themselves, but also to every other member of the human community. Suicide is thus not a purely private action, which has implications only for the suicidal agent:

> While Aquinas does not believe that society is sovereign over the individual, he does believe that individual decisions cannot be properly made in even so personal a matter as suicide without reference to the interests of other persons in the State.
>
> (Beauchamp, 1989, p. 192)

Robert Wennberg criticizes the claim that suicide is a sin against the human community. Wennberg interprets Aquinas's argument as asserting, "To commit suicide is to rob the community of one of its contributing members" (Wennberg, 1989, p. 68). Wennberg suggests that this assertion

> is not applicable to those contemplated cases of suicide-euthanasia in which the individual is in the latter stages of a terminal illness and therefore not in a position to make a contribution to society – indeed, may actually be a drain on its resources.
>
> (1989, p. 69)

Wennberg's interpretation does not agree with my own mentioned earlier. I made no reference to an individual's contribution to society. Aquinas would object to such a purely *utilitarian* analysis. Aquinas's appeal to the community is meant to call to mind the fact that no individual human being exists in isolation. A grave decision, such as suicide, is not an individual's decision alone. The whole community has a say in such serious types of conduct by its citizens. With respect to this particular point, suicide (or active euthanasia) does not appear to be summarily ruled out. It may be that the community feels that individuals should have the right to self-termination. If so, then, at least with respect to this particular indictment, suicide may be morally permissible given the community's consent. Community consent, however, or political decision is not sufficient to constitute what Aquinas considers "just law." Society may pass unjust laws that violate the objective principles of natural law (ST, Ia-IIae.95.2) – for example, laws that permit slavery or that do not provide for a liberal education. An individual is subservient to the community in which they live, but the community is subservient to the natural law.

An individual must be obedient to particular laws of their community only when those laws are just – that is, when they do not violate the natural law. Since a law permitting suicide would constitute a violation of the natural law, no community has the right to pass such a law, and no individual in a community that passes such a law is under obligation or permission to adhere to it.

Novak stresses this point by indicating Aquinas's twofold view of responsibility between a person and the community in which they live: "The person owes the community loyalty and service *in return* for the just distribution of society's goods he has received" (Novak, 1975, p. 66). The set of "goods" a community owes to its members is what counts toward the fulfillment of their nature – that is, satisfies their natural inclinations. Such goods include not only the fundamental good of life, but also various other goods that need to be cultivated within a person so that they may live to the fullest extent of their nature. Novak cites certain virtues as examples: "In a true communion of persons one can see a need for even the help-less and infirm. Their very presence enables us to practice the human virtues of benevolence and generosity" (Novak, 1975, p. 66). Even a "helpless and infirmed" member of the community can remain a contributing member by assisting others in the cultivation of fulfilling goods, while at the same time preserving the funda-mental good of their own existence. Every community owes its members the capacity to be of such service to others and to be served by others in return. It would thus violate a community's basic duty to its citizens if it permitted some to view themselves as useless, noncontributing members, for such would not be the truth of the matter.

Clinical attitude toward the dying

Due to a human being's nature as a soul-body unity, who experiences both physical and psychological suffering when stricken with a terminal illness and approaching death, the appropriate clinical attitude toward patients in such a condition includes the alleviation of suffering at both levels according to the limits of medical practice, but without violation of a human being's natural inclination to live. Human beings have a natural inclination toward bodily health so that they may fulfill their proper functions: "Health indeed is esteemed as a kind of virtue" (ST, Ia-IIae.71.1.ad 3). Given that illness and its attendant suffering go against the natural inclination toward health and proper functioning, as well as a human being's natural inclination toward pleasant sensual experiences and psychological "peace of mind," a number of means to alleviate suffering besides active euthanasia follow from the natural law. Such means include the administration of palliative treatment, even when it may hasten death, and the nonutilization of life-sustaining measures that unduly prolong a patient's experience of suffering and their process of dying – I will discuss in this chapter how these actions may be warranted and morally justified. At the same time, while a patient continues to suffer until the point at which they naturally expire, all available means of psychological and spiritual counseling should be made available to them, and a suitable environment provided for prolonged contact with family and friends. Several models of palliative and hospice care already reflect these ideals.

In caring for a suffering or dying person, it is important for the patient and their caregivers not to deny that suffering and death are unavoidable facets of human life. Though suffering and death are undesirable for their own sake, and thus can be justifiably avoided or delayed, when unavoidable or impending, they may provide a means by which certain benefits may be realized. Aquinas does not see bodily suffering as the greatest evil to be avoided at all costs. Rather, he holds that at least some pain is "from something apparently evil, which is truly good" (ST, Ia-IIae.39.4). Hence, such pain "cannot be the greatest evil, for it would be worse to be entirely alienated from what is truly good" (ST, Ia-IIae.39.4). But the value of pain is relative to its usefulness for producing some good:

> Someone's suffering adversity would not be pleasing to God except for the sake of some good coming from the adversity. And so although adversity is in itself bitter and gives rise to sadness, it should nonetheless be agreeable [to us] when we consider its usefulness, on account of which it is pleasing to God…For in his reason a person rejoices over the taking of bitter medicine because of the hope of health, even though in his senses he is troubled.
>
> (In Job, I.20–1; trans. Stump)

It is important to note that placing such value on suffering does not entail that one should seek suffering for its own sake. This would violate the first precept of natural law. Bodily pain is an evil because it interferes with the body's natural functioning; such evil should be avoided. Any good that comes from suffering does not make suffering good in itself:

> On Aquinas's view suffering is good *not simpliciter* but only *secundum quid*. That is, suffering is not good in itself but only conditionally, insofar as it is a means to an end. "The evils which are in this world," Aquinas says, "aren't to be desired for their own sake but insofar as they are ordered to some good" [In I Cor, XV.ii.925; trans. Stump]. In itself suffering is a bad thing; it acquires positive value only when it contributes to spiritual well-being.
>
> (Stump, 1999, pp. 201–2)

Aquinas's natural law ethic thus warrants the alleviation of suffering and supports palliative medicine. Care for the body also follows from Aquinas's contention that we should love our bodies (ST, IIa-IIae.25.5).

The overarching principle at work in the aforementioned considerations is that of nature and the natural law which follows from a consideration of, specifically, *human* nature. Goodness, with respect to the body, is the body's health and relief from suffering, which allows it to fulfill its proper functioning. This goodness is to be promoted by any means which do not themselves violate the natural law. I thus conclude that Aquinas supports palliative medicine and any medical treatment that promotes the body's health and relief from suffering, so long as such treatment does not violate the natural law. Since active euthanasia, as a form of suicide, is a violation of the natural law, it cannot be justified even as a means of alleviating suffering. When bodily suffering is unavoidably forced upon us, we can take what steps we can to lessen or eliminate it. But if suffering is part of the natural course of one's life, meaning that the only way to end the suffering is to end one's life, then it must be endured as it is now constitutive of one's existence. Due to the potential value of a human being's experience of suffering and impending death, Aquinas exhorts us to respect the fundamental natural inclination to live and not deny this inclination only for the sake of satisfying our other natural inclinations not to experience suffering and death.

Passive euthanasia

As alternatives to active euthanasia, two types of cases come to the fore at this point. One is a form of passive euthanasia, or "letting die," that involves the non-utilization[9] of life-sustaining treatment for a terminally ill patient. If the overarching principle at work in Aquinas's ethic is that of noninterference with one's nature, then if one's natural state is that of bodily decay toward death, interference with that natural course is not warranted. Hence, the utilization of artificial means to sustain a living body, which would otherwise be dead, is not required and may even be wrong on Aquinas's account. Since passive euthanasia is not suicide, nor homicide, it is not summarily dismissed as is active euthanasia. Furthermore, since passive euthanasia is, by definition, the allowance of nature to take its course without interference, it seems to be not only permissible according to natural law, but also demanded.

One must be careful, though, to keep in mind that Aquinas's natural law ethic is not a call for universal, absolute respect for the natural course of things. Rather, Aquinas is exhorting us to use a being's defined nature to determine what is "good" or "evil" for that type of being. Since it is constitutive of human nature to be living, then any action that sustains and promotes life is "good." Understood in this sense, passive euthanasia would not be consistent with the natural law. Rather, any possible means to sustain life would be warranted. On this construal of natural law, hooking a body up to respirators and other life-sustaining machines is apparently mandated. Nevertheless, as James Colbert, Jr notes, "To suggest that recognizing an absolute value in life in a Thomistic sense, would require that one use *all* imaginable means to conserve life, is a caricature" (Colbert, 1978, p. 196). I will return to this issue later.

The other type of case, which I will discuss first, involves the administration of palliative treatment that has the foreseen concomitant – that is, unavoidable – consequence of hastening a patient's death. I will discuss only the limited topic of palliative *treatment* – that is, the administration of analgesic medication – as opposed to the more expansive topic of palliative *care*, which is "the active total care of patients whose disease is not responsive to curative treatment" and involves "control of pain, of other symptoms, and of psychological, social and spiritual problems" (World Health Organization, 1990, p. 11). I will also limit my discussion to palliative treatment for patients who are terminally ill and have reached the limit of medicine's ability to cure them of their affliction.

Administration of palliative treatment and terminal sedation

The goal of palliative treatment is not only to minimize a patient's experience of pain, but also, by making the patient as comfortable as possible, to allow them to carry out whatever activities they are able to perform that contribute to the flourishing of their remaining life – conversing and emotionally sharing with family and friends, putting their final affairs in order, and preparing spiritually for death:

> Given that not even an approximation to health can be achieved, one aims to secure as *tolerable* a state of the organism as possible so that conscious living (with family and friends and others) may continue. Thus palliative medicine, in deploying techniques of pain control, is focused, just like other forms of medicine, on the organic component of our aptitude to share in other human goods.
>
> (Gormally, 1994, p. 134)

The most effective forms of palliative treatment, used in cases of the most severe pain, may have the concomitant negative effect of hastening a terminally ill patient's death. Hence, in order to judge the provision of such treatment to be morally permissible, Aquinas must hold some form of the Principle of Double Effect (PDE) – as I argue he does in Chapter 1 – since he is explicitly against active euthanasia. To be morally permissible, the forms of palliative treatment considered here must be distinguished as an act in which a patient's death is not directly intended (Cavanaugh, 1996).

An example would be a case in which a patient with end-stage lung cancer requires analgesic medication to control the intense suffering they endure with each successive breath. The only effective medication – usually an opiate such as morphine – has the known consequence of causing respiratory suppression, and this effect is even more acute in this case due to the patient being in the end stage of lung cancer. If administered, this medication will not only ease the patient's suffering, but also likely cut short the length of time that they are able to continue to respire, and hence to live. Recent development of nonopiate analgesic medications, as well as "antagonist" drugs – for example, Narcan – that can counteract the respiratory suppressant effect of morphine, limit the number of cases in which the administration of effective palliative treatment will actually hasten a patient's death (Barry and Maher, 1990, pp. 129–36). Nevertheless, James Bernat observes that, "Occasionally a patient's pulmonary failure is so severe that the small respiratory suppressant effect may become clinically significant. In these cases, it is conceivable that the high-dose opiates necessary to control pain or dyspnea might accelerate death" (Bernat, 2001, p. 977).

Another example is what is generally termed "terminal sedation." In some cases, a patient's condition is so severe that the only effective means of alleviating their suffering is to render them unconscious:

> In cases of intolerable and refractory suffering, adequate relief can be obtained only by sedating the patients, often into unconsciousness, so that they no

longer are able to feel their pain or other suffering. Although the frequency of intolerable and refractory symptoms is uncertain, studies have found their existence in 10–50% of terminally ill patients referred for palliative care.

(Orentlicher, 1997, p. 955; cf. Cherny and Portenoy, 1994, p. 32)

The use of terminal sedation is sometimes a necessary means of providing effective palliative treatment for terminally ill patients:

One report has suggested that more than 50% of patients with terminal cancer have physical suffering during the last days of their life controlled, as such, only by sedation. Another report shows that 40% of all dying patients in the United States die in pain. Recently, the Institute of Medicine (IOM) found that anywhere from 40% to 80% of patients with terminal illness report that their treatment for pain is inadequate and prolongs the very agony of death.

(Smith, 1998, p. 382)

Reported reasons for using sedation include pain (12%), anguish (14%), respiratory distress (12%), agitation/delirium/confusion/hallucinations (12%), fear/panic/anxiety/terror (10%), emotional/psychological/spiritual distress (10%), restlessness (10%), seizures/twitching (4%), and nausea/vomiting/retching (2%). Nevertheless, delirium appears to be the most common indication for terminal sedation.

(Lanuke *et al.*, 2003, p. 279)

To determine the moral permissibility of terminal sedation, it is first necessary to elaborate upon the nature of the act, its intended end, and the value of the intended end.

Terminal sedation involves the use of a high dose of sedatives that renders a patient unconscious: "Narcotics (e.g. morphine), benzodiazepine sedative drugs (e.g. Valium), barbiturates (e.g. amobarbital) and/or major tranquilizing drugs (e.g. Haldol or Thorazine) are used to sedate the patient" (Orentlicher, 1997, p. 955; cf. Truog *et al.*, 1992, p. 1678; Cherny and Portenoy, 1994, p. 35). The intended end of terminal sedation is to relieve patients' suffering either through removal of their conscious experience of pain, or by hastening their death as the sedatives typically used result in side-effects such as respiratory depression and hypotension. Herein lies the controversial nature of terminal sedation, for *either* intention may be at work in such acts. If the physician administering the sedative has the latter intention, then the act of terminal sedation is a form of active euthanasia. Sedation is a means whereby the patient's hastened death is not merely foreseen, but is willfully caused:

In terminal sedation, not only is the patient's death clearly foreseen, it is in fact the end point of what is being done. Clearly (and however it may be cloaked by the use of language), the intent here is more than just the clear goal of relieving pain and suffering. Because the goal of relieving pain and suffering adequately can be attained only by obtunding the patient until death ensues, the patient's death becomes the end point and, therefore, one of the intended goals. These goals do not differ from those of physician-assisted suicide or, for that matter, voluntary euthanasia.

(Loewy, 2001, p. 331)

On the other hand, a physician may have the intention of merely suppressing the patient's consciousness so that they will not experience pain that cannot be alleviated by other means:

> Although proponents of physician-assisted suicide and euthanasia contend that terminal sedation is covert physician-assisted suicide or euthanasia, the concept of sedating pharmacotherapy is based on informed consent and the principle of double effect. Double effect acknowledges that the intent and desired effect of treatment is mitigation of symptoms rather than cessation of life, even though life may be shortened. However, prior to initiation of sedation, clinicians must ascertain the need for sedating therapy, including the presence of a terminal disease with impending death, exhaustion of all other palliative treatments, agreement by patient and family members of the need for sedation, and a current do-not-resuscitate order.
>
> (Rousseau, 1996, p. 1785)

As noted in the preceding passage, the moral justification of an act of terminal sedation with the intention of merely alleviating suffering, and not hastening death, requires the applicability of PDE. I will demonstrate how PDE morally justifies the use of terminal sedation given the proper intention merely to alleviate suffering with the foreseen, but not directly intended, consequence of hastening a patient's death.

A further complication is that terminal sedation is sometimes exercised with the stated intention of merely alleviating suffering, but concurrent with the sedative's administration is the withdrawal of all life-sustaining treatment, including artificial nutrition and hydration (Quill and Byock, 2000). Therefore, a complete ethical assessment of terminal sedation must include an evaluation of the moral permissibility of withdrawing artificial nutrition and hydration, which I provide later in this section.

In order for the administration of palliative medication or terminal sedation to be justified, a physician must directly intend *only* to alleviate their patient's suffering. The physician must not directly intend that the treatment cause or hasten the patient's death as a means of alleviating their suffering. The former intention may be demonstrated by administering only enough of the medication to ease the patient's suffering effectively. Administrating more medication than is known to be minimally necessary to be effective would demonstrate a direct intention not only to ease suffering, but also to cause the patient's death.[10]

Furthermore, the proper application of Aquinas's form of PDE requires that the foreseen negative consequence is merely "risked" and not certain to occur

(Cavanaugh, 1997, pp. 116–19; Sullivan, 2000, p. 437). Robert Barry and James Maher thus conclude:

> The use of certainly lethal doses of analgesia would be wrong because they would be the means by which death would occur even if it was judged to be the only means available of relieving the patient's pain. If one gave a certainly lethal dose of painkillers to a patient, the hastening of death or shortening of life would be equivalent to causing death... The use of an analgesic that would be more lethal than therapeutic would make it the moral and physical direct cause of death.
>
> (1990, p. 139)

Any action that involves the direct intention of the patient's death would not be justified according to the Thomistic account of PDE described in Chapter 1. One could argue that the patient's death is not directly intended in this case because the overall purpose is to alleviate their suffering. Such an argument, however, conflates the "object" of an action – what is done – with its "end" – why is it done. Although the end – alleviation of suffering – is a good worth pursuing, the act that is willfully done to achieve this end is not good – causing the patient's death. Even if one could successfully argue that death is not directly intended by this action, it is nevertheless the means by which the patient's suffering is alleviated and thereby fails to fulfill the conditions of PDE.

Palliative treatment that merely increases the risk of a terminally ill patient's death, or hastens death without a direct intention to do so, is morally justified:

> If hastening death only implies a relatively minor increase in the *probability* of death or a minor reduction of the defenses of the body when there are other highly lethal threats already present, then it would seem that use of this form of analgesia would be permissible, as the good of alleviation of pain would compensate for the increased risk of death. This is a common occurrence in medicine, as virtually all medications increase one's risk of death.
>
> (Barry and Maher, 1990, p. 140)

Aquinas's account of the morality of human action allows an agent to directly intend a good end, while at the same time allowing for foreseen concomitant negative consequences. A physician may directly intend to alleviate their patient's suffering with the foreseen consequence of increasing the risk of the patient's death:

> Indirectly life-shortening analgesia would be in accord with the principle of double effect if the intention was only to relieve pain, if the analgesia were not *per se* lethal, and if the pain was so severe and intractable that it was proportionate to death itself.
>
> (Barry and Maher, 1990, p. 137;
> cf. Pellegrino, 1998, p. 1521)

This does not entail, however, that the physician, or any moral agent in such double-effect cases, is in no way responsible for their actions. The foreseen negative consequence is not completely removed from the physician's intention. Nevertheless, there is a window of opportunity for the physician to justify why they performed the directly intended action and thereby allowed the concomitant negative consequence to occur. Such justification would include the fact that, because it is not directly intended, the foreseen concomitant consequence does not render "evil" the good action of administering palliative treatment for the sake of alleviating suffering.

In cases of terminal sedation, a physician directly intends to alleviate their patient's suffering by the only effective means possible: rendering the patient unconscious. Once sedated, the patient will not regain consciousness again, unless the sedation is ceased and the patient is allowed to awaken and experience their suffering. Terminal sedation, understood as an act of rendering a patient unconscious until death naturally ensues with the foreseen side-effect of death being hastened, is clearly justified by appeal to PDE so long as no other means are available to alleviate the patient's intractable suffering effectively:

> Analyses of the morality of sedation in patients who are imminently dying, using the principle of double effect, conclude that it is morally permissible when there is no better alternative. Sedating a patient for palliative care is moral. The death of the patient may be a foreseen consequence but is not the intended consequence; only relief of pain or other symptoms is intended. The relief of pain does not require the death of the patient to be effective. The act is performed for a proportionately serious reason, namely to prevent suffering.
> (Bernat, 2001, p. 978; cf. Mount, 1996, pp. 34–5; Orentlicher, 1997, p. 957; Pellegrino, 1998, p. 1521; Sulmasy and Pellegrino, 1999, p. 547; Krakauer *et al.*, 2000, p. 60; Gauthier, 2001, p. 45; Williams, 2001, p. 50; Jansen and Sulmasy, 2002, p. 847; Lanuke *et al.*, 2003, p. 280)

Terminal sedation does not necessarily involve a physician directly intending that their patient's death be hastened. Furthermore, as argued in Chapter 3, Aquinas does not equate permanent unconsciousness with death, nor does he deny the intrinsic goodness of life itself. Death does not ensue until the body's integrated organic functioning ceases. Rendering a patient unconscious does not entail intending their death; the lack of this intention may be evidenced by the sedative being titrated to render the patient unconscious effectively, but not unduly hasten their death (Truog in Krakauer *et al.*, 2000, p. 59). A direct intention to hasten death, though, may underlie some acts of terminal sedation; thus rendering the act morally impermissible in such cases.

The value of intending to alleviate a patient's intractable suffering through terminal sedation is sufficiently obvious: relief of suffering. But the value of a patient's continued conscious existence is also worth noting. While Aquinas would consider it impermissible to inhibit a person's conscious rational activity for no good reason, there may be a sufficiently good reason to do so when a person's experience of pain is so severe as to inhibit their conscious rational activity already. While a person's conscious rational activity is a good worth promoting, an arguably proportionate good is relief from intense and intractable pain.

As mentioned earlier, an important corollary of terminal sedation is the withdrawal of artificial nutrition and hydration (ANH) because many cases of terminal sedation involve the latter as well. Though a number of authors recognize the justification of terminal sedation by PDE, some also warn that PDE does not justify the additional act of withdrawing ANH after unconsciousness has been induced:

> The principle of double effect, however, only justifies the sedation part of terminal sedation. We cannot justify the withdrawal of food and water component of terminal sedation, because that step does nothing to relieve the patient's suffering, but rather serves only to bring on the patient's death.
>
> (Orentlicher, 1997, p. 957)

> Whereas the goal of administering barbiturates to induce sleep to relieve suffering is good and beneficial to the patient, on no interpretation can the additional step of withdrawing artificial nutrition and hydration be considered a necessary condition of relieving pain... Accordingly withdrawing food and water from a terminally sedated patient cannot be justified under the principle of double effect. It must and should always be confined to excluding situations involving withdrawing artificial nutrition and hydration.
>
> (Williams, 2001, pp. 51–2)

David Orentlicher argues that terminal sedation accompanied by withdrawal of ANH implicates the physician in having a direct intention of hastening the patient's death (Orentlicher, 1997, p. 959). Two forms of terminal sedation must therefore be distinguished: (1) terminal sedation *simpliciter*, which involves only the titrated administration of analgesic medication to the point that a patient loses consciousness and is maintained in an unconscious state until death naturally ensues; and (2) terminal sedation accompanied by the withdrawal of ANH. (1) is clearly justified by appeal to PDE; but determining the moral permissibility of (2) requires a detailed ethical analysis of the withholding or withdrawal of artificial life support, including nutrition and hydration.

Nonutilization of life-sustaining treatment

Since Aquinas holds a form of PDE, then not only may palliative treatment and terminal sedation be justified actions, but the nonutilization of life-sustaining treatment may also be justified provided that the patient's death is not directly intended, but only that their suffering not be prolonged. In this case, the object of the action is the nonutilization of life-sustaining treatment. The directly intended end is not to prolong the patient's suffering; death is a foreseen concomitant consequence. One may question this description by asserting that, in this case, the patient's death is the direct means by which the end of not prolonging their suffering is achieved. I disagree and contend that the direct means of not prolonging the patient's suffering is by not employing measures to *sustain* their life indefinitely. The nonutilization of life-sustaining treatment does not cause the patient's death. Their death is due to the natural course of whatever disease or injury they suffer. This is truly a case of "passive" euthanasia, in which a patient's natural condition is allowed to be the cause of death.

Sustaining biological existence is a "good," however, as well as not prolonging suffering: "Human bodily life is a great good. It is a good *of* the person and intrinsic to the person and is not a mere instrumental good or good *for* the person" (May, 1990, p. 81; cf. May *et al.*, 1987, p. 204; May, 1998, p. 48). When only one of these goods can be pursued to the exclusion of the other, the paramount moral requirement is that "evil" not be perpetrated in the pursuance of either one. The questionable element is that the nonutilization of life-sustaining treatment has the concomitant consequence of not preventing the patient's death. Nevertheless, since Aquinas holds PDE and it is applicable to this type of case, the nonutilization of life-sustaining treatment may be morally permissible.

It is important, though, to consider the type of life-sustaining treatment that may be provided and the type of patient to whom it is being provided in determining if its nonutilization is permissible. I will discuss three relevant cases: nonutilization of artificial respiration for a whole-brain dead patient; nonutilization of ANH for a PVS patient; and nonutilization of ANH for a terminally ill patient whose death is imminent.

The nonutilization of artificial respiration for a whole-brain dead patient is a paradigm case of morally permissible passive euthanasia. First of all, such an action is not technically an act of "euthanasia" because a whole-brain dead patient is indeed *dead*. The nonutilization of artificial respiration merely brings about the total cessation of persistent, but not integrated, biological processes; the human organism has already ceased to exist. Second, as Patrick Hopkins notes, "The principle here is that a patient being artificially sustained is not being sustained in the *kind* of way that necessarily morally prohibits interrupting their physical processes, even if death may result" (Hopkins, 1997, p. 33).

Normally, interrupting the physical process of a person's respiration – for example, by strangling or suffocating them – would be morally impermissible because one is interfering with that person's "natural" vital metabolic processes. In the case at hand, though, one is interfering with something "artificial" that replaces one of a person's vital metabolic processes in order to sustain the rest. This characterization of the case involves, as Hopkins describes:

> thinking of the patient on a respirator as an artificially sustained being. Once the patient's breathing is artificial, once his or her vital processes are artificially maintained, once his or her very existence is perceived as a novel phenomenon, then certain alterations of physiological processes become merely the removal of artificial interventions.

(1997, p. 33)

Hopkins challenges this characterization and contends:

> The problem with the connection between passive euthanasia (or "acts of omission") and machines is that the age-old distinction between nature and artifice obscures the actual functional relevance of particular machines to particular bodies. What is often ignored is the constitutive function the machine plays in the coherence of the actual person.
>
> (1997, p. 33)

Hopkins considers the withdrawal of artificial respiration to constitute direct interference with a patient's vital metabolic processes:

> But the problem in the respirator case is that the machine we are going to remove is the pulmonary system of the sick patient (or more precisely, is an integral part of that system). That machine breathes for the patient; it is a basic functional component of her pulmonary system, just like lungs are a basic functional component of the pulmonary system of a healthy person.
>
> (1997, p. 34)

The basis for Hopkins's contention is the lack, he argues, of a morally relevant difference between an artificial respirator and a pair of lungs; the only difference between them, he asserts, is the material out of which they are constructed and this hardly constitutes a morally relevant difference (Hopkins, 1997, pp. 34–5). He thus concludes, "Only if one assumes that there is a metaphysical, essential, and intrinsic moral difference between machines and natural bodily organs can one claim that turning off a machine is merely an omission, merely a passive act" (Hopkins, 1997, p. 35).

Is there a morally relevant difference between natural organs and artifacts? As noted in Chapter 3, Aquinas holds that there is. Natural substances and artifacts are distinct grades of being (In DA, II.1). This ontological difference in their respective essences precludes an artifact becoming a "proper part" of a natural substance; an artifact cannot be informed by a natural substance's substantial form, especially an artifact that has its power source and locus of control outside the body. This conclusion is at odds with Hopkins's characterization of artificial respirators as ontologically similar to the lungs that constitute a person's body. While it is true that an artificial respirator can functionally "mimic" my own lungs, such functional similarity does not make that artifact *mine* in the sense that it is now part of my body. Part of the rationale underlying this assertion is that such an artifact is functionally disconnected from me because it is not coordinated by my brainstem. My natural respiratory and cardiac systems are coordinated by electrical signals sent from my brainstem, and this makes them constitutive of *me*. Thus, while interfering with my natural pulmonary or cardiac functioning does something directly to me, removing an artificial respirator only does something directly to an object external to me that consequently has an effect on me. Of course, if I am whole-brain dead, then my death does not result from the respirator's withdrawal since I am already dead. There may be cases, however, in which a patient is not whole-brain dead, but is nonetheless irreversibly dependent on a respirator. In this case, the respirator's nonutilization has the negative effect of bringing about the patient's death. Thus, for such an act to be morally permissible, it must be justified by PDE. This would require that the directly intended end of not utilizing the respirator is *not* to bring about the patient's death, but merely to avoid prolonging their suffering.[11]

If the nonutilization of artificial respiration is morally justifiable by appeal to PDE, then would the nonutilization of artificial nutrition and hydration be justified as well? According to J. P. Moreland and Scott Rae, the two actions are morally equivalent:

> In cases in which it is morally appropriate to remove a ventilator, it is similarly appropriate to withdraw medically provided nutrition and hydration, for withdrawing medically provided nutrition and hydration is not starving someone to death any more than removing a ventilator is suffocating someone. In both cases the underlying disease or injury, not the removal of the treatment, is the cause of death.
>
> (2000, p. 338)

In cases of whole-brain dead patients, the nonutilization of ANH is clearly justified because the patient is already dead and ANH sustains only individual biological processes that no longer constitute an integrated organism. Controversial cases of not utilizing ANH typically involve PVS patients who are not whole-brain dead. It could be argued that, for such patients, the nonutilization of ANH or artificial respiration (if necessary) is justifiable by appeal to PDE so long as the directly intended end is merely not to prolong their suffering. Fred Rosner, however, notes:

> Patients in a coma or a persistent vegetative state are not suffering. Their families, friends, care givers, and society may suffer emotionally and financially. But it is wrong to relieve the suffering of others by shortening the life of the patient.
>
> (1993, p. 1894)

If PVS patients are incapable of suffering, then what good is being served by their life not being prolonged? May and others argue that there is a fundamental good that is served by utilizing ANH for a PVS patient: "Human life itself" (May *et al.*, 1987, p. 210).

Aquinas asserts:

> It is prescribed that a human being sustains his body, for otherwise he murders himself… Therefore, one is bound to nourish his body, and we are bound likewise with respect to all other things without which the body cannot live.
>
> (In II Thes, III.2)

This passage can be interpreted to support the provision of ANH just as we are required to provide food and water to any hungry or thirsty person in need. A more widely applicable interpretation, however, would seem to follow because Aquinas requires the provision of "all other things without which the body cannot live." This implies that we ought to provide artificial respiration and any other medical treatments, such as radiation and chemotherapy for cancer patients, without which their bodies cannot live. Aquinas recognizes, though, that what he has asserted does not entail an absolutely binding obligation:

> It is inherent in everyone by nature that he loves his own life and whatever is ordered toward it, but in due measure, such that these things are loved not as if the end were determined in them, but insofar as they are to be used for the sake of his final end.
>
> (ST, IIa-IIae.126.1)

Hence, the use of ANH is not necessarily warranted in all cases. For example, when a terminally ill patient is facing imminent death, such that any effort to prolong their life would be *futile* (Miles, 1992; Zucker and Zucker, 1997; Atkinson, 2000; Bailey, 2003; Cantor *et al.*, 2003; Nelson, 2003), or such that their body cannot metabolize what is being provided, ANH is no longer medically or morally indicated (May *et al.*, 1987, p. 209; Gormally, 1999, p. 265). The use of ANH is not warranted in such cases because the patient's impending death is hardly affected by its provision.

A PVS patient may not be facing imminent death, but the provision of ANH may nonetheless be futile because it will not improve the prognosis for recovery of conscious rational thought. Kevin O'Rourke and Patrick Norris note Aquinas's distinction between a "human act" (*actus humanus*), which follows from a person's intellect and will, and an "act of a human" (*actus hominis*), which is an autonomic reflex or absent-minded action that does not follow from one's intellect and will (ST, Ia-IIae.1.1). They further note Aquinas's assertion that the purpose of a human being's life – the "final end" to which Aquinas refers in the preceding passage – is achieved only through the intentional human acts that follow from intellect and will (ST, Ia-IIae.5.1). They thus conclude:

> People who are not able to perform acts of cognitive-affective function because of some pathology are not less human, but the moral mandate to help them prolong their lives is no longer present because they will never again perform human acts, that is, acts proceeding directly from the intellect and will. Clearly people in this condition…may not be directly put to death nor mistreated in any way, but life support that keeps them alive need not be continued because it does not offer them any hope of benefit.
>
> (2001, p. 210; cf. Eberl, 2005c)

While a PVS patient's biological life has an inherent fundamental value, as May and others contend, its value relative to the patient's pursuit of ends that are consciously willed has been mitigated by their irreversibly unconscious condition. The patient still lives and is a person, and so one may not directly intend to end their life or mistreat them, but measures to prolong their life that are futile – in terms of failing to provide for some measure of recovery – or disproportionately burdensome[12] are not morally mandated.

In some cases, a patient has lost the swallowing reflex, which is a fatal pathology indicating the body's refusal of further nutrition so that death may naturally occur (O'Rourke, 1989). The provision of ANH, however, may induce this fatal pathology by allowing the esophageal muscles to atrophy.[13] If ANH is medically necessary to maintain a patient's life, then inducing this fatal pathology is justified by PDE as a foreseen concomitant consequence.[14] Once this pathology is present, the futile provision of ANH is no longer warranted as the body is preparing itself for death. Withdrawal of ANH in such a case, while hastening the patient's death, is justified by PDE because the direct intention is not to prolong their already protracted process of dying; the fundamental value of their continued bodily existence is contrasted by their body's own natural refusal of further nutrition. Even if the patient is not consciously suffering, the medical futility of providing ANH and the evidence that the patient's body is naturally preparing itself for death contraindicates further provision of ANH. Therefore, in the case of Terri Schiavo, if she were correctly diagnosed as a PVS patient and no longer had the swallowing reflex – and thus would not have benefited from hand-feeding – then the withdrawal of ANH was justified by PDE and the futility of continued treatment that would not have improved her condition and may have unduly prolonged her dying process.

Organ donation

Organ donation is an important end-of-life issue that has significant consequences for both donors and potential recipients. According to the United Network for Organ Sharing (UNOS), as of October 1, 2004, there are 87,012 patients on the transplant waitlist. UNOS also reports that there have been 13,226 transplants performed between January and June 2004 utilizing organs from 6,935 donors.[15] There is obviously a large gap between the amount of transplants occurring and the number of patients in need. The US Organ Procurement and Transplantation Network and the Scientific Registry of Transplant Recipients published in their 2003 Annual Report that more than 6,000 patients died while awaiting a transplant that year.[16]

It is not difficult to conceive of organ donation being an inherently good action from Aquinas's natural law perspective. First, organ donation promotes human life as its directly intended end. Second, participation in this form of communal giving can be arguably derived as a secondary natural law principle, based on humanity's inherently *social* nature and our natural inclination to promote the common good. Amitai Etzioni describes the goal of the "communitarian approach" to organ donation:

> The essence of the communitarian approach is that it seeks to make organ donation an act people engage in because they consider it their social responsibility, something a good person does, akin to volunteering, contributing to a cause, not parking in handicap spaces, recycling, not washing one's car when there is a water shortage, and so on.
>
> (2003, p. 5; cf. Nelson, 2001)

It would be a mistake, though, to conceive of organ donation as a mandate of natural law without considering some issues that arise given Aquinas's metaphysical view of human nature, as well as the fundamental good of the donor's life in addition to the lives of any potential organ recipients. Some of the particular issues that I will address are religious objections to organ donation based on belief in postmortem bodily resurrection, Aquinas's view of a human being's bodily integrity and when it is justifiable to violate such integrity in cases of "living" donation, and finally procurement of organs utilizing "non-heart-beating donor" protocols.

Organ donation and belief in bodily resurrection

Some religious believers object to organ donation due to their belief that human beings will enjoy a *bodily* existence postmortem, which comes about through the resurrection of the body that had been lain down in death. For orthodox Jews and fundamentalist Christians, this belief entails that all the body's parts must be present in order for human beings to be resurrected in their physical entirety:

> The traditional rabbinic belief in bodily resurrection is, for some Jews, the source of an important objection to organ donation. They believe that the body must be buried with all its parts so that they will all be there when it comes time for resurrection.
>
> (Dorff, 1996, p. 179)

> As the Pauline notion of the resurrection suggests, there is a grand economy in the universal matter of bodies. All the parts must be accounted for. Even when an organ is fatally diseased or not functioning, it cannot be thrown away.
>
> (Barkan, 1996, p. 243)

Robert Veatch contends, though, that "fundamentalist Christians who really understand their church's doctrine should not have a problem with organ donation as far as belief in a resurrection of the body is concerned" (Veatch, 2000, p. 7).

The understanding of the Christian belief in bodily resurrection to which Veatch refers is found within Aquinas's metaphysical account of human nature. Aquinas defines a human being's death as the separation of their rational soul from the body it informs (Eberl, 2000b, p. 216).[17] He contends that a human being's rational soul does not perish with its body, but persists as a separate immaterial thing that still composes a human being, albeit incompletely (Eberl, 2004, pp. 339–41). But a rational soul cannot persist forever in a state of separation from its body, for this condition is "unnatural" for it (CT, 151; SCG, IV.79; Eberl, 2000b, pp. 216–17). Aquinas thus concludes that a rational soul's reunion with the *same* body it informed premortem is mandated by natural necessity (CT, 153). He argues that the resurrected body's identity is effected through its being informed by the same soul that had previously informed it; the resurrected body is the same as the body that had died because it has the same substantial form (ST, Supp.79.2; Eberl, 2004, pp. 357–8).

A human being's resurrected body, Aquinas contends, need not be reconstituted from the exact same material particles that constituted the body premortem. Aquinas recognizes that the material constituents of a human being's body are constantly in flux throughout their life (SCG, IV.81; ST, Ia.119.1; Chandlish, 1968); bodies undergo cellular decay, and food is transformed by digestion into raw material to generate new cells and other bodily components. This does not render a human being's identity problematic because the same substantial form persists and functions as the "blueprint" for its body (Stump, 2003, p. 46; Eberl, 2004, pp. 353–9). Therefore, since a human being's rational soul persists between death and resurrection and will inform the resurrected body, it is inconsequential what matter composes the resurrected body. Regardless of where such matter originates, it is made to compose *this* human being's body because it is informed by *its* soul (Stump, 1995, p. 517; Eberl, 2000b, pp. 223–4; Eberl, 2004, pp. 357–8).

Therefore, religious believers in postmortem bodily resurrection need not oppose organ donation on that basis. Aquinas offers a clear and coherent metaphysical account of human nature that preserves a human being's identity after death by virtue of the soul alone; the matter that composes a human being premortem plays no essential, identity-preserving role either before or after death. If one donates their organs, it does not follow that they will fail to have those organs as parts of their resurrected body; any matter informed by their soul will be formed such that it has all the requisite organs functioning perfectly.

Living donation and the principle of totality

Another major issue that arises in regard to organ donation from a Thomistic perspective involves what scholars term the "principle of totality" (PT), which refers to the relationship between a human body's parts and the body as a whole. Aquinas formulates PT as follows:

> Since a member is part of the whole human body, it exists for the sake of the whole…Hence, the disposition of a human body's member is as it is advantageous for the whole. Now a human body's member is itself useful for the good of the whole body, but it may happen accidentally that it is harmful, as when a decayed member is corruptive of the whole body. If therefore a member were healthy and remaining in its natural disposition, it cannot be cut off without being detrimental to the whole human being.
>
> (ST, IIa-IIae.65.1; cf. ST, IIa-IIae.64.2; SCG, III.112)

Aquinas holds that a healthy organ or limb cannot be excised from the body unless it were to become detrimental to the body's overall health, and even then only as a last resort: "A member is not to be cut off for the sake of the bodily health of the whole except when nothing can aid the whole otherwise" (ST, IIa-IIae.65.1.ad 3).

Some interpreters of Aquinas and moral theologians hold that PT precludes "living" organ donation – that is, donation of a kidney or a lobe of the liver by a living donor as opposed to procurement from a cadaver (Ramsey, 1970, pp. 165–97; Gaffney, 1976). Others contend that living organ donation does not violate PT (McCormick, 1975; Lamb, 1990, p. 105; Cherry, 2000; DuBois, 2002a, pp. 435–6;). I agree with the latter position for several reasons. First, the functional integrity of the donor's body as a whole is not threatened by donating a kidney or a lobe of their liver:

> Because kidneys are paired and the body can function with one healthy kidney, the removal of a kidney does not seriously impair an essential function. Likewise, removal of a lobe of the liver typically does not impair function, largely because the surgically reduced liver amazingly regenerates to nearly its full size, doubling its mass in only seven days.
>
> (DuBois, 2002a, p. 436)

Second, although there is an associated risk of death by becoming a living organ donor due, for example, to complications from the transplant procedure or early failure of the remaining kidney, such risk can be justified by appeal to PDE. Nobody involved in a living donation procedure directly intends the donor's death, nor is their death a means toward the end of saving the recipient's life. The increased risk of death for the donor is a foreseen concomitant consequence of living donation, but is merely foreseen and not directly intended.

Finally, there is a positive reason supporting living donation based on the relationship between individual human beings and their communities. David Lamb contends:

> A "total" human being is essentially social, and when removed from a social environment psychological, and possibly physiological, dysfunction can be predicted. As a social being, it can be argued that the principle of totality must include a capacity to co-operate with others, respond to their needs, and receive help... Given that self-destruction is not an inevitable consequence of kidney donation, it would appear that the risks entailed and modest dysfunction are compatible with the principle of totality, especially when threats to social and psychological totality are apparent, such as the potential loss of a caring and loved relative.
>
> (Lamb, 1990, p. 105)

Living donation, as an act of "charity" (Cherry, 2000, p. 180), can thus be understood as consistent with, if not directly following from, humanity's fundamentally social nature.

Perhaps the moral mandate, however, is even stronger than just an exhortation to perform a charitable act. In formulating PT, Aquinas describes an apparent subordination of the good of a human being's whole body to the good of the community:

> But as the whole of a human being is ordained to the end of the whole community of which he is a part [ST, IIa-IIae.61.1, IIa-IIae.64.2, 5], it may

happen that cutting off a member, though it may tend toward the detriment of the whole body, may nevertheless be ordained toward the good of the community.

(ST, IIa-IIae.65.1)

This passage appears to be quite problematic because it seems to allow for the community to *require* than an individual donate their kidney or lobe of their liver if a matching recipient is located. Mark Cherry counters:

Persons exist neither for the sake of others nor for the sake of society. Citizens may have certain duties to society, but this is quite different from asserting that they are parts of a quasi social organism in the same sense as the kidney is part of the body.

(Cherry, 2000, p. 179; cf. Kelly, 1960, p. 247)

Cherry is right to warn against any extreme form of instrumentalization or subordination of individual human beings to their communities. Certainly any legislative mandate to be a living donor would go too far; as Aquinas affirms, not every type of virtuous act is to be enforced by human law (ST, Ia-IIae.96.4.ad 1).

Nevertheless, human beings have a fundamentally social nature and, to fulfill this aspect of human nature, Aquinas appeals to the virtue of charity. Charity has for its object first and foremost, according to Aquinas, God; but charity extends also to love of one's neighbor (ST, IIa-IIae.25.1). Pertinent to the issue of living organ donation, Aquinas exhorts that, despite PT, a person should bear bodily injury for their friend's sake (ST, IIa-IIae.26.4.ad 2) and that one ought to love one's neighbor out of charity more than one's own body (ST, IIa-IIae.26.5). He is careful, though, not to imply that such a moral obligation is absolute or should be externally forced upon someone:

Every human being is intent on the care of his own body, but not every human being is intent on the care of his neighbor's welfare, except perhaps in an emergency. And so it is not necessitated by charity that a human being offers his own body for his neighbor's welfare, except in a case where he is bound to care for his neighbor's welfare. But if someone voluntarily offers himself for that purpose, it pertains to the perfection of charity.

(ST, IIa-IIae.26.5.ad 3)

Therefore, an act of living donation is most properly construed as an act of charity and is morally permissible despite the apparent conflict with PT. I thus agree with Cherry when he argues:

(1) Persons are charitable beings and (2) such charity is good. Moreover, (3) the good of being charitable is often more important than the good of preserving the wholeness of the body. However, (4) directly intending to kill oneself is forbidden (e.g., donating one's heart while still living). Therefore: often

charity is sufficient to defeat the *prima facie* moral impermissibility of removing healthy human body parts, as long as this is not part of an act that intends directly to kill oneself.

(2000, p. 180)

The dead donor rule and non-heart-beating donation

The overriding principle in the donation of vital human organs – for example, heart, lungs, whole liver, or both kidneys – is what is known as the "dead donor rule" (DDR). DDR states quite simply that organ procurement should never kill a patient and may begin only after the donor has been declared dead (Robertson, 2000; DuBois, 2002a, p. 418). Given the conclusion reached in Chapter 3 regarding the proper Thomistic concept and criterion of death, it is clear that vital organs cannot be procured from a PVS patient. It also would not be permissible to withdraw life-sustaining treatment from PVS patients for the directly intended end of procuring their vital organs after they expire (Hoffenberg *et al.*, 1997).

I concluded in Chapter 3 that the optimal criterion by which to declare a patient dead is the *whole-brain* criterion. This criterion has the pragmatic advantage of allowing a patient's vital metabolic functions to be maintained artificially so that their organs are perfused with oxygenated blood and do not suffer the effects of warm ischemia. This allows multiple organs to be procured, as well as greater time to elapse between the declaration of death and organ procurement, which permits more time for families to arrive at a decision regarding donation, for transplant teams to organize, and for UNOS to find compatible recipients. Using the whole-brain criterion to declare a patient dead so that, among other things, their organs may be procured is not immune to criticism (Truog and Robinson, 2003).[18] Nevertheless, it has been widely accepted as *the* medical standard for declaring death and, as argued in Chapter 3, offers the best contemporary interpretation of the Thomistic view of human death.

Recently, a new debate has arisen regarding the procurement of vital organs from non-heart-beating (NHB) donors, so-called because death is declared in such cases by the traditional criterion of irreversible cessation of heartbeat and respiration, as opposed to the whole-brain criterion. The practice of procuring vital organs from NHB donors began at the University of Pittsburgh Medical Center, but has since spread both nationally and internationally, and has the potential to significantly increase the supply of vital organs for transplant (Institute of Medicine, 2000, p. 7). This practice has been ethically evaluated from various perspectives, but primarily in terms of whether it adheres to DDR given that NHB donors typically have not suffered cessation of whole-brain functioning (Arnold and Youngner, 1993; Youngner and Arnold, 1993; Arnold *et al.*, 1995; Campbell and Weber, 1995; DeVita *et al.*, 1995; Spielman and McCarthy, 1995).

Non-heart-beating donation is basically characterized as follows:

The patient who becomes a non-heart-beating organ donor cannot sustain life without continued medical intervention. When this medical intervention is stopped [or not utilized], cardiac and respiratory functions cease, death is declared, and organs are removed. The process must be carried out rapidly in order to remove organs before they become unsuitable for transplantation.

(Institute of Medicine, 2000, p. 8)

As noted in this passage, time is of the essence in NHB donation because the cessation of cardiac functioning entails that the organs are no longer perfused with oxygenated blood and are soon subject to functional deterioration due to warm ischemia.

Non-heart-beating donation may be either "controlled" or "uncontrolled" (Institute of Medicine, 2000, pp. 8–9, 1997, pp. 23–6). In uncontrolled cases, a patient suffers spontaneous cardiac arrest and death is declared sometime after the decision has been made to cease or not employ resuscitative efforts. In controlled cases, a decision is made to withdraw artificial life support from a patient, and then a separate decision is made to do so in a way that allows the patient's vital organs to be donated: the ventilator is turned off in an operating room after the patient has been prepped for organ procurement. Hence, there are four categories of NHB donors:

(1) patients who elect to have life-supporting therapy withdrawn and may become organ donors following death; (2) patients who suffer cardiac arrest and have a do-not-resuscitate (DNR) order; (3) patients who suffer cardiac arrest and are refractory to resuscitative efforts; and (4) patients who are pronounced dead using neurologic criteria, but suffer cardiac arrest prior to organ procurement.

(DeVita in Arnold *et al.*, 1995, p. 34)

Patients in category (4) do not present an ethical challenge because they have already been declared dead by the whole-brain criterion. The issue regarding patients in the other categories is whether death is declared too quickly after the cessation of cardiac functioning, before anoxia has resulted in irreversible neuro-logical damage. In other words, if a patient in cardiac arrest can be resuscitated and maintain whole-brain functioning, then are they actually dead if organ procure-ment occurs within two, five, or ten minutes – which a number of NHB donation protocols stipulate as a sufficient "wait time" – after the heart stops beating? In Thomistic terms, are the rational soul's vegetative capacities still present and actualizable – if resuscitative measures are used – in a patient whose heart has ceased functioning only two to ten minutes ago?

More specifically, the questions at hand are as follows: Is it legitimate to use the circulatory/respiratory criterion to determine death without establishing death using the whole-brain criterion as well? What standard of "irreversibility" should be adopted in determining the loss of cardiac functioning? How much time should be allotted between the cessation of cardiac functioning and organ procurement? The answers to the first two questions inform the answer to the third.

Jerry Menikoff and James Bernat both raise the following concern regarding the determination of death by the traditional criterion alone:

> At the time that the individual is declared dead, it is quite possible that substantial portions of that person's brain (including the higher brain, responsible for thoughts and emotions) have not yet permanently ceased to function. If one, for example, were to restart pulmonary and cardiac function in that person, the brain (including the higher brain) might then be brought back to some degree of function.
>
> (Menikoff, 2002, p. 14)

> It is not clear that patients are dead within the first few minutes of apnea and asystole. It takes considerably longer than a few minutes for the brain and other organs to be destroyed from cessation of circulation and lack of oxygen. Moreover, it takes longer than this time for the cessation of heartbeat and breathing to be unequivocally irreversible, a prerequisite for death. As proof of this assertion, if cardiopulmonary resuscitation were performed within the first few minutes of cardiorespiratory arrest, it is likely that some of the purportedly "dead" patients could be successfully resuscitated to spontaneous heartbeat and some intact brain function.
>
> (Bernat, 1998, p. 20)

James DuBois notes:

> From a regulatory perspective, it is not necessary to establish that non-heart-beating donors would meet brain-based criteria for determining death… Nevertheless, from an ontological or metaphysical perspective, we can still ask whether it is possible for a person to be dead before his or her brain has died. Given the centrality of the role the brain plays in human life… it is difficult to see how a person with a living brain could be dead
>
> (2002b, pp. 34–5; cf. DuBois, 2002a, pp. 430–1)

In its report, *Defining Death: Medical, Legal, and Ethical Issues in the Definition of Death*, the President's Commission for the Study of Ethical Problems in Medicine and Biomedical and Behavioral Research affirms two formulations of the whole-brain concept of death. The first defines death as the irreversible cessation of an organism's "integrated functions" (President's Commission, 1981, p. 37) and contends that loss of cardiopulmonary functioning and loss of whole-brain functioning are equally suitable criteria for declaring death. The second recognizes the brain as the "primary organ" that is both "the sponsor of consciousness" and "the complex organizer and regulator of bodily functions" (President's Commission, 1981, p. 34). This view asserts that the loss of whole-brain functioning is the primary criterion for declaring death and affirms the loss of cardiopulmonary functioning as a practical surrogate (President's Commission, 1981, p. 37).

The second formulation is more consistent with the Thomistic account of death described in Chapter 3, in which the brain is identified as the primary organ of the mature human body through which the soul exercises its capacities in the body's various parts. If the second formulation is thus adopted, it follows that NHB donation protocols should allow sufficient time for the brain to irreversibly cease functioning before declaring death. Menikoff asserts:

> It would indeed be disingenuous to claim that X [loss of cardiopulmonary functioning] is being used as a surrogate for Y [loss of whole-brain functioning] while interpreting the statute to allow reliance on X at a time when one is certain that Y has not yet occurred.
>
> (1998, p. 160)

But how long should one wait to ensure that irreversible cessation of whole-brain functioning has occurred? The original Pittsburgh protocol requires only two minutes of asystole for death to be declared. The Institute of Medicine, in its study of NHB donation protocols, calls for a five-minute waiting period before procurement begins (Institute of Medicine, 1997, p. 59, 2000, p. 22). Five minutes, however, may be "too short a period to cause sufficient ischemic damage to the brain to ensure that patients would meet brain death criteria. Probably ten to fifteen minutes would be required" (DuBois, 2002a, p. 430; cf. Lynn in Arnold and Youngner, 1993, p. 175; Menikoff, 1998, p. 161; Zamperetti *et al.*, 2003, p. 183). But waiting so long after the heart has stopped beating to procure vital organs is problematic because damage to the organs from warm ischemia may render them unsuitable for transplant; unless, as DuBois notes, available premortem interventions to preserve the organs are used. The issue of whether such interventions may justifiably be employed, insofar as they may hasten the donor's death, will be addressed below.

The final key concept that requires discussion is "irreversibility." In agreement with the Institute of Medicine's study regarding NHB donation protocols, DuBois claims that the heart's inability to "auto-resuscitate" is sufficient to declare cardiac function irreversible in cases where a patient has a "do-not-resuscitate" order or has otherwise refused further medical intervention (Institute of Medicine, 1997, pp. 58–9, 2000, pp. 24–5; DuBois, 2002a, pp. 431–2, 2002b, pp. 32–3). DuBois is quite correct that it would be "unethical and illegal" to resuscitate such patients. But the fact that patients should not be resuscitated does not entail that they have lost the *capacity* to be resuscitated and have their vegetative functions restored. DuBois admits this and refers to reported cases of "near-death experiences" to illustrate the possibility that one may be "clinically dead" once auto-resuscitation is no longer possible, and he uses the Thomistic language of the soul leaving the body at that point. If resuscitative measures are then employed and spontaneous heartbeat and respiration resumes, DuBois characterizes what occurs as "reanimation" – the soul returning to the body, its departure having been reversed (DuBois, 1999, p. 129, 2002b, p. 33).

DuBois offers a metaphysically complicated picture of the soul's separation from the body at death that does not cohere with the Thomistic understanding of the soul as the body's "substantial form." As articulated throughout this volume, a human rational soul is the principle of all the operations proper to human beings that are actualized in their bodies: rational, sensitive, and vegetative. Furthermore, a rational soul continues to inform its body until the capacity for vegetative operations is no longer actualizable in that body. While a patient whose spontaneous heartbeat and respiratory activity has ceased is no longer actualizing their soul's vegetative capacities, such capacities are evidently present so long as spontaneous heartbeat and respiration may be resumed.[19] To describe the soul as leaving and then being called back to the body by external resuscitation is significantly more complex than understanding the soul to remain in the body as its substantial form until its vegetative capacities are no longer actualizable *at all* in that body; the clinical sign of this is the loss of spontaneous heartbeat and respiration where resuscitation efforts would be futile. As Menikoff notes, "Irreversibility is a statement about the physical state of our world and our *ability* to alter it" (Menikoff, 1998, p. 158), not a statement about what we *elect* to alter.

There are further problems that arise from "basing the determination of death on moral judgments rather than ontological arguments or 'objective' biological phenomena" (Youngner *et al.*, 1999, p. 16). One of which is that biologically identical cases may end up being treated differently. A patient who has a DNR order and is a candidate for being a NHB donor will be declared dead sooner than a patient in cardiac arrest who wants to be resuscitated; and the same patient will be declared dead later than a patient who simply has a DNR order and is not a candidate for being a NHB donor (Youngner *et al.*, 1999, p. 17). I thus agree with Nereo Zamperetti and his colleagues, who argue that "the fact that one is bound to die without active intervention does not mean that one is dead" and that those who advocate waiting only two to five minutes after cardiac arrest to declare death in NHB donation cases "mistake the 'prognosis of death' for the 'diagnosis of death' " (Zamperetti *et al.*, 2003, p. 183).

As mentioned earlier, some interventions may be undertaken to prepare a NHB donor's vital organs so that more time may be allowed to pass between cardiac arrest and the declaration of death:

> Anticoagulants (e.g., heparin) and vasodilators (e.g., phentolamine) are sometimes given to a donor shortly before the person's death in order to "improve" the quality of the donated organs. These drugs are not beneficial to the patient, however, and in fact may be harmful. In some circumstances, they may even hasten the death of the patient.
>
> (Menikoff, 2002, p. 18)

The Institute of Medicine's 1997 report discusses the possibility of such pharmacological interventions being justified by PDE, just as the withdrawal of life-sustaining treatment in NHB donation cases is justifiable by PDE in other cases of terminally ill patients (Childress in Arnold and Youngner, 1993). The report concludes that justifying the premortem use of such drugs "is a heavy burden for the principle of double effect, and there is no consensus about whether the principle can bear it" (Institute of Medicine, 1997, p. 52).

Veatch, on the other hand, demonstrates how this action can be justified by PDE:

> It seems obvious that if the drug is given, the purpose is not to hasten the patient's death. It is not the quicker death that preserves the organs...the purpose of administering the heparin or phentolamine is not to get the donor dead more quickly.
>
> (2000, p. 219)

The first conditions of PDE are satisfied because the patient's death is not directly intended as the end, nor is their death the means by which the directly intended end − the preservation of viable organs − is brought about. Furthermore, it is arguable that the positive effect of procuring viable vital organs for transplant, which will likely save numerous lives, outweighs the negative effect of the patient's death being hastened. Of course, for Aquinas, the inherent fundamental value of the donor's life is incommensurable with the sum total of any number of other lives. Hence, it is always wrong to act from a direct intention to end the donor's life. In NHB donation, however, a decision is previously made to withhold (uncontrolled) or withdraw (controlled) life-sustaining treatment based on the futility of providing such treatment or in compliance with a patient's DNR order; this decision is justified by PDE. The donor's death, caused by their underlying illness or injury, is imminent and risking the side-effect of hastening their death through the use of heparin or phentolamine is not equivalent to negating the value of the donor's life (Veatch, 2000, pp. 219–20; cf. DuBois, 2002a, pp. 432–4, 2002b, pp. 37–8).

I thus conclude that organ donation is a morally virtuous act that is strongly supported by the Thomistic natural law ethic, even if it is not morally or legally mandated. Neither the religious belief in postmortem bodily resurrection, nor the concern for preserving the integrity of a human being's body as a whole, preclude donating one's organs in either living or cadaveric cases. Finally, organ procurement from NHB donors is *prima facie* morally permissible provided that a sufficient waiting time − at least ten to fifteen minutes − is allowed to pass between the onset of cardiac asystole and the declaration of death to ensure that neurological function has been irreversibly lost. While such a significant waiting period seems to contradict the pragmatic value of using NHB donation protocols to procure viable organs, the morally legitimate use of pharmacological preserving agents to maintain maximum organ viability, prior to death being declared, alleviates this concern.

Conclusion

In this chapter, I have argued that PVS patients are persons despite the irreversible loss of consciousness. They thus merit care that does not involve the direct intention to terminate their inherently valuable life. Nevertheless, in cases of PVS and other terminally ill patients, the prolongation of a life defined by intractable suffering, or in which further medical treatment would be futile in staving off imminent death or in restoring conscious rational activity, is not warranted. Aquinas's adherence to PDE allows for various actions to be morally permissible that have the foreseen concomitant consequence of risking a terminally ill or PVS patient's death being hastened. These actions include the administration of palliative treatment, such as titrated morphine or terminal sedation, as well as the nonutilization of life-sustaining treatment, such as artificial respiration and ANH. Not all of these options, however, are permissible in every case. For example, withdrawal of ANH is not permissible in cases of terminally ill, but conscious, patients whose death is not imminent.

Finally, with respect to organ donation, there is an unequivocally inherent good in donating one's organs. This good can be satisfied either as a living donor – in which a kidney or lobe of the liver is donated – or as a cadaver once death has been properly declared. Death should be declared either by using the whole-brain criterion, or by waiting a sufficient amount of time after the onset of cardiac asystole to ensure that both the brain and the heart have irreversibly ceased functioning and cannot be restored through resuscitative efforts. These are the only clinical means of demonstrating that the donor's rational soul has ceased to inform their body and thereby satisfying DDR.

Notes

Introduction

1 This condemnation was later annulled by Tempier's successor, Stephen Bourret, on February 14, 1325.

2 A brief note regarding pronoun use: For the sake of fidelity to the Latin of Aquinas's texts, I use masculine pronouns in all my translations; however, because Aquinas's thought is generally as relevant today as it was in the thirteenth century, I use the gender-neutral plural pronouns throughout the volume to highlight Aquinas's audience being gender-inclusive. In fact, whereas Aquinas is generally considered to have a negative view of the nature of women in comparison to men – following Aristotle and the predominant attitude among his contemporaries – he actually contends that women are *not* of an inferior nature to men and have an equal status to men as rational beings, as persons created in the *imago Dei* (ST, Ia.93.6.ad 2, Ia.93.4.ad 1; for further correctives on Aquinas's view of women, see Nolan, 2000; Finnis, 1998, pp. 171–6). This is not to say, though, that Aquinas would be a "feminist" by contemporary standards or that all his views regarding women are relevant, or palatable, today.

1 Aquinas's account of human nature and natural law theory

1 This section is derived from Eberl (2004).

2 I use the terms "mind" and "intellect" interchangeably. The former term, though, does not precisely correspond to Aquinas's understanding of the latter. As will be shown, the mind includes certain capacities, such as the estimative capacity, that are distinct from the intellective capacity to understand universal concepts. Hence, the intellect is but one capacity of the mind. Contemporary philosophers, however, often understand the concept of mind in a fashion similar to Aquinas's concept of intellect and thus I propose the interchangeability of these terms.

3 Aquinas recognizes different types of beings as persons. In addition to human beings, Aquinas claims that angels are persons and that God exists as three distinct persons. Since my interest here is solely with *human* persons, I will not entertain any further discussion of such other types of persons.

4 Following Aristotle, Aquinas defines a "rational soul" as a soul that has the relevant capacities for life, sensation, and rational thought and as the type of soul proper to the human species. A "sensitive soul," on the other hand, has the relevant capacities for only life and sensation, and is the type of soul proper to all nonhuman species of the animal genus. A "vegetative soul" has the relevant capacities for life alone and is proper to all nonanimal living organisms (Aristotle, 1984, 414a30–415a14).

5 Examples of things that Aquinas counts as *unum simpliciter* are elemental substances, certain mixtures of elemental substances, immaterial substances, and living organisms (Pasnau, 2002, p. 88).

6 Aquinas states that two things that are joined by a "contact of power" [*contactus virtutis*] – that is, one thing is the efficient cause of change in the other – do not result in an unqualified unity (SCG, II.56).

7 The qualifier, "typically," is used here due to Aquinas's understanding of the Incarnation of Christ, in which the unified substantial existence of both human and divine natures precludes a new ontological entity having come into existence when Christ's soul assumed a human body (CT, 211).

8 The purpose of phantasms is to be available for the mind to use in abstracting the universal, intelligible forms of perceived things. Phantasms are thus between the immediate mental impression of an object perceived by sensation and the rational understanding of that object's nature as abstracted from any individuating characteristics (Kretzmann, 1999, pp. 350–64; Pasnau, 2002, pp. 278–95).

9 "Reduction" of a human being to their animal nature entails that they are nothing "over and above" their material body. As will be shown, Aquinas argues that a human being's essential rational capacities entail that they are more than their body alone.

10 For detailed explanations of Aquinas's account of rational cognition, see Kretzmann, (1999, pp. 350–68); Pasnau (2002, chs 9–10); Stump (2003, ch. 8).

11 This is not to say that there are no clear bioethical implications of Aquinas's virtue theory, but I will leave the elucidation of his virtue theory and such implications for another occasion.

12 A number of recent scholars – most notably, Grisez (1965); Finnis (1980, 1998), Hittinger (1987); McInerny (1993, 1997); and Lisska (1996) – have offered various contemporary interpretations of Aquinas's natural law theory, though not all in agreement with one another. I will not adjudicate the interpretive debates among these scholars in this chapter.

13 For an account of the continued development of natural law theory beyond Aquinas, see Rommen (1948, pp. 57–109, 135–58). For an analysis of natural law theory in comparison to the antithetical legal positivist theory, see Henle (1993) and Rommen (1948, ch. 6).

14 My intention here is to endorse Aquinas's general natural law principles, but not to underwrite all of his explicit applications of such principles. I apply these principles for my own purposes in Chapters 4 and 5.

15 Aquinas does not hold that every principle of divine law reflects the natural law. Some are revealed and ought to be followed because they pertain to an article of faith – for example, the commandment not to make any graven image or to take God's name in vain (ST, Ia-IIae.100.1).

16 The only exceptions are those principles of divine law that pertain to articles of faith.

17 This section is derived from Eberl (2003).

18 This is illustrated in an example from ST, Ia-IIae.73.8, in which Aquinas contends that a person who takes a shortcut through a field in order to commit fornication, which results in their knowingly injuring the crops growing in the field, aggravates their sin of fornication, even though they did not directly intend to injure the crops.

19 I discuss the moral permissibility of abortion and the use of abortifacient contraceptives in Chapter 4.

2 The beginning of a human person's life

1 Since Aquinas holds that all human beings are persons, I will use the terms "human being" and "person" interchangeably.

2 Completion of the fertilization process is at "syngamy," when the 23 chromosomes contributed by each of the parental gametes are fused into a unique 46-chromosome combination. The terms "fertilization," "conception," and "syngamy" may be used interchangeably for the most part.

3 This is Aquinas's definition of "person," which applies to, among other types of beings, a body informed by a rational soul (ST, Ia.29.1); see Chapter 1.

4 This section is derived from Eberl (2005b).

5 See Chapter 1, p. 5.

6 See Chapter 1, note 4.

7 See Chapter 1, pp. 7–8.

8 Aquinas, following Aristotle, understands conception to involve male semen acting upon female menstrual blood to form an embryo (ST, Ia.118.1.ad 4; Aristotle, 1984, 736a24–737b6). Neither Aristotle nor Aquinas had knowledge of sperm, ova, and DNA.

9 Since Aquinas holds that rational operations do not require the use of a bodily organ (QDA, II), the requisite "organic complexity" here is that which allows for the operations of sensation and imagination to generate phantasms of perceived objects from which the intellect can abstract intelligible forms.

10 Aquinas contends, following Aristotle, that a developing embryo is first informed by a rational soul at the time of "quickening," which occurs 40 days after conception if it is male and 90 days after conception if it is female (In Sent, III.3.v.2; Aristotle, 1984, 583b3–5).

11 Unlike vegetative and sensitive souls, which naturally inform properly organized matter, Aquinas holds that God directly creates each human being's rational soul (QDP, III.9; SCG, II.86–7; ST, Ia.90.2, Ia.118.2; CT, 93). Nevertheless, he also contends that God does not create a rational soul unless an appropriate body exists for it to inform; for a rational soul has its natural perfection only by informing such a body to compose a human being (ST, Ia.90.4).

12 Aquinas claims that a rational soul includes sensitive and vegetative capacities, and that the sensitive and vegetative souls that had previously informed a developing embryo are annihilated once a rational soul is created. He does so to counter the claim by some of his contemporaries that there are three souls – vegetative, sensitive, and rational – existing at the same time in a fully developed human being.

13 This section is derived from Eberl (2005b).

14 See Chapter 1, p. 9.

15 For further discussion of the "formative power" transmitted by semen to guide embryonic development, and its conceptual relationship to DNA, see Eberl (2005b).

16 This contention may sound as if I am concluding that an embryo's genetic identity is sufficient evidence of its having an active potentiality for rational thought and thus being a person. As will be explained below when discussing Ashley's account, however, genetic identity is not sufficient evidence of an embryo's being a person. Donceel rightly notes that, if such were the case, then hydatidiform moles – masses of placental tissue with the same genetic identity as an embryo – would also count as persons (Donceel, 1970, p. 96). Hence, it is not the case that merely possessing human DNA is sufficient for something to be a person.

17 Aristotle defines four causes of any being. The "material cause" is the matter that composes it, that out of which it is produced. The "formal cause" is the substantial or accidental form that defines it as the type of thing it is. The "efficient cause" is the agent or activity that instantiates the form in the matter, that which produces the thing. The "final cause" is the end or purpose for which the thing is produced (Aristotle, 1984, 194b24–195a3).

18 For further discussion of Pasnau's view, see Haldane and Lee (2003a), and the subsequent responses by Pasnau (2003) and Haldane and Lee (2003b).

19 An "epigenetic primordium" is that from which a particular tissue, organ, or organ system will naturally develop if unimpeded. The tissue, organ, or organ system does not exist actually, but virtually, in its epigenetic primordium insofar as a developmental continuity can be traced from one to the other.

20 The cells in this conglomeration are individual living substances, each informed by a vegetative soul (Eberl, 2000a, pp. 151–2).

21 "Totipotentiality" refers to a preimplantation embryo's cells, each having the capacity to divide and form any tissue or organ of a human body, or even a whole other body.

22 "Pluripotentiality," as opposed to totipotentiality, refers to a cell's having the capacity to divide and form a range of tissues or perhaps even an organ, but not *any* tissue, organ, or an entire human body.

23 An ovarian teratoma is a growth that arises from an ovum parthenogenetically – that is, without fertilization by a sperm cell. A teratoma, after cleaving spontaneously from an unfertilized ovum, "progresses to form a morula and a blastocyst; then it becomes disorganized and develops into a tumor composed of well-differentiated cells and tissues" (Suarez, 1990, p. 628).

24 Unlike the substantial form of, say, a flatworm, which may be divisible if the worm's body is divided into two distinct living worms (QDSC, IV.ad 19; QDP, III.12.ad 5; In M, VII.16.1635; In DA, II.4), Aquinas argues that a human being's rational soul is indivisible, simple, and one (QDP, V.10.ad 6; SCG, II.86; QDSC, IV.ad 9; QDA, X.ad 15).

25 This way of construing the twinning phenomenon makes it the case that the proximate progenitor of one of the twins, *B* or *C*, is *A*; whereas the proximate progenitor of *A* and the other twin is *A*'s mother and father. This conclusion may be technically true, but unproblematic because, for all practical purposes and due to the epistemic uncertainty regarding which of the twins is identical to *A*, *A*'s mother and father can be considered as the parents of both *B* and *C*.

26 I do not see any possible epistemic criteria for determining which of the twins, *B* or *C*, has the same substantial form as *A* and which is the new organism generated by a new substantial form informing matter that previously composed *A*. Epistemic uncertainty regarding which twin is identical with *A*, however, does not preclude the metaphysical claim that one of the twins is identical with *A* while the other is not.

27 Practically, this is not how cloning would be carried out today. The process rather involves "somatic cell nuclear transfer," which refers to the nucleus of one of an adult human being's undifferentiated cells, say, from their bone marrow, being extracted and infused in an enucleated ovum. Induced parthenogenetic reproduction of the ovum could then result in a genetically identical organism. The metaphysical implication, though, of a portion of an individual organism's matter being removed and used to produce a being with the same genetic identity, but a distinct substantial form, remains the same as the theoretical process Lee describes.

28 Aquinas, following Aristotle, understands the primary organ to be the heart; though contemporary science understands it to be the brain. For further discussion, see Chapter 3.

29 A hydatidiform mole, as described earlier, is a mass of placental tissue with the same genetic identity as an embryo. What separates a hydatidiform mole and a developing embryo is that the former can never, despite its intrinsic genetic structure and even if it is placed in a supportive uterine environment, develop into an organism with a functioning cerebral cortex; the latter can.

30 A zygote's "unilateral" development into a mature human being presumes that it has a supportive uterine environment and no external factors impede its development.

31 For similar arguments for this conclusion, see Gerber (1966), Heaney (1992), Johnson (1995), De Koninck (1999), Bracken (2001), Mirkes (2001),

32 This point is discussed further in Chapter 3.

3 The end of a human person's life

1 This chapter, except for the section entitled "Circulatory/respiratory criterion," is derived from Eberl (2005a).

2 My concern here is with the concept of death for human beings only. I will not address any proposed concept of death for nonhuman organisms.

3 Originally, this criterion was linked with the cessation of cardiopulmonary functioning, though such functioning can now be artificially stimulated or replaced.

4 The whole-brain criterion has received legislative approval in several nations, including the United States (President's Commission, 1981). In addition, it has received moral approval from the Roman Catholic Church (White, *et al.*, 1992; John Paul II, 2001).

5 For Aquinas's assertion of (3), see QDSC, IV; In DA, II.1.

6 This passage elucidates the second sense of "to live" stated in the previous passage.

7 By "individual contrary parts," Aquinas is referring to a human body's diverse organs and the basic elements constituting them.

8 Aquinas considers such "defects" to be the result of original sin and not from the fact *simpliciter* of a human being's natural embodiment (ST, Supp.75.1.ad 5).

9 It is clear in both this passage and the preceding one that Aquinas is referring to a *rational* soul, as opposed to a vegetative or sensitive soul. For only a rational soul is incorruptible, as the soul is described in the preceding passage, and Aquinas does not entertain any discussion of vegetative or sensitive souls until QDA, XI, which comes after this passage.

10 Once again, the context of this passage – in ST, Ia.76, which concerns the union of a rational soul to a body – makes it clear that Aquinas is not referring to either a vegetative or a sensitive soul.

11 Shewmon no longer holds this position. As will be explained later, after briefly advocating the whole-brain criterion (Shewmon, 1992), he now argues for a return to the circulatory/respiratory criterion for establishing when death occurs (Shewmon, 1997, 1998a, 2001).

12 See Chapter 2, p. 25.

13 See Chapter 1, pp. 7–8.

14 The loss of higher-brain functioning does not preclude a rational soul from continuing to engage in rational activity, but this would require the soul to have separated from its body and thus for death to have occurred; see Eberl (2005c).

15 Similar interpretations of Aquinas are argued by Eike-Henner Kluge (Kluge, 1981) and Robert Pasnau (Pasnau, 2002, p. 124). For a critique, see Eberl (2005a, pp. 36–9).

16 The story of Patricia White Bull was reported by The Associated Press and appeared in, among other publications, the *Saint Louis Post Dispatch*, January 5, 2000, A4; see Kavanaugh (2001, p. 68, n. 25).

17 See Chapter 2, pp. 34–5.

18 See Chapter 2, pp. 27–8.

19 While the essential form of artificial life support that precludes a patient having the capacity for vital metabolic functions is a mechanical ventilator or a cardiopulmonary bypass machine, additional supportive treatment may need to be provided, such as the use of vasopressive drugs and other pharmaceuticals, to maintain the homeostatic conditions of body temperature, fluid and electrolyte balance, etc.

20 The term "whole-brain functioning" does not refer to the functioning of *every* part of the brain, but of the set of critical neural systems – defined by Bernat – present in the cerebral cortex, cerebellum, and brainstem that constitute the brain's role as an "integrator" for its body. All three components must be irreversibly nonfunctional in order for the brain *as a whole*, and thus the patient, to be considered dead. There is, however, general recognition that random electrical activity may persist in a brain that is nonetheless dead.

21 Shewmon provides a detailed analysis of 56 cases of whole-brain dead patients with prolonged survival and persistence of these apparently somatically integrative functions (Shewmon, 1998b).

22 Cases of whole-brain dead adults with prolonged somatic survival have been reported, but with more medical complications than the cases of young children Shewmon cites, thereby indicating that integrative unity was not maintained despite persistent, artificially stimulated, cardiac functioning (Parisi *et al.*, 1982).

23 This conclusion, though, remains merely *apparent*, because it is inconclusive whether the random electrical signals that may persist in a "dead" brain – and are usually discounted as being correlated with any integrative functioning – are indeed not constitutive of somatic integrative unity. The possibility that they are may mandate a revision to the clinical criteria for establishing whole-brain death; requiring the cessation of all electrical activity in any brain structure. I am willing, though, to take the standard understanding of whole-brain death and Shewmon's description of these cases as adequate for now.

24 While, for Aquinas, an artificial conductor joining the brainstem to the rest of the body would not be a proper part of the patient, because it is not suitable for being informed by their rational soul; it nevertheless can function as a "facilitator" to bring about functional unity of the brainstem with the rest of the body. The artificial conductor would be akin to a pacemaker in that it assists integrative functioning rather than replacing such functioning, as in the case of a mechanical ventilator or cardiopulmonary bypass machine.

4 Issues at the beginning of human life: abortion, embryonic stem cell research, and cloning

1 For Aquinas, the existence of any human being entails the existence of a person (ST, IIIa.16.12.ad 1). Hence, I use the terms "human being" and "person" interchangeably.

2 I will not address here the moral permissibility of utilizing nonabortifacient contraceptives. For an analysis of this issue from a Thomistic natural law perspective, see Rhonheimer (2000, pp. 109–38). Even if the general use of nonabortifacient contraceptives is morally questionable, though, it is recognized – by even the most ardent pro-life advocates – that a rape victim may protect herself from a resultant pregnancy by nonabortifacient means (Ashley and O'Rourke, 1997, p. 305; Ford, 2002, pp. 94–5).

3 For discussions of the role of "risk" in Aquinas's formulation of PDE, see Sullivan (2000, p. 437) and Cavanaugh (1997, pp. 116–19).

4 For further information, visit http://stemcells.nih.gov/info/basics/basics3.asp.

5 An ESC "line" is a self-renewing cluster of ESCs that have been derived from the ICM of an embryo and are cultured on mouse embryonic fibroblast feeder layers (Thomson, 2001, pp. 17–20).

6 See Chapter 2. Ford's argument on twinning in particular has been utilized on several occasions to support ESC research (Robertson, 1999, p. 117; Eberl, 2000a; Lanza *et al.*, 2000; Shannon, 2001, p. 178; Green, 2002, p. 22; McCartney, 2002, pp. 604–8).

7 Michael Burke illuminated to me another distinction in potentiality that Peters fails to note: "strong" versus "weak." A somatic cell is potentially a human being, in the strong sense, only if it could come to be a human being while preserving its numerical identity – that is, it remains the *same* substance identical with itself throughout its development from a cell to a fully actualized human being. A change, however, from a somatic cell to a human being does not appear to be an identity-preserving transformation. Aquinas denies that a vegetative substance – a somatic cell – can change into a rational substance – a human being – and remain the same substance, because vegetative and rational substances are of distinct species with quite different substantial forms. The only sense in which a somatic cell is plausibly a potential human being is in the weak sense that it provides the "makings" of a human being; and such weak potentiality clearly does not confer a right to life.

8 Aquinas would thus support the use of animals for food or medical research when it is unavoidably necessary for human survival, but would presumably not support the testing of cosmetic products on animals since such testing is potentially harmful to them and does not serve a human good that is essential for our survival or flourishing as rational beings.

9 Geron Corporation is a primary locus of ESC research and was one of the first bodies to announce the establishment of human ESC culture lines on November 5, 1998.

10 I am grateful to John Tilley for raising this objection to me in correspondence.

11 For a critique of this facet of consequentialism, see Williams and Smart (1973, pp. 98ff).

12 An analogous example is provided by Gene Hackman's character in Michael Apted's film *Extreme Measures* (1996), who performs illicit experiments on homeless persons by severing their spinal cords and then attempting to grow neural tissue to reestablish the connection.

13 Advanced Cell Technology utilized SCNT with 17 enucleated ova. Three cloned embryos were produced that developed up to the six-cell stage.

14 My concern here is with only the moral permissibility of *human* cloning. Therefore, any references to cloning, or the creation of embryos for reproductive or research purposes, should be understood to include the modifier "human." The permissibility of nonhuman cloning merits its own discussion, but I will not address it here.

15 Although (4) is sometimes cited as a reason for wishing to engage in reproductive cloning, it is usually recognized as an impractical reason to clone, because, first, the replication of a genotype does not entail the replication of an individual human being, and second, the phenotypic expression of, say, an innate talent for music, has as much to do with environmental influences as it does with one's genotype.

16 See the discussion of the metaphysics of twinning in Chapter 2, pp. 37–9.

17 A somatic cell that has been separated from a human being's body is not a proper part of them as it is no longer informed by their rational soul; it has its own substantial form. Such a cell, though, could not be considered to have the same potentiality as a cloned embryo either, because it is not totipotential. External intervention is required to enucleate the cell and implant its nucleus into an enucleated ovum in order for a human being to be produced from it. This process, as I argued above, alters the cell's metaphysical identity. Therefore, there are no grounds for asserting that a somatic cell which has been separated from its body and may be enucleated for the purpose of generating a cloned human being has in itself an active potentiality to become a fully actualized human being.

18 Aquinas does not refer to human females here since women bear their children and thus their biological relationship to their children is not subject to question, at least prior to the advent of surrogate motherhood practices and IVF utilizing donated gametes.

19 A large number of recent studies regarding the derivation and potential therapeutic use of ASCs – with mixed, but promising results – are cited by David A. Prentice (Prentice in PCB, 2004, pp. 309–46).

5 Issues at the end of human life: PVS patients, euthanasia, and organ donation

1 By "ability" here, I take Moreland and Rae to intend something akin to Pasnau's concept of a "capacity in hand" discussed in Chapter 2, p. 27. As noted in that chapter, there is a level of active potentiality that precedes a capacity in hand to actually perform some operation. It is arguable that a PVS patient continues to have this preceding level of active potentiality for rational thought because their body is informed by a rational soul – as evidenced by continued vegetative operations – despite their inability to ever actualize that potentiality unless they experience postmortem bodily resurrection.

2 I use the terms "human being" and "person" interchangeably since, for Aquinas, all human beings are persons; see Chapter 2, p. 23.

3 Aquinas also claims that there are "immaterial" beings: God and angels.

4 This section is derived from Eberl (2003).

5 A patient may kill themselves; kill themselves with the medical assistance of a physician or some other person; or be killed by another in accordance with either the patient's

expressed wish to die, or what the homicidal agent determines would be in the patient's best interest in cases where the patient is unconscious or unable to communicate their wishes effectively.

6 Aquinas's third indictment is based on God's sovereignty over human life, which is a theological premise that falls outside the scope of my focus in this volume; see Eberl (2003).

7 Aquinas holds that human beings are capable of postmortem existence in a disembodied state, but this form of existence would be atypical and deficient because a human being cannot actualize all of their proper capacities without their physical body; see Eberl (2000b, 2004).

8 The reference to Aristotle, from his *Nicomachean Ethics*, is as follows: "Now if someone murders himself because of anger, he does so willingly, in violation of correct reason, when the law forbids it; hence he does injustice. But injustice to whom? Surely to the city, not to himself, since he suffers it willingly, and no one willingly suffers injustice" (Aristotle, 1984, 1138a10–12).

9 I use the term "nonutilization" to refer to either the withholding or withdrawal of life-sustaining treatment, thus making no ethical distinction between the two types of acts – either both are permissible or both are impermissible (AMA, 1992, p. 2233; Bernat, 2001, p. 971).

10 Terminal sedation can be considered the upper limit of permissibility. Any further palliative medication administered after the patient has been rendered unconscious is unnecessary unless hastening their death is directly intended.

11 This explains why, in an example Hopkins raises, it would be murder to "to blow out the computer chip in a person's pacemaker with an electromagnetic pulse" (Hopkins, 1997, p. 35). Such an act would not be justified by PDE because the agent's direct intention is the person's death; not by interfering with their cardiac system, as Hopkins would put it, but by interfering with an object upon which their cardiac system depends to function normally.

12 The judgment that some forms of treatment may not be morally mandated because they are "disproportionately burdensome" is based on the distinction between "ordinary" and "extraordinary" care that was developed by Roman Catholic moral theologians and philosophers beginning in the sixteenth century (Cronin, 1989). This distinction has since been adopted in magisterial Catholic teachings (Pius XII, 1958; Sacred Congregation for the Doctrine of the Faith, 1980), and its moral significance was recognized by the President's Commission for the Study of Ethical Problems in Medicine and Biomedical and Behavioral Research (President's Commission, 1983, p. 88). Since Aquinas does not explicitly recognize or employ this distinction, I have refrained from using it in the present ethical analysis; see Eberl (2005c).

13 I am grateful to James DuBois for raising this point with me.

14 The provision of ANH would not be justified if the patient may benefit from hand-feeding – usually in cases of dementia as opposed to PVS. If the patient is capable of reflexive swallowing once food is manually provided, then this – admittedly resource-consuming (Mitchell *et al.*, 2004) – form of care should be provided to avoid introducing the fatal pathology of loss of the swallowing reflex (Li, 2002). I am grateful to Fr. John Kavanaugh for comments regarding the value of hand-feeding.

15 This information can be found at http://www.unos.org (accessed October 1, 2004).

16 This report can be found at http://www.optn.org/AR2003/default.htm (accessed October 1, 2004).

17 See Chapter 3, pp. 43–5.

18 A significant criticism of the Ad Hoc Committee of the Harvard Medical School that first proposed the whole-brain criterion (Ad Hoc Committee, 1968) is that the pragmatic concern over organ donation was their primary motivation in re-defining death. Gary Belkin, however, convincingly demonstrates that this was not the case (Belkin, 2003).

19 Note that this case is different from one in which heartbeat and respiratory activity is replaced by an artificial respirator or cardiopulmonary bypass machine. Such replacement would not preserve a human being's proper vegetative capacities, as discussed in Chapter 3, pp. 51–3. The external intervention relevant here is no more than what is necessary to restore *spontaneous* heartbeat and respiration.

Bibliography

Ad Hoc Committee of the Harvard Medical School (1968) "A definition of irreversible coma," *Journal of the American Medical Association*, 205: 337–40.

Ahmann, J. (2001) "Therapeutic cloning and stem cell therapy," *The National Catholic Bioethics Quarterly*, 1: 145–50.

American Medical Association (AMA) (1992) "Decisions near the end of life," *Journal of the American Medical Association*, 267: 2229–33.

Andrews, K., Murphy, L., Munday, R., and Littlewood, C. (1996) "Misdiagnosis of the vegetative state: retrospective study in a rehabilitation unit," *British Medical Journal* 313: 13–16.

Aristotle (1984) *The Complete Works of Aristotle*, in J. Barnes (ed.), 2 vols, Princeton, NJ: Princeton University Press.

Armstrong, R.A. (1966) *Primary and Secondary Precepts in Thomistic Natural Law Teaching*, The Hague: Martinus Nijhoff.

Arnold, R.M. and Youngner, S.J. (eds) (1993) "Special issue: ethical, psychosocial, and public policy implications of procuring organs from non-heart-beating cadaver donors," *Kennedy Institute of Ethics Journal*, 3: 103–278.

Arnold, R.M., Youngner, S.J., Schapiro, R., Spicer, C.M. (eds) (1995) *Procuring Organs for Transplant: The Debate Over Non-Heart-Beating Cadaver Protocols*, Baltimore, MD: Johns Hopkins University Press.

Ashley, B. (1976) "A critique of the theory of delayed hominization," in D. McCarthy and A. Moraczewski (eds) *An Ethical Evaluation of Fetal Experimentation: An Interdisciplinary Study*, St. Louis: Pope John XXIII Center.

—— (2001) "Integrative unity and the human soul," *The National Catholic Bioethics Quarterly*, 1: 7–9.

Ashley, B. and Moraczewski, A. (2001) "Cloning, Aquinas, and the embryonic person," *The National Catholic Bioethics Quarterly*, 1: 189–201.

Ashley, B. and O'Rourke, K. (1997) *Health Care Ethics*, 4th edn, Washington, DC: Georgetown University Press.

Atkinson, A. (2000) "Artificial nutrition and hydration in patients in persistent vegetative state: continuing reflections," *Ethics and Medicine*, 16: 73–5.

Austriaco, N. (2002) "On static eggs and dynamic embryos: a systems perspective," *The National Catholic Bioethics Quarterly*, 2: 659–83.

Austriaco, N., Cole, B., and May, W. (2001) "Reply to Fr. Ashley," *The National Catholic Bioethics Quarterly*, 1: 9–11.

Bailey, S. (2003) "The concept of futility in health care decision making," *Nursing Ethics*, 11: 77–83.

Barad, J. (1988) "Aquinas's inconsistency on the nature and the treatment of animals," *Between the Species*, 4: 102–11.

Barkan, L. (1996) "Cosmas and Damian: of medicine, miracles, and the economies of the body," in S. Younger, R. Fox, and L. O'Connell (eds) *Organ Transplantation: Meanings and Realities*, Madison, WI: University of Wisconsin Press.

Barry, R. and Maher, J.E. (1990) "Indirectly intended life-shortening analgesia: clarifying the principles," *Issues in Law and Medicine*, 6: 117–51.

Baylis, F. (2001) "Human embryonic stem cell research: comments on the NBAC report," in S. Holland, K. Lebacqz, and L. Zoloth (eds) *The Human Embryonic Stem Cell Debate: Science, Ethics, and Public Policy*, Cambridge, MA: MIT Press.

Beauchamp, T. (1989) "Suicide in the age of reason," in B.A. Brody (ed.) *Suicide and Euthanasia: Historical and Contemporary Themes*, Dordrecht: Kluwer.

Bedate, C. and Cefalo, R. (1989) "The zygote: to be or not be a person," *The Journal of Medicine and Philosophy*, 14: 641–5.

Beddington, R. and Robertson, E. (1999) "Axis development and early asymmetry in mammals," *Cell*, 96: 195–209.

Belkin, G.S. (2003) "Brain death and the historical understanding of bioethics," *Journal of the History of Medicine*, 58: 325–61.

Berkman, J. (2003) "Gestating the embryos of others," *The National Catholic Bioethics Quarterly*, 3: 309–29.

Bernat, J. (1998) "A defense of the whole-brain concept of death," *Hastings Center Report*, 28: 14–23.

—— (1999) "Refinements in the definition and criterion of death," in S. Youngner, R. Arnold, and R. Shapiro (eds) *The Definition of Death: Contemporary Controversies*, Baltimore, MD: Johns Hopkins University Press.

—— (2001) "Ethical and legal issues in palliative care," *Neurologic Clinics*, 19: 969–87.

—— (2002) "The biophilosophical basis of whole-brain death," *Social Philosophy and Policy*, 19: 324–42.

Bernstein, I., Watson, M., Simons, G., Catalano, P., Davis, G., and Collins, R. (1989) "Maternal brain death and prolonged fetal survival," *Obstetrics and Gynecology*, 74: 434–7.

Boethius, A.M.S. (1918) "Contra Eutychen et Nestorium," in H.F. Stewart, E.K. Rand, and S.J. Tester (trans.) *Tractates and The Consolation of Philosophy*, Cambridge, MA: Harvard University Press.

Bopp, J. (1994) "Fetal tissue transplantation and moral complicity with induced abortion," in P.J. Cataldo and A. Moraczewski (eds) *The Fetal Tissue Issue: Medical and Ethical Aspects*, Braintree, MA: The Pope John Center.

Boyle, J. (1978) "*Praeter intentionem* in Aquinas," *The Thomist*, 42: 649–65.

—— (1980) "Toward understanding the principle of double effect," *Ethics*, 90: 527–38.

—— (1989) "Sanctity of life and suicide: tensions and developments within common morality," in B.A. Brody (ed.) *Suicide and Euthanasia: Historical and Contemporary Themes*, Dordrecht: Kluwer.

Boyle, J. and Sullivan, T. (1977) "The diffusiveness of intention principle: a counter-example," *Philosophical Studies*, 31: 357–60.

Boyle, J., Finnis, J., and Grisez, G. (2001) " 'Direct' and 'indirect': a reply to critics of our action theory," *The Thomist*, 65: 1–44.

Bracken, W.J. (2001) "Is the early embryo a person?," *Linacre Quarterly*, 68: 49–70.

Brock, S. (1998) *Action and Conduct: Thomas Aquinas and the Theory of Action*, Edinburgh: T & T Clark.

Burke, M. (1996) "Sortal essentialism and the potentiality principle," *Review of Metaphysics*, 49: 491–514.

Bush, G.W. (2001) "Remarks by the President on stem cell research," televised address delivered August 9. Online. Available HTTP: //www.whitehouse.gov/news/releases/2001/08/20010809-2.html (accessed September 27, 2004).

Byrne, P. and Rinkowski, G. (1999) " 'Brain death' is false," *Linacre Quarterly*, 66: 42–8.

Cahill, L.S. (1977) "A 'natural law' reconsideration of euthanasia," *Linacre Quarterly*, 44: 47–63.

Campbell, M.L. and Weber, L.J. (1995) "Procuring organs from a non-heart-beating cadaver: commentary on a case report," *Kennedy Institute of Ethics Journal*, 5: 35–42.

Cantor, M.D., Braddock, C.H., III, Derse, A.R., Edwards, D.M., Logue, G.L., Nelson, W., Prudhomme, A.M., Pearlman, R.A., Reagan, J.E., Wlody, G.S., and Fox, E. (2003) "Do-not-resuscitate orders and medical futility," *Archives of Internal Medicine*, 163: 2689–94.

Cataldo, P.J. (2002) "A cooperation analysis of embryonic stem cell research," *The National Catholic Bioethics Quarterly*, 2: 35–41.

Cavanaugh, T.A. (1996) "The ethics of death-hastening or death-causing palliative analgesic administration to the terminally ill," *Journal of Pain and Symptom Management*, 12: 248–54.

—— (1997) "Aquinas's account of double effect," *The Thomist*, 61: 107–12.

Chandlish, J. (1968) "St. Thomas and the dynamic state of body constituents," *Journal of the History of Medicine and Applied Sciences*, 23: 272–5.

Charo, R.A. (2001) "Every cell is sacred: logical consequences of the argument from potential in the age of cloning," in P. Lauritzen (ed.) *Cloning and the Future of Human Embryo Research*, New York: Oxford University Press.

Cherny, N.I. and Portenoy, R.K. (1994) "Sedation in the management of refractory symptoms: guidelines for evaluation and treatment," *Journal of Palliative Care*, 10: 31–8.

Cherry, M.J. (2000) "Body parts and the market place: insights from Thomistic philosophy," *Christian Bioethics*, 6: 171–93.

Childs, N.L., Mercer, W.N., and Childs, H.W. (1993) "Accuracy of diagnosis of persistent vegetative state," *Neurology*, 43: 1465–7.

Cibelli, J.B., Kiessling, A.A., Cunniff, K., Richards, C., Lanza, R.P., and West, M.D. (2001) "Somatic cell nuclear transfer in humans: pronuclear and early embryonic development," *E-Biomed: The Journal of Regenerative Medicine*, 2: 25–31. Online. Available HTTP: http://lysander.ingentaselect.com/vl=2024512/cl=102/nw=1/rpsv/~549/v2n5/s5/p25 (accessed September 21, 2004).

Cibelli, J.B., Lanza, R.P., West, M.D., and Ezzell, C. (2002) "The first human cloned embryo," *Scientific American*, 286: 44–51.

Coad, N.R. and Byrne, A.J. (1990) "Guillain-Barré syndrome mimicking brainstem death," *Anaesthesia*, 45: 456–7.

Colbert, J.G., Jr (1978) "Euthanasia and natural law," *Linacre Quarterly*, 45: 187–98.

Cole-Turner, R. (1997) "At the beginning," in R. Cole-Turner (ed.) *Human Cloning: Religious Responses*, Louisville, KY: Westminster John Knox Press.

Conner, P. (2002) "The indignity of human cloning," *The National Catholic Bioethics Quarterly*, 2: 635–58.

Coors, M.E. (2002) "Therapeutic cloning: from consequences to contradiction," *Journal of Medicine and Philosophy*, 27: 297–317.

Cronin, D.A. (1989) "The moral law in regard to the ordinary and extraordinary means of conserving life," in R.E. Smith (ed.) *Conserving Human Life*, Braintree, MA: The Pope John Center.

Crosby, J. (1993) "The personhood of the human embryo," *The Journal of Medicine and Philosophy*, 18: 399–418.

Davidson, J.L. (2001) "Case study: a successful embryo adoption," *The National Catholic Bioethics Quarterly*, 1: 229–33.

De Koninck, T. (1999) "Persons and things," in T. Hibbs and J. O'Callaghan (eds) *Recovering Nature: Essays In Natural Philosophy, Ethics, and Metaphysics in Honor of Ralph McInerny*, Notre Dame: University of Notre Dame Press.

de Melo-Martín, I. (2002) "On cloning human beings," *Bioethics*, 16: 246–65.

DeVita, M.A., Vukmir, R., Snyder, J.V., and Graziano, C. (1995) "Non-heart-beating organ donation: a reply to Campbell and Weber," *Kennedy Institute of Ethics Journal*, 5: 43–9.

Dillon, W.P., Lee, R.V., Tronolone, M.J., Buckwald, S., and Foote, R.J. (1982) "Life support and maternal brain death during pregnancy," *Journal of the American Medical Association*, 248: 1089–91.

Doerflinger, R.M. (2003) "Testimony on embryo research and related issues," *The National Catholic Bioethics Quarterly*, 3: 767–86.

Donceel, J. (1970) "Immediate animation and delayed hominization," *Theological Studies*, 31: 76–105.

Dorff, E.N. (1996) "Choosing life: aspects of Judaism affecting organ transplantation," in S. Younger, R. Fox and L. O'Connell (eds) *Organ Transplantation: Meanings and Realities*, Madison, WI: University of Wisconsin Press.

Drury, I., Westmoreland, B.F. and Sharbrough, F.W. (1987) "Fulminant demyelinating polyradiculoneuropathy resembling brain death," *Electroencephalography and Clinical Neurophysiology*, 67: 42–3.

DuBois, J.M. (1999) "Non-heart-beating organ donation: a defense of the required determination of death," *Journal of Law, Medicine, and Ethics*, 27: 126–36.

—— (2002a) "Organ transplantation: an ethical road map," *The National Catholic Bioethics Quarterly*, 2: 413–53.

—— (2002b) "Is organ procurement causing the death of patients," *Issues in Law and Medicine*, 18: 21–41.

Eberl, J.T. (2000a) "The beginning of personhood: a Thomistic biological analysis," *Bioethics*, 14: 134–57.

—— (2000b) "The metaphysics of resurrection: issues of identity in Thomas Aquinas," *Proceedings of the American Catholic Philosophical Association*, 74: 215–30.

—— (2003) "Aquinas on euthanasia, suffering, and palliative care," *The National Catholic Bioethics Quarterly*, 3: 331–54.

—— (2004) "Aquinas on the nature of human beings," *Review of Metaphysics*, 58: 333–65.

—— (2005a) "A Thomistic understanding of human death," *Bioethics*, 19: 29–48.

—— (2005b) "Aquinas's account of human embryogenesis and recent interpretations," *Journal of Medicine and Philosophy*, 30: 379–94.

—— (2005c) "Extraordinary care and the spiritual goal of life," *The National Catholic Bioethics Quarterly*, 5: 491–501.

Etzioni, A. (2003) "Organ donation: a communitarian approach," *Kennedy Institute of Ethics Journal*, 13: 1–18.

Evers, K. (1999) "The identity of clones," *Journal of Medicine and Philosophy*, 24: 67–76.

Farmer, L. (1996) "Human is generated by human and created by God," *American Catholic Philosophical Quarterly*, 70: 413–27.

Field, D.R., Gates, E.A., Creasy, R.K., Jonsen, A.R., and Laros, R.K. (1988) "Maternal brain death during pregnancy: medical and ethical issues," *Journal of the American Medical Association*, 260: 816–22.

Finnis, J. (1980) *Natural Law and Natural Rights*, Oxford: Clarendon Press.

—— (1998) *Aquinas: Moral, Political, and Legal Theory*, New York: Oxford University Press.

—— (1999) "Abortion and health care ethics," in H. Kuhse and P. Singer (eds) *Bioethics: An Anthology*, Oxford: Blackwell.

Fisher, A. (1991) " 'When did I begin?' Revisited," *Linacre Quarterly*, 58: 59–68.

FitzPatrick, W. (2003) "Surplus embryos, nonreproductive cloning, and the intend/foresee distinction," *Hastings Center Report*, 33: 297–317.

Flaman, P. (1991) "When did I begin? Another critical response to Norman Ford," *Linacre Quarterly*, 58: 39–55.

Fletcher, J. (1971) "Ethical aspects of genetic controls," *New England Journal of Medicine*, 285: 776–83.

Ford, N.M. (1988) *When Did I Begin? Conception of the Human Individual in History, Philosophy and Science*, New York: Cambridge University Press.

—— (2001) "The human embryo as person in Catholic teaching," *The National Catholic Bioethics Quarterly*, 1: 155–60.

—— (2002) *The Prenatal Person: Ethics from Conception to Birth*, Oxford: Blackwell.

Foster, J. (2001) "A brief defense of the Cartesian view," in K. Corcoran (ed.) *Soul, Body, and Survival: Essays on the Metaphysics of Human Persons*, Ithaca, NY: Cornell University Press.

Gaffney, J. (1976) "The over-extended principle of totality and some underlying issues," *Journal of Religious Ethics*, 4: 259–67.

Gardner, R.L. (1997) "The early blastocyst is bilaterally symmetrical and its axis of symmetry is aligned with the animal-vegetal axis of the zygote in the mouse," *Development*, 124: 289–301.

—— (2001) "Specification of embryonic axes begins before cleavage in normal mouse development," *Development*, 128: 839–47.

—— (2002) "Thoughts and observations on patterning in early mammalian development," *Reproductive Biomedicine Online*, 4 (Suppl.): 46–51. Online. Available HTTP: //www.rbmonline.com/4DCGI/Article/2001/162/RB162 Gardner.pdf (accessed September 21, 2004).

Gauthier, C.C. (2001) "Active voluntary euthanasia, terminal sedation, and assisted suicide," *Journal of Clinical Ethics*, 12: 43–50.

Gerber, R. (1966) "When is the human soul infused?," *Laval Theologique et Philosophique*, 22: 234–47.

Geron Ethics Advisory Board (1999) "Research with human embryonic stem cells: ethical considerations," *Hastings Center Report*, 29: 31–6.

Gillett, G. (1990) "Consciousness, the brain, and what matters," *Bioethics*, 4: 181–98.

Gilson, E. (1956) *The Christian Philosophy of St. Thomas Aquinas*, Notre Dame: University of Notre Dame Press.

Gómez-Lobo, A. (2002) *Morality and the Human Goods: An Introduction to Natural Law Ethics*, Washington, DC: Georgetown University Press.

Gormally, L. (ed.) (1994) *Euthanasia, Clinical Practice and the Law*, London: The Linacre Center for Health Care Ethics.

—— (1999) "Palliative treatment and ordinary care," in J. Vial Correa and E. Sgreccia (eds) *The Dignity of the Dying Person*, Vatican City: Libreria Editrice Vaticana.

Green, R.M. (2001) *The Human Embryo Research Debates: Bioethics in the Vortex of Controversy*, New York: Oxford University Press.

—— (2002) "Determining moral status," *American Journal of Bioethics*, 2: 20–30.

Grisez, G. (1965) "The first principle of practical reason: a commentary on the *Summa Theologiae*, Question 94, Article 2," *Natural Law Forum*, 10: 168–201.

—— (1989) "When do people begin?," *Proceedings of the American Catholic Philosophical Association*, 63: 27–47.

Grisez, G. and Boyle, J. (1979) *Life and Death with Liberty and Justice: A Contribution to the Euthanasia Debate*, Notre Dame: University of Notre Dame Press.

Gustafson, G.J. (1944) *The Theory of Natural Appetency in the Philosophy of St. Thomas*, Washington, DC: Catholic University of America Press.

Haldane, J. (2000) "Being human: science, knowledge and virtue," in J. Haldane (ed.) *Philosophy and Public Affairs*, New York: Cambridge University Press.

Haldane, J. and Lee, P. (2003a) "Aquinas on human ensoulment, abortion and the value of life," *Philosophy*, 78: 255–78.

—— (2003b) "Rational souls and the beginning of life: a reply to Robert Pasnau," *Philosophy*, 78: 532–40.

Hall, J.L., Engel, D., Gindoff, P.R. *et al.* (1993) "Experimental cloning of human polypoid embryos using an artificial zona pellucida," paper presented at The American Fertility Society conjointly with the Canadian Fertility and Andrology Society.

Hassan, T. and Mumford, C. (1991) "Guillain-Barré syndrome mistaken for brain stem death," *Postgraduate Medical Journal*, 67: 280–1.

Hawking, S. (1996) *The Illustrated A Brief History of Time*, New York: Bantam.

Heaney, S. (1992) "Aquinas on the presence of the human rational soul in the early embryo," *The Thomist*, 56: 19–48.

Henle, R.J. (1993) *The Treatise on Law*, Notre Dame: University of Notre Dame Press.

Hittinger, R. (1987) *A Critique of the New Natural Law Theory*, Notre Dame: University of Notre Dame Press.

Hoffenberg, R., Lock, M., Tilney, N., Casabona, C., Daar, A.S., Guttman, R.D., Kennedy, I., Nundy, S., Radcliffe-Richards, J., and Sells, R.A. (1997) "Should organs from patients in permanent vegetative state be used for transplantation?" *The Lancet*, 350: 1320–1.

Hopkins, P.D. (1997) "Why does removing machines count as 'passive' euthanasia?," *Hastings Center Report*, 27: 29–37.

Howsepian, A. (1997) "Lockwood on human identity and the primitive streak," *Journal of Medical Ethics*, 23: 38–41.

Hughes, G.J. (1976) "Natural law," *Journal of Medical Ethics*, 2: 34–6.

Institute of Medicine (1997) *Non-Heart-Beating Organ Transplantation: Medical and Ethical Issues in Procurement*, Washington, DC: National Academy Press.

—— (2000) *Non-Heart-Beating Organ Transplantation: Practice and Protocols*, Washington, DC: National Academy Press.

Iozzio, M. (2002) "It is time to support embryo adoption," *The National Catholic Bioethics Quarterly*, 2: 585–93.

Irving, D.N. (2000) "Abortion: correct application of natural law theory," *Linacre Quarterly*, 67: 45–55.

Jansen, L.A. and Sulmasy, D.P. (2002) "Sedation, alimentation, hydration, and equivocation: careful conversations about care at the end of life," *Annals of Internal Medicine*, 136: 845–9.

Jennett, B. and Plum, F. (1972) "Persistent vegetative state after brain damage: a syndrome in search of a name," *Lancet*, 1: 734–7.

John Paul II (1998) *Fides et Ratio*. Online. Available HTTP: //www.vatican.va/edocs/ENG0216/_INDEX.HTM (accessed December 1, 2004).

—— (2001) "Address to the International Congress on Transplants," *The National Catholic Bioethics Quarterly*, 1: 89–92.

Johnson, M. (1995) "Delayed hominization: reflections on some recent Catholic claims for delayed hominization," *Theological Studies*, 56: 743–63.

Jones, D.A. (2000) "Metaphysical misgivings about 'brain death'," in M. Potts, P. Byrne, and R. Nilges (eds) *Beyond Brain Death: The Case Against Brain Based Criteria for Human Death*, Dordrecht: Kluwer.

Jonsen, A. (1998) *The Birth of Bioethics*, New York: Oxford University Press.

Juengst, E. and Fossel, M. (2000) "Now and forever, cells without end," *Journal of the American Medical Association*, 284: 3180–4.

Kant, I. (1785) *Grundlegung zur Metaphysik der Sitten*; H.J. Paton (trans.) (1964) *Groundwork of the Metaphysic of Morals*, New York: Harper Torchbooks.

Kavanaugh, J.F. (2001) *Who Count as Persons: Human Identity and the Ethics of Killing*, Washington, DC: Georgetown University Press.

Kelly, G. (1960) *Medico-Moral Problems*, Dublin: Clonmore and Reynolds Ltd.

Klima, G. (2001) "Aquinas' proofs of the immateriality of the intellect from the universality of human thought," *Proceedings of the Society for Medieval Logic and Metaphysics*, 1: 19–28.

Klubertanz, G. (1953) *The Philosophy of Human Nature*, New York: Appleton-Century-Crofts.

Kluge, E.-H. (1981) "St. Thomas, abortion, and euthanasia: another look," *Philosophy Research Archives*, 7: 312–44.

Kondziolka, D., Wechsler, L., Goldstein, S., Meltzer, C., Thulborn, K.R., Gebel, J., Jannetta, P., De Cesare, S., Elder, E.M., McGrogan, M., Reitman, M.A., and Bynum, L. (2000) "Transplantation of cultured human neuronal cells for patients with stroke," *Neurology*, 55: 565–9.

Krakauer, E.L., Penson, R.T., Truog, R.D., King, L.A., Chabner, B.A., and Lynch, T.J., Jr (2000) "Sedation for intractable distress of a dying patient: acute palliative care and the principle of double effect," *The Oncologist*, 5: 53–62.

Kretzmann, N. (1997) *The Metaphysics of Theism: Aquinas's Natural Theology in Summa Contra Gentiles I*, Oxford: Clarendon Press.

—— (1999) *The Metaphysics of Creation: Aquinas's Natural Theology in Summa Contra Gentiles II*, Oxford: Clarendon Press.

Krueger, C. (2003) "Understanding Terri Schiavo," *St. Petersburg Times*, October 28. Online. Available HTTP: //www.sptimes.com/2003/10/28/news_pf/Tampabay/ Understanding_Terri_S.shtml (accessed June 29, 2004).

Kuhse, H. (1998) "Why killing is not always worse – and sometimes better – than letting die," *Cambridge Quarterly of Healthcare Ethics*, 7: 371–4.

Lamb, D. (1990) *Organ Transplants and Ethics*, New York: Routledge.

Langendorf, F., Mallin, J., Masdeu, J., Moshe, S., and Lipton, R. (1986) "Fulminant Guillain-Barré syndrome simulating brain death: clinical and electrophysiological findings," abstract in *Electroencephalography and Clinical Neurophysiology*, 64: 74P.

Lanuke, K., Fainsinger, R.L., DeMoissac, D., and Archibald, J. (2003) "Two remarkable dyspneic men: when should terminal sedation be administered?," *Journal of Palliative Medicine*, 6: 277–81.

Lanza, R.P., Caplan, A.L., Silver, L.M., Cibelli, J.B., West, M.D., and Green, R.M. (2000) "The ethical validity of using nuclear transfer in human transplantation," *Journal of the American Medical Association*, 284: 3175–9.

LaRock, E.F. (2001) "Dualistic interaction, neural dependence, and Aquinas's composite view," *Philosophia Christi*, 3: 459–72.

Lee, P. (1996) *Abortion and Unborn Human Life*, Washington, DC: Catholic University of America Press.

Leftow, B. (2001) "Souls dipped in dust," in K. Corcoran (ed.) *Soul, Body, and Survival: Essays on the Metaphysics of Human Persons*, Ithaca, NY: Cornell University Press.

Leo XIII (1879) *Aeterni Patris*. Online. Available HTTP: //www.vatican.va/holy_father/leo_xiii/encyclicals/documents/hf_l-xiii_enc_04081879_aeterni-patris_en.html (accessed December 1, 2004).

Li, I. (2002) "Feeding tubes in patients with severe dementia," *American Family Physician*, 65: 1605–10.

Lisska, A. (1996) *Aquinas's Natural Law Theory: An Analytic Reconstruction*, Oxford: Clarendon Press.

Loeb, J. (1916) *The Organism as a Whole*, New York: Putnam.

Loewy, E.H. (2001) "Terminal sedation, self-starvation, and orchestrating the end of life," *Archives of Internal Medicine*, 161: 329–32.

Lutz, M. (1999) "Statement against the 'A report on cerebral death' by Prof. Corrado Manni," in J. Vial Correa and E. Sgreccia (eds) *The Dignity of the Dying Person*, Vatican City: Libreria Editrice Vaticana.

McCartney, J.J. (2002) "Embryonic stem cell research and respect for human life philosophical and legal reflections," *Albany Law Review*, 65: 597–624.

McCormick, R.A. (1975) "Transplantation of organs: a comment on Paul Ramsey," *Theological Studies* 17: 322–44.

—— (1991) "Who or what is the preembryo?," *Kennedy Institute of Ethics Journal*, 1: 1–15.

MacDonald, S. (ed.) (1991) *Being and Goodness: The Concept of the Good in Metaphysics and Philosophical Theology*, Ithaca, NY: Cornell University Press.

McInerny, R. (1993) "Ethics," in N. Kretzmann and E. Stump (eds) *The Cambridge Companion to Aquinas*, New York: Cambridge University Press.

—— (1997) *Ethica Thomistica: The Moral Philosophy of Thomas Aquinas*, rev. ed., Washington, DC: Catholic University of America Press.

McMahan, J. (1999) "Cloning, killing, and identity," *Journal of Medical Ethics*, 25: 77–86.

—— (2002) *The Ethics of Killing: Problems at the Margins of Life*, New York: Oxford University Press.

Maienschein, J. (2002) "What's in a name: embryos, clones, and stem cells," *American Journal of Bioethics*, 2: 12–19.

Manni, C. (1999) "A report on cerebral death," in J. Vial Correa and E. Sgreccia (eds) *The Dignity of the Dying Person*, Vatican City: Libreria Editrice Vaticana.

Mappes, T.A. (2003) "Persistent vegetative state, prospective thinking, and advance directives," *Kennedy Institute of Ethics Journal*, 13: 119–39.

Marti-Masso, J., Suarez, J., Lopez de Munain, A., and Carrera, N. (1993) "Clinical signs of brain death simulated by Guillain-Barré syndrome," *Journal of the Neurological Sciences*, 120: 115–17.

Matthews, G. (1999) "Saint Thomas and the principle of double effect," in S. MacDonald and E. Stump (eds) *Aquinas's Moral Theory: Essays in Honor of Norman Kretzmann*, Ithaca, NY: Cornell University Press.

Maurer, A. (1993) "Descartes and Aquinas on the unity of a human being: revisited," *American Catholic Philosophical Quarterly*, 67: 497–511.

May, W.E. (1990) "Criteria for withholding or withdrawing treatment," *Linacre Quarterly*, 57: 81–90.

—— (1992) "The moral status of the embryo," *Linacre Quarterly*, 59: 76–83.

—— (1998) "Bioethics and human life," in D.F. Forte (ed.) *Natural Law and Contemporary Public Policy*, Washington, DC: Georgetown University Press.

May, W.E., Barry, R., Griese, O., Grisez, G., Johnstone, B., Marzen, T.J., McHugh, J.T., Meilaender, G., Siegler, M., and Smith, W. (1987) "Feeding and hydrating the permanently unconscious and other vulnerable persons," *Issues in Law and Medicine*, 3: 203–11.

Menikoff, J. (1998) "Doubts about death: the silence of the Institute of Medicine," *Journal of Law, Medicine and Ethics*, 26: 157–65.

—— (2002) "The importance of being dead: non-heart-beating organ donation," *Issues in Law and Medicine*, 18: 3–20.

Michejda, M. (2002) "Spontaneous miscarriages as source of fetal stem cells," *The National Catholic Bioethics Quarterly*, 2: 401–11.

Miles, S.H. (1992) "Medical futility," *Law, Medicine and Health Care*, 20: 310–15.

Mirkes, R. (2001) "NBAC and embryo ethics," *The National Catholic Bioethics Quarterly*, 1: 163–87.

Mitalipov, S.M., Nusser, K.D., and Wolf, D.P. (2001) "Parthenogenetic activation of rhesus monkey oocytes and reconstructed embryos," *Biology of Reproduction*, 65: 256–8.

Mitchell, S.L., Buchanan, J.L., Littlehale, S., and Hamel, M.B. (2004) "Tube-feeding versus hand-feeding nursing home residents with advanced dementia: a cost comparison," *Journal of the American Medical Directors Association*, 5: S22–9.

Montaldi, D. (1986) "A defense of St. Thomas and the principle of double effect," *Journal of Religious Ethics*, 14: 296–332.

Moraczewski, A. (2002) "May one benefit from the evil deeds of others?," *The National Catholic Bioethics Quarterly*, 2: 43–7.

Moreland, J.P. (1995) "Humanness, personhood, and the right to die," *Faith and Philosophy*, 12: 95–112.

Moreland, J.P. and Rae, S.B. (2000) *Body and Soul: Human Nature and the Crisis in Ethics*, Downers Grove, IL: InterVarsity Press.

Moreland, J.P. and Wallace, S. (1995) "Aquinas versus Locke and Descartes on the human person and end-of-life ethics," *International Philosophical Quarterly*, 35: 319–30.

Mount, B. (1996) "Morphine drips, terminal sedation, and slow euthanasia: definitions and facts, not anecdotes," *Journal of Palliative Care*, 12: 31–7.

Munsie, M.J., Michalska, A.E., O'Brien, C.M., Trounson, A.O., Pera, M.F., and Mountford, P.S. (2000) "Isolation of pluripotent embryonic stem cells from reprogrammed adult mouse somatic cell nuclei," *Current Biology*, 10: 989–92.

National Advisory Board on Ethics in Reproduction (1994) "Report on human cloning through embryo splitting: an amber light," *Kennedy Institute of Ethics Journal*. 4: 251–82.

National Bioethics Advisory Commission (NBAC) (1997) *Cloning Human Beings*, Vol. 1. Online. Available HTTP: //www.bioethics.gov/reports/past_commissions/nbac_cloning.pdf (accessed May 23, 2004).

—— (1999) *Ethical Issues in Human Stem Cell Research*, Vol. 1. Online. Available HTTP: //www.bioethics.gov/reports/past_commissions/nbac_stemcell1.pdf (accessed March 31, 2004).

Nelson, D.M. (1992) *The Priority of Prudence: Virtue and Natural Law in Thomas Aquinas and the Implications for Modern Ethics*, University Park, PA: The Pennsylvania State University Press.

Nelson, J.L. (2001) "Do we all have a responsibility to donate our organs?," in W. Shelton and J. Balint (eds) *The Ethics of Organ Transplantation*, Amsterdam: Elsevier Science Ltd.

Nelson, S.N. (2003) " 'Do everything!' Encountering 'futility' in medical practice," *Ethics and Medicine*, 19: 103–13.

Nolan, M. (2000) "The Aristotelian background to Aquinas's denial that 'Woman is a defective male'," *The Thomist*, 64: 21–69.

Novak, D. (1975) *Suicide and Morality*, New York: Scholars Studies Press.

Olson, E. (1997) *The Human Animal: Personal Identity Without Psychology*, New York: Oxford University Press.

Orentlicher, D. (1997) "The Supreme Court and terminal sedation: rejecting assisted suicide, embracing euthanasia," *Hasting Constitutional Law Quarterly*, 24: 947–68.

O'Rourke, K. (1989) "Should nutrition and hydration be provided to permanently unconscious and other mentally disabled persons," *Issues in Law and Medicine*, 5: 181–96.

O'Rourke, K. and Norris, P. (2001) "Care of PVS patients: Catholic opinion in the United States," *Linacre Quarterly*, 68: 201–17.

Orr, R.D. (2002) "The moral status of the embryonal stem cell: inherent or imputed?," *American Journal of Bioethics*, 2: 57–9.

Panicola, M. (2002) "Three on the preimplantation embryo," *The National Catholic Bioethics Quarterly*, 2: 69–97.

Parisi, J., Kim, R., Collins, G., and Hilfinger, M. (1982) "Brain death with prolonged somatic survival," *New England Journal of Medicine*, 306: 14–16.

Pasnau, R. (2002) *Thomas Aquinas on Human Nature*, New York: Cambridge University Press.

—— (2003) "Souls and the beginning of life: a reply to Haldane and Lee," *Philosophy*, 78: 521–31.

Pegis, A. (1978; orig. 1934) *St. Thomas and the Problem of the Soul in the Thirteenth Century*, Toronto: Pontifical Institute of Mediaeval Studies.

Pellegrino, E.D. (1998) "Emerging ethical issues in palliative care," *Journal of the American Medical Association*, 279: 1521–2.

Peters, T. (1997) "Cloning shock: a theological reaction," in R. Cole-Turner (ed.) *Human Cloning: Religious Responses*, Louisville, KY: Westminster John Knox Press.

—— (2001) "Embryonic stem cells and the theology of dignity," in S. Holland, K. Lebacqz, and L. Zoloth (eds) *The Human Embryonic Stem Cell Debate: Science, Ethics, and Public Policy*, Cambridge, MA: MIT Press.

Piontelli, A. (2002) *Twins: From Fetus to Child*, New York: Routledge.

Piotrowska, K. and Zernicka-Goetz, M. (2001) "Role for sperm in spatial patterning of the early mouse embryo," *Nature*, 409: 517–21.

Piotrowska, K., Wianny, F., Pedersen, R.A., and Zernicka-Goetz, M. (2001) "Blastomeres arising from the first cleavage division have distinguishable fates in normal mouse development," *Development*, 128: 3739–48.

Pius XII (1958) "The prolongation of life," *The Pope Speaks*, 4: 393–8.

Potts, M. (2001) "A requiem for whole brain death: a response to D. Alan Shewmon's 'The brain and somatic integration'," *Journal of Medicine and Philosophy*, 26: 479–91.

Prentice, D.A. (2003) "Adult stem cells." Online. Available HTTP: //stemcellresearch. org/facts/prentice.htm (accessed April 10, 2004).

President's Commission for the Study of Ethical Problems in Medicine and Biomedical and Behavioral Research (1981) *Defining Death: Medical, Legal, and Ethical Issues in the Definition of Death*, Washington, DC: US Government Printing Office.

—— (1983) *Deciding to Forego Life-Sustaining Treatment: Ethical, Medical, and Legal Issues in Treatment Decisions*, Washington, DC: US Government Printing Office.

President's Council on Bioethics (PCB) (2002) *Human Cloning and Human Dignity: An Ethical Inquiry*. Online. Available HTTP: //www.bioethics.gov/reports/cloningreport/ pcbe_cloning_report.pdf (accessed March 24, 2004).

—— (2004) *Monitoring Stem Cell Research*. Online. Available HTTP: //www.bioethics.gov/reports/stemcell/index.html (accessed July 5, 2004).

Quill, T.E. and Byock, I.R. (2000) "Responding to intractable terminal suffering: the role of terminal sedation and voluntary refusal of food and fluids," *Annals of Internal Medicine*, 132: 408–14.

Rachels, J. (1975) "Active and passive euthanasia," *New England Journal of Medicine*, 292: 78–80.

—— (1986) *The End of Life: Euthanasia and Morality*, New York: Oxford University Press.

Ramsey, P. (1970) *The Patient as Person*, New Haven, CT: Yale University Press.

Reeve, C. and Rosenblatt, R. (1998) *Still Me*, New York: Random House.

Reichlin, M. (1997) "The argument from potential: a reappraisal," *Bioethics*, 11: 1–23.

Rhonheimer, M. (2000) *Natural Law and Practical Reason: A Thomist View of Moral Autonomy*, New York: Fordham University Press.

Robertson, J.A. (1999), "Ethics and policy in embryonic stem cell research," *Kennedy Institute of Ethics Journal*, 9: 109–36.

—— (2000) "The dead donor rule," *Hastings Center Report*, 29: 6–14.

Rolston, H., III (1982) "The irreversibly comatose: respect for the subhuman in human life," *Journal of Medicine and Philosophy*, 7: 337–54.

Rommen, H.A. (1948) *The Natural Law: A Study in Legal and Social History And Philosophy*, trans. T.R. Hanley, St. Louis: Herder.

Rosner, F. (1993) "Why nutrition and hydration should not be withheld from patients," *Chest*, 104: 1892–6.

Ross, E. (2003) "Cloned sheep Dolly euthanized," Associated Press wire. Online. Available HTTP: //www.newsday.com/news/nationworld/nation/sns-cloning.story (accessed September 9, 2004).

Rousseau, P. (1996) "Terminal sedation in the care of dying patients," *Archives of Internal Medicine*, 156: 1785–6.

Sacred Congregation for the Doctrine of the Faith (1980) *Declaration on Euthanasia*, Boston, MA: St. Paul Books and Media.

Savulescu, J. (2001) "Should we clone human beings? Cloning as a source of tissue transplantation," in M. Ruse and A. Sheppard (eds) *Cloning: Responsible Science or Technomadness?*, Amherst, NY: Prometheus Books.

Shamblott, M.J., Axelman, J., Wang, S., Bugg, E.M., Littlefield, J.W., Donovan, P.J., Blumenthal, P.D., Huggins, G.R., and Gearhart, J.D. (1998) "Derivation of pluripotent stem cells from cultured human primordial germ cell," *Proceedings of the National Academy of Sciences USA*, 95: 13726–31.

Seifert, J. (1992) "Is 'brain death' actually death? A critique of redefining man's death in terms of 'brain death'," in R. White, H. Angstwurm, and I. Carrasco de Paula (eds) *Working Group on the Determination of Brain Death and Its Relationship to Human Death*, Vatican City: Pontificia Academia Scientiarum.

—— (1993) "Is 'brain death' actually death," *The Monist*, 76: 175–202.

—— (2000) "Brain death and euthanasia," in M. Potts, P. Byrne, and R. Nilges (eds) *Beyond Brain Death: The Case Against Brain Based Criteria for Human Death*, Dordrecht: Kluwer.

Serra, A. and Colombo, R. (1998) "Identity and status of the human embryo: the contribution of biology," in J. Vial Correa and E. Sgreccia (eds) *Identity and Statute of Human Embryo*, Vatican City: Libreria Editrice Vaticana.

Shannon, T. (2001) "From the micro to the macro," in S. Holland, K. Lebacqz, and L. Zoloth (eds) *The Human Embryonic Stem Cell Debate: Science, Ethics, and Public Policy*, Cambridge, MA: MIT Press.

Shannon, T. and Wolter, A. (1990) "Reflections on the moral status of the pre-embryo," *Theological Studies*, 51: 603–26.

Shewmon, D.A. (1985) "The metaphysics of brain death, persistent vegetative state, and dementia," *The Thomist*, 49: 24–80.

—— (1992) " 'Brain death': a valid theme with invalid variations, blurred by semantic ambiguity," in R. White, H. Angstwurm, and I. Carrasco de Paula (eds) *Working Group on the Determination of Brain Death and Its Relationship to Human Death*, Vatican City: Pontificia Academia Scientiarum.

—— (1997) "Recovery from brain death: a neurologist's *Apologia*," *Linacre Quarterly*, 64: 30–96.

—— (1998a) " 'Brainstem death', 'brain death' and death: a critical re-evaluation of the purported equivalence," *Issues in Law and Medicine*, 14: 125–45.

—— (1998b) "Chronic 'brain death': meta-analysis and conceptual consequences," *Neurology*, 51: 1538–45.

—— (1999) "Spinal shock and 'brain death': somatic pathophysiological equivalence and implications for the integrative-unity rationale," *Spinal cord*, 37: 313–40.

—— (2001) "The brain and somatic integration: insights into the standard biological rationale for equating 'brain death' with death," *Journal of Medicine and Philosophy*, 26: 457–78.

Siegler, M. and Wikler, D. (1982) "Brain death and live birth," *Journal of the American Medical Association*, 248: 1101–2.

Singer, P. and Dawson, K. (1990) "IVF technology and the argument from potential," in P. Singer, H. Kuhse, S. Buckle, K. Dawson, P. Kasimba (eds) *Embryo Experimentation: Ethical, Legal, and Social Issues*, New York: Cambridge University Press.

Smith, G.P., II (1998) "Terminal sedation as palliative care: revalidating a right to a good death," *Cambridge Quarterly of Healthcare Ethics*, 7: 382–7.

Smith, P. (1983) "The beginning of personhood: a Thomistic perspective," *Laval Théologique et Philosophique*, 39: 195–214.

—— (1990a) "Personhood and the persistent vegetative state," *Linacre Quarterly*, 57: 49–57.

—— (1990b) "Transient natures at the edges of human life: a Thomistic exploration," *The Thomist*, 54: 191–227.

—— (1990c) "Brain death: a Thomistic appraisal," *Angelicum*, 67: 3–35.

Spielman, B. and McCarthy, C.S. (1995) "Beyond Pittsburgh: protocols for controlled non-heart-beating cadaver organ recovery," *Kennedy Institute of Ethics Journals*, 5: 323–33.

Steinbock, B. (1989) "Recovery from persistent vegetative state?: the case of Carrie Coons," *Hastings Center Report*, 19: 14–15.

Stojkovic, T., Verdin, M., Hurtevent, J.F., Laureau, E., Krivosic-Horber, R., and Vermersch, P. (2001) "Guillain-Barré syndrome resembling brainstem death in a patient with brain injury," *Journal of Neurology*, 248: 430–2.

Stump, E. (1995) "Non-Cartesian substance dualism and materialism without reductionism," *Faith and Philosophy*, 12: 505–31.

—— (1999) "Aquinas on the sufferings of Job," in F.M. McClain and W.M. Richardson (eds) *Human and Divine Agency*, New York: University Press of America.

—— (2003) *Aquinas*, New York: Routledge.

Suarez, A. (1990) "Hydatidiform moles and teratomas confirm the human identity of the preimplantation embryo," *Journal of Medicine and Philosophy*, 15: 627–35.

Sullivan, D. (2000) "The doctrine of double effect and the domains of moral responsibility," *The Thomist*, 64: 423–48.

Sulmasy, D.P. and Pellegrino, E.D. (1999) "The rule of double effect: clearing up the double talk," *Archives of Internal Medicine*, 159: 545–50.

Swinburne, R. (1997) *The Evolution of the Soul*, rev. ed., New York: Oxford University Press.

Thomson, J.A., J. Itskovitz-Eldor, S.S. Shapiro, M.A. Waknitz, J.J. Swiergiel, V.S. Marshall, J.M. Jones (1998) "Embryonic stem cell lines derived from human blastocysts," *Science*, 282: 1145–7.

Tonti-Filippini, N. (1991) "Determining when death has occurred," *Linacre Quarterly*, 58: 25–49.

—— (2003) "The embryo rescue debate," *The National Catholic Bioethics Quarterly*, 3: 111–37.

Torchia, J. (2003) "Artificial hydration and nutrition for the PVS patient: ordinary care or extraordinary intervention," *The National Catholic Bioethics Quarterly*, 3: 719–30.

Torrell, J.-P. (1996) *Saint Thomas Aquinas, Volume 1: The Person and His Work*, R. Royal (trans.), Washington, DC: Catholic University of American Press.

Truog, R.D. (1997) "Is it time to abandon brain death?," *Hastings Center Report*, 27: 29–37.

Truog, R.D. and Robinson, W.M. (2003) "Role of brain death and the dead-donor rule in the ethics of organ transplantation," *Critical Care Medicine*, 31: 2391–6.

Truog, R.D., Berde, C.B., Mitchell, C., and Grier, H.E. (1992) "Barbiturates in the care of the terminally ill," *New England Journal of Medicine*, 327: 1678–82.

Vacek, E.C. (1992) "Catholic 'natural law' and reproductive ethics," *Journal of Medicine and Philosophy*, 17: 329–46.

van Inwagen, P. (1990) *Material Beings*, Ithaca, NY: Cornell University Press.

Veatch, R.M. (1988) "Whole-brain, neocortical, and higher brain related concepts," in R. Zaner (ed.) *Death: Beyond Whole-Brain Criteria*, Dordrecht: Kluwer.

—— (2000) *Transplantation Ethics*, Washington, DC, Georgetown University Press.

Vial Correa, J. and Dabike, M. (1998) "The embryo as an organism," in J. Vial Correa and E. Sgreccia (eds) *Identity and Statute of Human Embryo*, Vatican City: Libreria Editrice Vaticana.

Wade, F. (1975) "Potentiality in the abortion discussion," *Review of Metaphysics*, 29: 239–55.

Waters, B. (1997) "One flesh? Cloning, procreation, and the family," in R. Cole-Turner (ed.) *Human Cloning: Religious Responses*, Louisville, KY: Westminster John Knox Press.

Watt, H. (1999) "Are there any circumstances in which it would be morally admirable for a woman to seek to have an orphan embryo implanted in her womb?," in L. Gormally (ed.) *Issues for a Catholic Bioethic*, London: Linacre Centre.

—— (2001) "A brief defense of frozen embryo adoption," *The National Catholic Bioethics Quarterly*, 1: 151–4.

Wennberg, R. (1989) *Terminal Choices: Euthanasia, Suicide, and the Right to Die*, Grand Rapids: Eerdmans.

White, K. (1995) "Aquinas on the immediacy of the union of soul and body," in P. Lockey (ed.) *Studies in Thomistic Theology*, Houston, TX: Center for Thomistic Studies.

White, R., Angstwurm, H., and Carrasco de Paula, I. (1992) *Working Group on the Determination of Brain Death and Its Relationship to Human Death*, Vatican City: Pontificia Academia Scientiarum.

Williams, G. (2001) "The principle of double effect and terminal sedation," *Medical Law Review*, 9: 41–53.

Williams, B. and Smart, J.J.C. (1973) *Utilitarianism: For and Against*, New York: Cambridge University Press.

Wilmut, I., Schnieke, A.E., McWhir, J., Kind, A.J., and Campbell, K.H.S. (1997) "Viable offspring derived from fetal and adult mammalian cells," *Nature* 385: 810–13.

World Health Organization (1990) *Cancer Pain Relief and Palliative Care*, Technical report series 804, Geneva: World Health Organization.

Youngner, S.J. and Arnold, R.M. (1993) "Ethical, psychosocial, and public policy implications of procuring organs from non-heart-beating cadaver donors," *Journal of the American Medical Association*, 269: 2769–74.

Youngner, S.J. and Bartlett, E.T. (1983) "Human death and high technology: the failure of the whole-brain formulations," *Annals of Internal Medicine*, 99: 252–8.

Youngner, S.J., Arnold, R.M., and DeVita, M.A. (1999) "When is 'dead'?," *Hastings Center Report*, 29: 14–21.

Zamperetti, N., Bellomo, R., and Ronco, C. (2003) "Defining death in non-heart beating organ donors," *Journal of Medical Ethics*, 29: 182–5.

Zucker, M.B. and Zucker, H.D. (1997) *Medical Futility and the Evaluation of Life-Sustaining Interventions*, New York: Cambridge University Press.

Index

CPSIA information can be obtained
at www.ICGtesting.com
Printed in the USA
BVHW040845180221
600493BV00010B/198

9 780415 654579